SCHOOLCRAFT COLLEGE LIBRARY

3 3013 00054 1379

W9-ANI-698

D
113
.D3
v.1

Davis, Charles
The eagle, the cres-
cent, and the cross

DATE DUE

BRADNER LIBRARY
SCHOOLCRAFT COLLEGE
LIVONIA, MICHIGAN 48152

940.14

4. 95

The Eagle, the Crescent, and the Cross

A GOLDENTREE BOOK

Edited by

Charles T. Davis
Tulane University

The Eagle, the Crescent, and the Cross

SOURCES OF MEDIEVAL HISTORY
VOLUME I (*c. 250 - c. 1000*)

New York

Appleton - Century - Crofts
Division of Meredith Publishing Company

Copyright © 1967 by

MEREDITH PUBLISHING COMPANY

All rights reserved. This book, or parts thereof,
must not be used or reproduced in any manner
without written permission. For information address the publisher, Appleton-Century-Crofts,
Division of Meredith Publishing Company,
440 Park Avenue South, New York, N. Y.
10016.

6126-1

Library of Congress Card Number: 67-12163

PRINTED IN THE UNITED STATES OF AMERICA

E 25519

D
113/S
.D3
v.1

PREFACE

This anthology of source readings attempts to provide both a chronological and a topical approach to some of the main aspects of medieval history. The first volume, *The Eagle, the Crescent, and the Cross*, covers the period from approximately A.D. 250 to 1000; the second volume, *Western Awakening*, from approximately A.D. 1000 to 1500. The selections in each are usually arranged chronologically within large subject headings. Dates printed in roman type refer to periods, events, or laws; dates in italics refer to time of composition of the letter, chronicle, biography, treatise, or poem from which the selection has been taken. The decision to choose many fairly long selections made inevitable a number of gaps, but seemed preferable to putting together a mosaic composed entirely of small bits and pieces. The student should find here sufficient primary material on large, central themes to enable him to attempt historical judgments of his own.

No material has been drawn from certain fundamental but readily available masterpieces, best read in their entirety. They include the *Confessions of St. Augustine*, the *Consolation of Philosophy*, the *Chanson de Roland*, the *Divina Commedia*, the *Decameron*, and the *Canterbury Tales*. Despite such omissions, the compiler hopes that some impression of the energy and variety of the age is conveyed and that nothing trivial or dull has been included.

I am grateful to all the publishers and translators who have allowed me to reprint material from their books. Detailed acknowledgments are supplied in the footnotes. My own translations from St. Columban, Widukind, Otto III, Salimbene, and Brunetto Latini have profited from the kind help of Mr. Colin Hardie, Professor Graydon Regenos, and Professor William S. Woods. I wish also to thank particularly my mother, who read the manuscript and made many useful suggestions. For her help and counsel at every stage of the work, I owe a special debt of gratitude to my wife.

C.T.D.

CONTENTS

INTRODUCTION

Some framework is necessary in studying history, even if it is dictated by prejudice and reinforced by convention. This is the case with the terms *Middle Ages* and *medieval*, which imply that a *Dark Age* had intervened between two periods of high cultural and political achievement. These terms were born of the disdain of Renaissance humanists for most of the historical developments after the decline of Rome. They serve to denote, together with the adjectives *ancient* and *modern*, that tripartite division of history which long ago passed into general usage.

Of course, the process of dividing history into periods reflects only the attempt of "moderns" to understand their own past. They try to do this by classifying, according to later and largely subjective criteria, those men who went before them and who also thought of themselves as "moderns" while they were alive. This practice, however indefensible, has at least the virtue of convenience and the status of a universal custom. But if everyone uses the term *medieval*, not everyone applies it to the same stretch of time. When did the Middle Ages begin? Some historians point to the sack of Rome by the Visigoths in 410, some to the deposition of the western emperor Romulus Augustulus in 476, some to the conquest of the southern half of the Mediterranean basin by the Moslems in the seventh century, and some to various other dates. But the most convenient dividing line between the ancient and the medieval worlds is the transformation of the former's leading political institution: the Christianizing of the Roman Empire.

Rome was not, however, the only focal point of early medieval history, which may be regarded as the period from the fourth through the tenth centuries. Rather it revolved around three centers: Byzantium, Islam, and the Western Church. The highly-organized universal empire of Rome gradually yielded to a new world, indeed to three new worlds, characterized by radical and turbulent change. The Byzantine state, facing constant attacks from barbarians without and frequent upheavals from rebels within, stood often on the verge of destruction. Yet it succeeded in preserving much of the military and legal heritage of Rome and in combining it with cultural and religious legacies from Greece and Asia. Islamic expansion, so astonishingly dynamic and successful, was matched by the violence of its internal dissensions. Yet a remarkable degree of cultural and religious unity, at least in the beginning, prevailed. Only in the West, the weakest of the three power centers, was it doubtful that a true civilization could emerge. Classical culture and the Christian religion exerted diverse and often discordant influences on the by no means passive raw material of the new barbarian peoples. Heir to Caesar as well as to Christ, the Church was a supremely formative force, resisting, converting, and refining the savage tribes. It found strong allies in the barbarian kings, and under the Frankish monarch Charles the Great western Christendom achieved a remarkable consolidation, culturally permanent even if politically transitory.

The period ended much as it had begun, with Byzantium resurgent, Islamic marauding still rampant, and the West suffering new waves of invasion at the hands of the Vikings and Magyars. Only the sturdy defense of the Wessex kings and the Saxon emperors gave promise of brighter days. Their accomplishments gave at least a hint of that epochal shift in power, from the Mediterranean East to the northern West, which cleared the way for the rise of the civilization we call European.

I

EMPIRE AND CHURCH

Pagan Rome extended tolerance to a bewildering variety of alien religious cults but considered Christianity to be a threat to the state. Just as Pilate was afraid that Christ wanted to set up an earthly kingdom, so later Roman officials feared the uncompromising claims of the religion he had founded and thought that Christians were traitors to the Emperor because they recognized a higher authority. Christians were often unwilling to participate in the normal ceremonies that expressed Roman patriotism: many refused to sacrifice on public altars or to show reverence to imperial images. They formed, moreover, what was in effect a secret society with branches in the major cities of the Empire; they were suspected of harboring dark designs against the political society of which they were numerically an increasingly important part. Even though many Christians served in the army and the civil service, some were reluctant to do so, and they were very generally suspected of disloyalty and sedition. It was natural that their ideological intolerance—their assertion that Christianity was the only true religion—should be answered by the active legal intolerance of the Roman government.

Outbreaks of persecution were, however, only sporadic until the late third century. Then a systematic attempt was made to eliminate this supposed cancer of the body politic. But Christianity was too firmly rooted in the Empire to be dislodged. The conversion of the Emperor Constantine in the early fourth century marked a turning point. Roman Empire and Christian Church, hitherto enemies, became allies. Yet grave issues still remained. The Empire was compelled to try to draw strength for the dilemmas of this world from a religion mainly concerned with the next. The Church was compelled to struggle not only to achieve internal unity but also to keep from being secularized and made into an instrument of state. It is with such problems as these that the following section deals.

1. ST. CYPRIAN: *LETTER 80:* VALERIAN'S PERSECUTION (258)[1]

Before the second half of the third century A.D. persecution of Christians had been intermittent and had occurred under good emperors and bad, under, for example, both Nero, the notorious tyrant, and Marcus Aurelius, the Stoic philosopher-king. The historian Tacitus had summed up the hostility of the cultivated classes to the new movement by calling Christians "enemies of the human race." Not until 257, however, under the Emperor Valerian (reigned 253-260) did a really systematic persecution begin. Seeking a scapegoat for his defeats at the hands of the Persians, he arrested leading Christian churchmen and forbade their religious services and access to their cemeteries under pain of death. He was not so much interested in forcing them to renounce their religion as in compelling them to participate in the rites of the state. For their resistance to his orders Xystus, the Bishop of Rome, his deacons, and many clerics and laymen were executed. It is clear, however, that Christians were punished more for their alleged disloyalty to the state than for their adherence to a religious cult.

St. Cyprian, Bishop of Carthage, who later died in this same persecution, won fame not only for his martyrdom but also for his theological and pastoral writings, his exaltation of the office of bishop, and his uncompromising attitude to those who had abjured their faith during a previous persecution under the Emperor Decius in 249-250. Against the opinion of Stephen, Bishop of Rome, Cyprian held that rebaptism was necessary before they could be received again into the Church. His account of the new persecution under Valerian reflects his indomitable spirit.

The reason why I did not write to you immediately, dearest brother, was that the whole body of the clergy were detained by the stress of the conflict, and could not depart thence at all, being prepared by the devotion of their

[1] St. Cyprian, *Letter 80*, trans. by D. C. Munro and E. Bramhall, *Translations and Reprints from the original Sources of European History*, Series I, Vol. IV, No. 1 (Philadelphia, University of Pennsylvania Press, 1898), pp. 22-23.

spirits for everlasting and heavenly glory. Be it known to you that those have returned whom I had sent to the City to discover and report to us as to the nature of the truth of the rescript concerning us. For many, various and uncertain were the rumors circulated. But the truth of the matter is this: Valerian had sent a rescript to the senate, that bishops, presbyters and deacons should be punished immediately, but that senators, nobles, and Roman knights should be degraded from their dignity, and furthermore despoiled of their goods, and if, after they had been deprived of their property, they should persist in being Christians, they too should be beheaded. Matrons should be deprived of their goods and sent into exile. Those of Caesar's household, whoever had confessed formerly or should confess now, should have their property confiscated and should be sent in chains by assignment to Caesar's estates. To his discourse, moreover, the Emperor Valerian added a copy of the letter which he sent to the governors of the provinces concerning us. This letter we hope daily will arrive, prepared according to the strength of the faith, ready to endure martyrdom, and expecting by the might and grace of God the crown of eternal life. Be it known to you, moreover, that Xistus was executed in the cemetery on the eighth before the Ides of August, and together with him four deacons. Indeed, the prefects in the city insist daily on this persecution. If any are brought before them, they are punished and their goods confiscated to the treasury.

I beg that this may be made known through you to the rest of our associates, so that everywhere by their encouragement the brotherhood may be strengthened and prepared for the spiritual conflict, that each of us may not think more of death than of immortality, and that, consecrated to the Lord, in full faith and all virtue, they may rejoice rather than fear in this confession in which they know that, as soldiers of God and Christ, they will not be destroyed but be crowned. I hope that you, dearest brother, will ever be strong in the Lord.

2.   ST. CYPRIAN'S MARTYRDOM (258)[1]

This account of the martyrdom of St. Cyprian furnishes a moving testimony to the courage of the persecuted. It also gives interesting evidence of the hesitations and waverings of the persecutors. Despite his defiance, St. Cyprian was at first only driven into exile. Before his final condemnation, he was entertained hospitably by a high public official. He was given every chance to reconsider his

[1] *Acta Proconsularia Cypriani,* trans. by D. C. Munro and E. Bramhall, *op. cit.,* Series I, Vol. IV, No. 1, pp. 23-26.

attitude and to perform the patriotic gesture of sacrificing on the public altars. His stubborn refusal ultimately led to his execution. The embarrassment of the governmental functionaries and the open desire of the Bishop for a martyr's crown should be noted. It was no wonder that many pagans thought of the Christians as men in love with death. Heroes like Cyprian are a minority in any movement, but there were enough Christians with a similar attitude in the third century to made the failure of the governmental policy of repression inevitable.

In the fourth consulship of the Emperor Valerian and the third of Gallienus, on the third before the Kalends of September, in the council chamber of Carthage, Paternus, the proconsul, said to Bishop Cyprian: "The most sacred Emperors, Valerian and Gallienus, have thought fit to give me a letter according to which they have ordered that those, who do not practice the Roman religion, should recognize the Roman rites. I have asked, therefore, concerning your name; what do you answer me?" Bishop Cyprian said: "I am a Christian and a bishop. I have known no other gods except the true and only God, who made heaven and earth, the sea, and all that in them is. To this God we Christians yield ourselves; to Him we pray by day and night for you, for all men, and for the safety of the Emperors themselves." Paternus, the proconsul said: "Do you, then, persist in this purpose?" Bishop Cyprian replied: "A good purpose, which has known God, cannot be changed." Paternus, the proconsul, said: "Will you be able to depart into exile, then, to the city of Curubitana (Curubis) according to the decree of Valerian and Gallienus?" Bishop Cyprian said: "I depart." Paternus, the proconsul, said: "They have thought fit to write to me concerning not only bishops, but also presbyters. I wish, therefore, to learn from you who the presbyters are who abide in the city." Bishop Cyprian replied: "By your laws you have rightly and profitably decreed that there should be no informers; and hence they cannot be betrayed and denounced by me. But in their own cities they will be found." Paternus, the proconsul, said: "To-day, in this place, I am going to seek them." Cyprian said: "Since custom forbids that any one offer himself voluntarily, and this is displeasing to your judgment, they cannot give themselves up; but, if you seek them, you shall find them." Paternus, the proconsul, said: "They will be found by me;" and added: "It has also been ordered that they should not hold assemblies in any place nor enter the cemeteries. If any one does not observe this so wholesome ordinance he is to be beheaded." Bishop Cyprian replied: "Do as you are ordered."

Then Paternus, the proconsul, ordered the blessed bishop Cyprian to be led into exile. When he had remained there for a long time, the proconsul Galerius Maximus succeeded the proconsul Aspasius Paternus and ordered the holy bishop Cyprian to be recalled from exile and brought before him. When the holy martyr Cyprian, chosen by God, had returned from the city of Curubitana, where he had been sent into exile by the order of Aspasius Paternus, proconsul at that time, he remained in his gardens according to holy injunction, and thence daily hoped that it would happen to him as had been revealed. While he was waiting here, there suddenly came to him, on the Ides of September in the consulship of Tuscus and Bassus, two men of high rank, one the curator of the official Galerius Maximus, the proconsul, who had succeeded Aspasius Paternus, and the other the groom from the guards of this same official. And they put him between them, and brought him to Sexti, where Galerius Maximus, the proconsul, had retired for the sake of recovering his health. And so the proconsul Galerius Maximus ordered Cyprian to be reserved for him until the next day. And at the same time, the blessed Cyprian retired, led away to the chief and curator of this same official, Galerius Maximus, the proconsul, a most illustrious man; and he stayed with this man, enjoying his hospitality in the village, called Saturni, which is between Venerea and Salutaria. Thither the whole company of brethren came; and, when the holy Cyprian learned this, he ordered the maidens to be protected, since all had remained in the village before the gate of the hospitable officer.

And thus on the next day, the eighteenth before the Kalends of October, early in the morning, a great crowd came to Sexti according to the order of Galerius Maximus, the proconsul. And accordingly Galerius Maximus, the proconsul, ordered Cyprian to be brought before him that day, while he was sitting in the Sauciolian court. And when he had been brought, Galerius Maximus, the proconsul, said to Bishop Cyprian: "You are Thascius Cyprian?" Bishop Cyprian replied: "I am." Galerius Maximus, the proconsul said: "The most sacred Emperors have commanded you to sacrifice." Bishop Cyprian said: "I will not." Galerius Maximus said: "Reflect on it." Bishop Cyprian replied: "Do what you are ordered to do. In such a just case there is no need of reflection."

Galerius Maximus, having spoken with the council, pronounced the sentence weakly and reluctantly in the following words: "For a long time you have lived in sacrilege, you have gathered about you many associates in your impious conspiracy, you have put yourself in hostility to the Roman gods and to the sacred rites, nor could the pious and most sacred princes, Valerian and Gallienus, Emperors, and Valerian, the most noble Caesar, bring you back to the practice of their worship. And therefore, since you are found to be the author of the vilest crimes, and the standard bearer, you shall be a warning to those whom you have gathered about you in your crime; by your blood, discipline shall be established." And having said this he read out the decree from his tablet: "We command that Thascius Cyprian be executed by the sword." Bishop Cyprian said: "Thank God."

After this sentence the crowd of brethren kept saying: "And we will be beheaded with him." On account of this a commotion arose among the brethren and a great crowd followed him. And thus Cyprian was brought in to the country near Sexti; here he laid aside his red cloak, kneeled on the ground, and prostrated himself before the Lord in prayer. And when he had laid aside his priestly robe and given it to the deacons, he stood in his linen under-garments and waited for the executioner. Moreover, when the executioner had come, he ordered his followers to give this executioner twenty-five pieces of gold. Indeed, linen cloths and handkerchiefs were being set before him by the brethren. After this the blessed Cyprian covered his eyes with his hand. When he could not bind the handkerchiefs to himself, Julian, the presbyter, and Julian, the subdeacon, bound them. Thus the blessed Cyprian died, and his body was placed near at hand on account of the curiosity of the heathen. Hence, being borne away in the night with tapers and torches, it was brought with prayers and great triumph to the courts of the procurator Macrobius Candidianus, which are on the Via Mappaliensis, near the fish ponds. Moreover, after a few days, Galerius Maximus, the proconsul, died.

The blessed martyr Cyprian suffered on the eighteenth before the Kalends of October[2] under the Emperors Valerian and Gallienus, Jesus Christ, the true God, reigning, to whom be honor and glory for ever and ever.   Amen.

3.   LACTANTIUS: BEGINNING OF THE GREAT PERSECUTION (302-303)[1]

According to Lactantius (*c.* 240-*c.* 320), a Christian apologist who certainly cannot be accused of tenderness towards the persecutors of his faith, it was not the great Diocletian (reigned 284-313) but his co-emperor Galerius (reigned 293-311) who was the real instigator of the final large-scale persecution of the Christians. Under Diocletian Christians had begun to enter the army and the civil service in increasing numbers; they were not generally compelled to participate in the sacrificial ceremonies connected with the cult of patriotism though Galerius forced his Christian officers to do so. Comprising some ten percent of the population of the Empire, the Christians were already a powerful and well-organized minority. Political realism would have suggested toleration, but Galerius was an extremist. The persecution that he set in motion was an anachronism, and common sense, as well as a growing conviction of the truth of the Christian religion, seems to have persuaded the new emperor Constantine to end it.

The mother of Galerius, an exceedingly superstitious woman, was a votary of the gods of the mountains. Being of such a character, she made sacri-

2 September 26, 258.

1 Lactantius, *On the Deaths of the Persecutors,* from *A New Eusebius,* ed. by J. Stevenson (London, S.P.C.K., 1957), pp. 285-286.

fices with sacred banquets almost every day, and she feasted her servants on the meat offered to idols; but the Christians would not partake, and while she feasted with the Gentiles, they continued in fasting and prayer. On this account she conceived hatred against the Christians, and by woman-like complaints instigated her son, no less superstitious than herself, to destroy them. So during the whole winter Diocletian and Galerius took counsel together; no one else was admitted, and it was the universal opinion that their conferences concerned the most momentous affairs of the empire. The old man long opposed the fury of Galerius, and showed how pernicious it would be to raise disturbances throughout the world and to shed so much blood; that the Christians were wont to meet death with eagerness; and that it would be enough if officials at the court and the armed forces were forbidden to practise Christianity. Yet he could not restrain the madness of that headstrong man. He resolved, therefore, to take the opinion of his friends. Now this was a trait in the evil disposition of Diocletian that whenever he determined to do good, he did it without advice, that the praise might be all his own; but whenever he determined to do ill, which he was sensible would be blamed, he called in many advisers that his own fault might be imputed to other men. A few civil magistrates therefore and a few military commanders were admitted to give their counsel; and the question was put to them according to priority of rank. Some, through personal ill-will towards the Christians, were of opinion that they ought to be destroyed as enemies of the gods and adversaries of the state religion. Others thought differently; but, having understood the will of Galerius, they, either from dread of displeasing him or from a desire of gratifying him, concurred in the opinion given against the Christians. Yet not even then could the Emperor be prevailed upon to yield his assent. He determined that the best plan was to consult his gods, and to that end he despatched a soothsayer to inquire of Apollo of Miletus, whose answer was such as might be expected from an enemy of the divine religion. So Diocletian was drawn over from his purpose. And although he could struggle no longer against his friends and against his Caesar (i.e., Galerius) and Apollo, yet still he attempted to observe such moderation as to command the business to be carried through without bloodshed; whereas Galerius would have had all persons burnt alive who refused to sacrifice.

A fit and auspicious day was sought for the accomplishment of this undertaking, and the festival of the god Terminus, celebrated on the twenty-third of February, was chosen, in preference to all others, to "terminate," as it were, the Christian religion.

> That day, the harbinger of death, arose,
> First cause of ill, and long-enduring woes,

which befell not only the Christians, but the whole earth. When that day dawned, in the eighth consulship of Diocletian and seventh of Maximian, suddenly, while it was yet hardly light, the prefect, together with chief com-

manders, tribunes and officers of the treasury, came to the church in Nicome-
dia; they forced the doors and searched everywhere for an image of the god.
The Holy Scriptures were found and burnt; the church was abandoned to
general pillage: all was rapine, confusion, tumult. That church, situated on
rising ground, was within view of the palace, and Diocletian and Galerius
stood on a watch-tower, disputing long whether it ought to be set on fire. The
sentiment of Diocletian prevailed, who was afraid that once so great a blaze
had started, some part of the city might be burnt; for there were many large
buildings round the church. Then Praetorian Guards came in battle array,
with axes and other tools; they were let loose everywhere, and in a few hours,
levelled that very lofty edifice with the ground.

Next day an edict was published, depriving the Christians of all honours
and dignities; ordaining also that, without any distinction of rank or degree,
they should be subject to torture, and that every suit at law should be received
against them; while, on the other hand, they were debarred from being plain-
tiffs in questions of wrong, adultery, or theft; and, finally, that they should
neither be capable of freedom, nor have right of suffrage.

4.   CONFISCATION OF BOOKS AT CIRTA (303)[1]

Most episodes of the Great Persecution were probably quite prosaic, involving
no great brutality on the part of government officials and no great courage on the
part of their victims. Preserved in the *Gesta apud Zenophilum,* this official record
of the inquisition at Cirta (the modern Constantine in Algeria) indicates the
reluctance of many Christians either to yield up their Scriptures or to face torture
and death. Often the second reluctance proved stronger than the first, as in this
case. It was natural that those who were willing to suffer should regard such
weaker brethren with contempt, but it was also imperative, after Constantine's
accession, that the Church should allow them to receive absolution without exaggerated penance or delay. Those rigorists who wished to exclude them, like the
Donatists, usually became schismatics and heretics and ended by excluding
themselves.

In the eighth and seventh consulships of Diocletian and Maximian, 19th
May, from the records of Munatius Felix, high priest of the province for life,
mayor of the colony of Cirta. Arrived at the house where the Christians used

[1] A. H. M. Jones, *Constantine and the Conversion of Europe* (London, **English**
Universities Press Ltd., 1948), pp. 51-54.

to meet, the Mayor said to Paul the bishop: "Bring out the writings of the law and anything else you have here, according to the order, so that you may obey the command."

The Bishop: "The readers have the scriptures, but we will give what we have here."

The Mayor: "Point out the readers or send for them."

The Bishop: "You all know them."

The Mayor: "We do not know them."

The Bishop: "The municipal office knows them, that is, the clerks Edusius and Junius."

The Mayor: "Leaving over the matter of the readers, whom the office will point out, produce what you have."

Then follows an inventory of the church plate and other property, including large stores of male and female clothes and shoes, produced in the presence of the clergy, who include three priests, two deacons, and four subdeacons, all named, and a number of "diggers."

The Mayor: "Bring out what you have."

Silvanus and Carosus (two of the subdeacons): "We have thrown out everything that was here."

The Mayor: "Your answer is entered on the record."

After some empty cupboards had been found in the library, Silvanus then produced a silver box and a silver lamp, which he said he had found behind a barrel.

Victor (the mayor's clerk): "You would have been a dead man if you hadn't found them."

The Mayor: "Look more carefully, in case there is anything left here."

Silvanus: "There is nothing left. We have thrown everything out."

And when the dining-room was opened, there were found there four bins and six barrels.

The Mayor: "Bring out the scriptures that you have so that we can obey the orders and command of the emperors."

Catullinus (another subdeacon) produced one very large volume.

The Mayor: "Why have you given one volume only? Produce the scriptures that you have."

Marcuclius and Catullinus (two subdeacons): "We haven't any more, because we are subdeacons; the readers have the books."

The Mayor: "Show me the readers."

Marcuclius and Catullinus: "We don't know where they live."

The Mayor: "If you don't know where they live, tell me their names."

Marcuclius and Catullinus: "We are not traitors: here we are, order us to be killed."

The Mayor: "Put them under arrest."

They apparently weakened so far as to reveal one reader, for the Mayor now moved on to the house of Eugenius, who produced four books.

The Mayor now turned on the other two subdeacons, Silvanus and Carosus:

The Mayor: "Show me the other readers."

Silvanus and Carosus: "The bishop has already said that Edusius and
Junius the clerks know them all: they will show you the way to their houses."

Edusius and Junius: "We will show them, sir."

The Mayor went on to visit the six remaining readers. Four produced
their books without demur. One declared he had none, and the Mayor was
content with entering his statement on the record. The last was out, but his
wife produced his books; the Mayor had the house searched by the public
slave to make sure that none had been overlooked. This task over, he addressed
the subdeacons: "If there has been any omission, the responsibility is yours."

5. EUSEBIUS OF CAESAREA: ON CONSTANTINE THE GREAT[1]

With the rescript of Milan, issued in 313 by Constantine (reigned 306-337)
and by his imperial colleague Licinius, Christianity received the legal privileges
of a recognized religious cult. Even before his victory in 312 over the usurper
Maxentius at the Battle of the Milvian Bridge, Constantine had followed Constantius, his father, in a policy of toleration for Christians. No such vision as that
recounted by Eusebius in his *Life of Constantine* would have been necessary to
make the Emperor issue his famous rescript. According to Eusebius, Constantine
himself told of his vision of a cross in the sky with the inscription, *Conquer by
This*. No other contemporary writer confirms the Eusebian story. Lactantius, however, writes of a dream which directed Constantine, before the Battle of the Milvian Bridge, to mark "the heavenly sign of Christ" on his soldiers' shields, and in
310 a pagan orator spoke of Apollo the sun god's appearance to Constantine.
Perhaps in the beginning Constantine thought of Christ only as an especially
potent manifestation of the Unconquered Sun, long an object of imperial veneration, and as the saviour of his army in the surprising victory over Maxentius. It is
significant in this connection that for many years after 312 various pagan gods
continued to be honored on imperial coins, a representation of the Unconquered
Sun, traditional companion of emperors, appearing as late as 323. But it must be
remembered that the vast majority of Constantine's subjects were still pagans, and
ancient modes of expressing patriotism could not wisely be abandoned at once.

[1] Eusebius, *Life of Constantine* and *Tricennial Oration*, trans. by E. C. Richardson,
A Select Library of Nicene and Post-Nicene Fathers of the Christian Church, Series II,
ed. by P. Schaff and H. Wace (reprinted Grand Rapids, Mich., Wm. B. Eerdmans
Publishing Company, 1952), I, 482-483, 489-491, 584, 585-586.

All this evidence might give some support to the old view that Constantine was not a sincere Christian. It is difficult to account for his ecclesiastical legislation, however, in any other way. He did not extend mere toleration to the Christians but also subsidies and special privileges; he presided over the First Ecumenical Council of Nicaea; he was formally baptized before his death. Considering the prevalence of visions in the fourth century and Constantine's own emotional nature, we have no real reason to doubt the truth of Eusebius' account.

Eusebius became bishop of Caesarea *c.* 315 and died *c.* 340. He was an intimate friend of the Emperor Constantine and played a leading, though moderate, part in the First Ecumenical Council of Nicaea in 325. His most famous work is the *Ecclesiastical History*, which relates the vicissitudes of the Church from the time of Christ to 324. Selections from his *Life of Constantine* and from his *Oration* celebrating the thirtieth anniversary of the Emperor's accession are given below.

FROM *LIFE OF CONSTANTINE* (c. 337)

Mankind, devising some consolation for the frail and precarious duration of human life, have thought by the erection of monuments to glorify the memories of their ancestors with immortal honors. Some have employed the vivid delineations and colors of painting; some have carved statues from lifeless blocks of wood; while others, by engraving their inscriptions deep on tablets and monuments, have thought to transmit the virtues of those whom they honored to perpetual remembrance. All these indeed are perishable, and consumed by the lapse of time, being representations of the corruptible body, and not expressing the image of the immortal soul. And yet these seemed sufficient to those who had no well-grounded hope of happiness after the termination of this mortal life. But God, that God, I say, who is the common Saviour of all, having treasured up with himself, for those who love godliness, greater blessings than human thought has conceived, gives the earnest and first-fruits of future rewards even here, assuring in some sort immortal hopes to mortal eyes. The ancient oracles of the prophets, delivered to us in the Scripture, declare this; the lives of pious men, who shone in old time with every virtue, bear witness to posterity of the same; and our own days prove it to be true, wherein CONSTANTINE, who alone of all that ever wielded the Roman power was the friend of God the Sovereign of all, has appeared to all mankind so clear an example of a godly life.

And God himself, whom Constantine worshiped, has confirmed this truth by the clearest manifestations of his will, being present to aid him at the commencement, during the course, and at the end of his reign, and holding him up to the human race as an instructive example of godliness. Accordingly, by the manifold blessings he has conferred on him, he has distinguished him alone of all the sovereigns of whom we have ever heard as at once a mighty luminary and most clear-voiced herald of genuine piety.

With respect to the duration of his reign, God honored him with three complete periods of ten years, and something more, extending the whole term of his mortal life to twice this number of years. And being pleased to make him a representative of his own sovereign power, he displayed him as the conqueror of the whole race of tyrants, and the destroyer of those God-defying giants of the earth who madly raised their impious arms against him, the supreme King of all. They appeared, so to speak, for an instant, and then disappeared: while the one and only true God, when he had enabled his servant, clad in heavenly panoply, to stand singly against many foes, and by his means had relieved mankind from the multitude of the ungodly, constituted him a teacher of his worship to all nations, to testify with a loud voice in the hearing of all that he acknowledged the true God, and turned with abhorrence from the error of them that are no gods.

Thus, like a faithful and good servant, did he act and testify, openly declaring and confessing himself the obedient minister of the supreme King. And God forthwith rewarded him, by making him ruler and sovereign, and victorious to such a degree that he alone of all rulers pursued a continual course of conquest, unsubdued and invincible, and through his trophies a greater ruler than tradition records ever to have been before. So dear was he to God, and so blessed; so pious and so fortunate in all that he undertook, that with the greatest facility he obtained the authority over more nations than any who had preceded him, and yet retained his power, undisturbed, to the very close of his life.

.   .   .   .   .

While, therefore, he regarded the entire world as one immense body, and perceived that the head of it all, the royal city of the Roman empire, was bowed down by the weight of a tyrannous oppression,[2] at first he had left the task of liberation to those who governed the other divisions of the empire, as being his superiors in point of age. But when none of these proved able to afford relief, and those who had attempted it had experienced a disastrous termination of their enterprise,[3] he said that life was without enjoyment to him as long as he saw the imperial city thus afflicted, and prepared himself for the overthrowal of the tyranny.

Being convinced, however, that he needed some more powerful aid than his military forces could afford him, on account of the wicked and magical enchantments which were so diligently practiced by the tyrant, he sought Divine assistance, deeming the possession of arms and a numerous soldiery

---

[2] Maxentius, son of the retired emperor Maximianus, seized Rome in 306.
[3] Valerius Severus was killed by Maxentius, and Galerius was driven out of Italy.

of secondary importance, but believing the co-operating power of Deity invincible and not to be shaken. He considered therefore, on what God he might rely for protection and assistance. While engaged in this enquiry, the thought occurred to him, that, of the many emperors who had preceded him, those who had rested their hopes in a multitude of gods, and served them with sacrifices and offerings, had in the first place been deceived by flattering predictions, and oracles which promised them all prosperity, and at last had met with an unhappy end, while not one of their gods had stood by to warn them of the impending wrath of heaven; while one alone who had pursued an entirely opposite course, who had condemned their error, and honored the one Supreme God during his whole life, had found him to be the Saviour and Protector of his empire, and the Giver of every good thing. Reflecting on this, and well weighing the fact that they who had trusted in many gods had also fallen by manifold forms of death, without leaving behind them either family or offspring, stock, name, or memorial among men: while the God of his father had given to him, on the other hand, manifestations of his power and very many tokens: and considering farther that those who had already taken arms against the tyrant, and had marched to the battle-field under the protection of a multitude of gods, had met with a dishonorable end (for one[4] of them had shamefully retreated from the contest without a blow, and the other,[5] being slain in the midst of his own troops, became, as it were, the mere sport of death; reviewing, I say, all these considerations, he judged it to be folly indeed to join in the idle worship of those who were no gods, and, after such convincing evidence, to err from the truth; and therefore felt it incumbent on him to honor his father's God alone.

Accordingly he called on him with earnest prayer and supplications that he would reveal to him who he was, and stretch forth his right hand to help him in his present difficulties. And while he was thus praying with fervent entreaty, a most marvelous sign appeared to him from heaven, the account of which it might have been hard to believe had it been related by any other person. But since the victorious emperor himself long afterwards declared it to the writer of this history, when he was honored with his acquaintance and society, and confirmed his statement by an oath, who could hesitate to accredit the relation, especially since the testimony of after-time has established its truth? He said that about noon, when the day was already beginning to decline, he saw with his own eyes the trophy of a cross of light in the heavens, above the sun, and bearing the inscription, Conquer by this. At this sight he himself was struck with amazement, and his whole army also, which followed him on this expedition, and witnessed the miracle.[6]

[4] Galerius.

[5] Valerius Severus.

[6] Another account of this vision is given by Lactantius (*On the Deaths of the Persecutors,* 44), who says that it occurred in a dream.

He said, moreover, that he doubted within himself what the import of this apparition could be. And while he continued to ponder and reason on its meaning, night suddenly came on; then in his sleep the Christ of God appeared to him with the same sign which he had seen in the heavens, and commanded him to make a likeness of that sign which he had seen in the heavens, and to use it as a safeguard in all engagements with his enemies.

At dawn of day he arose, and communicated the marvel to his friends: and then, calling together the workers in gold and precious stones, he sat in the midst of them, and described to them the figure of the sign he had seen, bidding them represent it in gold and precious stones. And this representation I myself have had an opportunity of seeing.

Now it was made in the following manner. A long spear, overlaid with gold, formed the figure of the cross by means of a transverse bar laid over it. On the top of the whole was fixed a wreath of gold and precious stones; and within this, the symbol of the Saviour's name, two letters indicating the name of Christ by means of its initial characters, the letter P[7] being intersected by X[8] in its centre: and these letters the emperor was in the habit of wearing on his helmet at a later period. From the cross-bar of the spear was suspended a cloth, a royal piece, covered with a profuse embroidery of most brilliant precious stones; and which, being also richly interlaced with gold, presented an indescribable degree of beauty to the beholder. This banner was of a square form, and the upright staff, whose lower section was of great length, bore a golden half-length portrait of the pious emperor and his children on its upper part, beneath the trophy of the cross, and immediately above the embroidered banner.

The emperor constantly made use of this sign of salvation as a safeguard against every adverse and hostile power, and commanded that others similar to it should be carried at the head of all his armies.

These things were done shortly afterwards. But at the time above specified, being struck with amazement at the extraordinary vision, and resolving to worship no other God save Him who had appeared to him, he sent for those who were acquainted with the mysteries of His doctrines, and enquired who that God was, and what was intended by the sign of the vision he had seen.

They affirmed that He was God, the only begotten Son of the one and only God: that the sign which had appeared was the symbol of immortality, and the trophy of that victory over death which He had gained in time past when sojourning on earth. They taught him also the causes of His advent, and explained to him the true account of His incarnation. Thus he was instructed in these matters, and was impressed with wonder at the divine manifestation which had been presented to his sight. Comparing, therefore, the heavenly vision with the interpretation given, he found his judgment con-

[7] The Greek letter Rho.
[8] The Greek letter Chi.

firmed; and, in the persuasion that the knowledge of these things had been imparted to him by Divine teaching, he determined thenceforth to devote himself to the reading of the Inspired writings.

Moreover, he made the priests of God his counselors, and deemed it incumbent on him to honor the God who had appeared to him with all devotion. And after this, being fortified by well-grounded hopes in Him, he hastened to quench the threatening fire of tyranny.

FROM *TRICENNIAL ORATION* (335)

. . . And thus our emperor, like the radiant sun, illuminates the most distant subjects of his empire through the presence of the Caesars, as with the far piercing rays of his own brightness. To us who occupy the eastern regions he has given a son worthy of himself; a second and a third respectively to other departments of his empire, to be, as it were, brilliant reflectors of the light which proceeds from himself. Once more, having harnessed, as it were, under the self-same yoke the four most noble Caesars as horses in the imperial chariot, he sits on high and directs their course by the reins of holy harmony and concord; and, himself every where present, and observant of every event, thus traverses every region of the world. Lastly, invested as he is with a semblance of heavenly sovereignty, he directs his gaze above, and frames his earthly government according to the pattern of that Divine original, feeling strength in its conformity to the monarchy of God. And this conformity is granted by the universal Sovereign to man alone of the creatures of this earth: for he only is the author of sovereign power, who decrees that all should be subject to the rule of one. And surely monarchy far transcends every other constitution and form of government: for that democratic equality of power, which is its opposite, may rather be described as anarchy and disorder. Hence there is one God, and not two, or three, or more: for to assert a plurality of gods is plainly to deny the being of God at all. There is one Sovereign; and his Word and royal Law is one: a Law not expressed in syllables and words, not written or engraved on tablets, and therefore subject to the ravages of time; but the living and self-subsisting Word, who himself is God, and who administers his Father's kingdom on behalf of all who are after him and subject to his power.

. . . . .

And by an indescribable power he filled the world in every part with his doctrine, expressing by the similitude of an earthly kingdom that heavenly one to which he earnestly invites all mankind, and presents it to them as a worthy object of their hope.

And in this hope our divinely-favored emperor partakes even in this present life, gifted as he is by God with native virtues, and having received into his soul the out-flowings of his favor. His reason he derives from the great Source of all reason: he is wise, and good, and just, as having fellowship with perfect Wisdom, Goodness, and Righteousness: virtuous, as following the pattern of perfect virtue: valiant, as partaking of heavenly strength. And truly may he deserve the imperial title, who has formed his soul to royal virtues, according to the standard of that celestial kingdom. But he who is a stranger to these blessings, who denies the Sovereign of the universe, and owns no allegiance to the heavenly Father of spirits; who invests not himself with the virtues which become an emperor, but overlays his soul with moral deformity and baseness; who for royal clemency substitutes the fury of a savage beast; for a generous temper, the incurable venom of malicious wickedness; for prudence, folly; for reason and wisdom, that recklessness which is the most odious of all vices, for from it, as from a spring of bitterness, proceed the most pernicious fruits; such as inveterate profligacy of life, covetousness, murder, impiety and defiance of God; surely one abandoned to such vices as these, however he may be deemed powerful through despotic violence, has no true title to the name of Emperor. For how should he whose soul is impressed with a thousand absurd images of false deities, be able to exhibit a counterpart of the true and heavenly sovereignty? Or how can he be absolute lord of others, who has subjected himself to the dominion of a thousand cruel masters? a slave of low delights and ungoverned lust, a slave of wrongfully-extorted wealth, of rage and passion, as well as of cowardice and terror; a slave of ruthless demons, and soul-destroying spirits? Let, then, our emperor, on the testimony of truth itself, be declared alone worthy of the title; who is dear to the Supreme Sovereign himself; who alone is free, nay, who is truly lord: above the thirst of wealth, superior to sexual desire; victorious even over natural pleasures; controlling, not controlled by, anger and passion. He is indeed an emperor, and bears a title corresponding to his deeds; a VICTOR in truth, who has gained the victory over those passions which overmaster the rest of men: whose character is formed after the Divine original of the Supreme Sovereign, and whose mind reflects, as in a mirror, the radiance of his virtues. Hence is our emperor perfect in discretion, in goodness, in justice, in courage, in piety, in devotion to God: he truly and only is a philosopher, since he knows himself, and is fully aware that supplies of every blessing are showered on him from a source quite external to himself, even from heaven itself. Declaring the august title of supreme authority by the splendor of his vesture, he alone worthily wears that imperial purple which so well becomes him. He is indeed an emperor, who calls on and implores in prayer the favor of his heavenly Father night and day, and whose ardent desires are fixed on his celestial kingdom.

6. CONSTANTINE: LAWS CONCERNING CLERICS (313-329)[1]

Although Constantine did not persecute pagans, refuse the title of Pontifex Maximus, or delete pagan symbolism from his coinage immediately after his conversion, his favoring of the Christian religion is clearly revealed by his legislation, both in the Theodosian Code and in the documents preserved by Eusebius. Constantine did not, however, desire that Christianity should be used as a wholesale excuse for flight from the heavy financial burdens of public service, as the third edict reprinted below shows.

EMPEROR CONSTANTINE AUGUSTUS.

We have learned that clerics of the Catholic Church are being so harassed by a faction of heretics that they are being burdened by nominations[2] and by service as tax receivers, as public custom demands, contrary to the privileges granted them. It is Our pleasure, therefore, that if Your Gravity should find any person thus harassed, another person shall be chosen as a substitute for him and that henceforward men of the aforesaid religion shall be protected from such outrages.

Given on the day before the kalends of November in the year of the third consulship of Constantine Augustus and of Licinius Caesar.—October 31, 313 (?).

THE SAME AUGUSTUS TO OCTAVIANUS, GOVERNOR OF LUCANIA
AND OF BRUTTIUM.

Those persons who devote the services of religion to divine worship, that is, those who are called clerics, shall be exempt from all compulsory public services whatever, lest, through the sacrilegious malice of certain persons, they should be called away from divine services.

Given on the twelfth day before the kalends of November in the year of the fifth consulship of Constantine Augustus and the consulship of Licinius Caesar.—October 21, 319; 313.

[1] *The Theodosian Code and Novels,* Book XVI, Title 2, ed. and trans. by C. Pharr, pp. 440-441. Reprinted by permission of the Princeton University Press. Copyright 1952 by Princeton University Press.
[2] To office.

THE SAME AUGUSTUS TO ABLAVIUS, PRAETORIAN F   ECT.

Exemption from compulsory public services shall not be   anted by popular consent, nor shall it be granted indiscriminately to all who petition under the pretext of being clerics, nor shall great numbers be added to the clergy rashly and beyond measure, but rather, when a cleric dies, another shall be selected to replace the deceased, one who has no kinship with a decurion family and who has not the wealth of resources whereby he may very easily support the compulsory public services. Thus, if there should be a dispute about the name of any person between a municipality and the clergy, if equity claims him for public service and if he is adjudged suitable for membership in the municipal council through either lineage or wealth, he   ll be removed from the clergy and shall be delivered to the municipality. For the wealthy must assume secular obligations, and the poor must be supported by the wealth of the churches.

Posted on the kalends of June in the year of the seventh consulship of Constantine Augustus and the consulship of Constantius Caesar.—June 1, 326; 329.

7.   FIRST COUNCIL OF NICAEA[1]

Constantine defeated his colleague and rival Licinius in 324 and extended his authority over the East; in the same year he began to transform Byzantium into the new capital of Constantinople. Having imposed political unity by force, he next tried to achieve religious concord by persuasion. For this purpose he summoned Christian bishops for the first ecumenical council. Though most of them came from Greek-speaking provinces of the Empire, there were some from the West, and even a few from lands outside the Empire. The main problem before them was the settlement of the Arian controversy. Arius (c. 256-c. 336), a priest of Alexandria, had propagated the doctrine that the Son was subordinate to the Father. Constantine's aim was peace, and he was relatively uninterested in theology. Therefore, when Eusebius of Caesarea, a moderate sympathizer with the Arian position, proposed the unimpeachably orthodox though rather neutral creed of his church, it was favorably received. But the majority of the bishops wanted a formula which would specifically exclude Arianism. Constantine, therefore, probably at the instigation of Hosius, Bishop of Cordova, proposed the controversial word *homoousios,* which declared Christ to be of one substance with the Father. Most of the council accepted this imperial intervention, although Eusebius' reservations are apparent in the letter he wrote to his congregation, attempting to

[1] *A New Eusebius,* ed. by J. Stevenson (London, S.P.C.K., 1957), pp. 358-367.

justify his actions at Nicaea. The letter is reprinted below. If Constantine thought his solution would be sufficient to end the strife of rival theologians, he was mistaken.

The council enacted important canons deciding a wide variety of disciplinary and organizational matters. They, also, are given below.

EUSEBIUS OF CAESAREA: LETTER TO HIS CHURCH CONCERNING THE CREED (325)

What was transacted concerning the faith of the Church at the Great Council assembled at Nicaea, you have probably learned, Beloved, from other sources, rumour being wont to precede the accurate account of what is doing. But lest in such reports the circumstances of the case have been misrepresented, we have been obliged to transmit to you, first, the formula of faith presented by ourselves; and next, the second, which they have published with additions to our words. Our own formulary, then, which was read in the presence of our most pious Emperor, and declared to be good and unexceptionable:—

As we have received from the Bishops who preceded us, and in our first catechizings, and when we received baptism, and as we have learned from the divine Scriptures, and as we constantly believed and taught as presbyter and bishop, so believing also at the time present, we report to you our faith, and it is this:—

"We believe in One God, Father Almighty, the Maker of all things visible and invisible. And in One Lord Jesus Christ, the Word of God, God from God, Light from Light, Life from Life, Only-begotten Son, first-born of all creation, before all the ages begotten from the Father, by Whom also all things were made; Who for our salvation was incarnate, and lived among men, and suffered, and rose again the third day, and ascended to the Father, and will come again in glory to judge living and dead. And we believe also in One Holy Spirit":

Believing each of these to be and to exist, the Father truly Father, and the Son truly Son, and the Holy Spirit truly Holy Spirit, as also our Lord, sending forth His disciples for the preaching, said, *Go, teach all nations, baptizing them in the Name of the Father and of the Son and of the Holy Spirit.* Concerning whom we confidently affirm that so we hold, and so we think, and so we have held aforetime, and we maintain this faith unto the death, anathematizing every godless heresy. That this we have ever thought from our heart and soul, from the time we recollect ourselves, and now think and say in truth, before God Almighty and our Lord Jesus Christ do we witness, being able by proofs to show and to convince you that, in times past also, we constantly believed and preached thus.

On this faith being publicly put forth by us, no room for contradiction appeared; but our most pious Emperor, before any one else, testified that it was most orthodox. He confessed, moreover, that such were his own sentiments; and he advised all present to agree to it, and to subscribe its articles and to assent to them, with the insertion of the single word Consubstantial (ὁμοούσιος) which, moreover, he interpreted himself saying that the Son is consubstantial not according to bodily affections, and that the Son subsisted from the Father neither according to division, nor severance: for the immaterial, and intellectual, and incorporeal nature could not be the subject of any bodily affection, but that it became us to conceive of such things in a divine and ineffable manner. And our most wise and most religious Emperor reasoned in this way; but they, because of the addition of consubstantial, drew up the following formulary:

We believe in One God, the Father, Almighty, Maker of all things visible and invisible:

And in One Lord Jesus Christ, the Son of God, begotten of the Father, Only-begotten, that is, from the substance of the Father; God from God, Light from Light, Very God from Very God, begotten not made, Consubstantial with the Father, by Whom all things were made, both things in heaven and things in earth; Who for us men and for our salvation came down and was incarnate, was made man, suffered, and rose again the third day, ascended into heaven, and is coming to judge living and dead.

And in the Holy Ghost.

And those who say "There was when He was not," and "Before His generation He was not," and "He came to be from nothing," or those who pretend that the Son of God is "Of other *hypostasis* or substance," or "created," or "alterable," or "mutable," the Catholic and Apostolic Church anathematizes.

On their suggesting this formula, we did not let it pass without inquiry in what sense they used the expressions "of the substance of the Father" and "Consubstantial with the Father." Accordingly, questions and explanations took place, and the discussion tested the meaning of these phrases. And they professed that the phrase "of the substance" was indicative of the Son's being indeed from the Father, yet without being as if a part of Him. And with this understanding, we thought good to assent to the meaning of the pious teaching suggesting that the Son was from the Father, not, however, a part of His substance. On this account, we assented to the meaning ourselves, without declining even the term "Consubstantial," peace being the aim which we set before us, and fear of deviating from the correct meaning.

In the same way, we also admitted "begotten, not made," since they said that "made" was an appellation common to the other creatures which came to be through the Son, to whom the Son had no likeness. Wherefore, He was not a work resembling the things which through Him came to be, but was of an essence which is too high for the level of any work; and which the Divine Oracles teach to have been generated from the Father, the mode of generation being ineffable and inexplicable to every originated nature.

And so too on examination there are grounds for saying that the Son is

"Consubstantial" with the Father; not in the way of bodies, nor like mortal beings, for He is not such by division of essence, or by severance, no, nor by any affection, or alteration, or changing of the Father's substance and power (since from all such the unoriginate nature of the Father is alien); but because "Consubstantial with the Father" suggests that the Son of God bears no resemblance to the originated creatures, but that to His Father alone Who begat Him is He in every way assimilated, and that He is not of any other *hypostasis* and substance, but from the Father. To this term also, thus interpreted, it appeared well to assent; since we were aware that even among the ancients some learned and illustrious bishops and writers have used the term "Consubstantial," in their theological teaching concerning the Father and Son.

So much then be said concerning the Faith which was published; to which all of us assented, not without inquiry, but according to the specific meanings, mentioned before the most religious Emperor himself, and justified by the fore-mentioned considerations. And as to the anathemas published by them at the end of the Faith, we thought it without offence because it forbade to use words not in Scripture, from which almost all the confusion and disorder in the Church have come. Since then no divinely inspired Scripture has used the phrases, "out of nothing" and "once He was not," and the rest which follow, there appeared no ground for using or teaching them; to which also we assented as a good decision, since it had not been our custom hitherto to use these terms.

Moreover, to anathematize "Before His generation He was not" did not seem preposterous, in that it is confessed by all, that the Son of God was before the generation according to the flesh.

Nay, our most religious Emperor did, at the time, prove, in a speech, that He was in being even according to His divine generation which is before all ages, since even before He was generated in actuality, He was potentially with the Father ingenerately, the Father being always Father, as King always, and Saviour always, being all things potentially, and being always in the same respects and in the same way.

This we have been forced to transmit to you, Beloved, as making clear to you the deliberation of our inquiry and assent, and how reasonably we resisted even to the last minute, as long as we were offended at statements which differed from our own, but received without contention what no longer pained us as soon as, on a candid examination of the sense of the words, they appeared to us to coincide with what we ourselves have professed in the faith which we previously declared.

CANONS OF NICAEA (325)

If any one has been obliged to undergo a surgical operation from disease, or has been castrated by barbarians, let him continue in the clergy. But if any one in good health has so mutilated himself, it is right that, if he be enrolled amongst the clergy, he should cease from his ministrations; and that from henceforth no such person should be promoted. As, however, it is plain that this is said with reference to those who dare to mutilate themselves, therefore, if any persons have been so mutilated by barbarians, or by their own masters, and in other respects are found worthy, the canon allows them to be admitted to the clerical office.

Since many things have been done by men either from necessity, or some other pressing cause, contrary to the canon of the Church, as that persons who have lately come over to the faith from a heathen life, and have been taught for a short time, have been presently brought to the spiritual laver, and at the same time that they have been baptized, have been promoted to the episcopate or presbyterate—it appears right to determine that nothing of the sort shall be done for the future; for some time is necessary for the state of a catechumen,[2] and a fuller probation after baptism; for the Apostolic decree is clear, which says, *Not a novice, lest being lifted up with pride he fall into a snare and the judgment of the devil.*[3] But if, in process of time, any natural fault be discovered about the person, and he be convicted by *two or three witnesses,*[4] let him be deposed from the clergy. Whosoever shall act contrary to these rules will endanger his own orders, as boldly opposing the great Synod.

The great Synod altogether forbids any bishop, presbyter or deacon, or any one of the clergy, to have a woman dwelling with him, excepting a mother, a sister, or aunt, or such persons only as are above all suspicion.

It is most proper that a bishop should be constituted by all the bishops of the province; but, if this be difficult on account of some urgent necessity, or the length of the way, that at all events three should meet together at the same place, those who are absent also giving their suffrages and their consent in writing, and then the ordination be performed. The confirming, however, of what is done in each province belongs to the Metropolitan of it.

Concerning those, whether of the clergy or laity, who have been excommunicated by the bishops in the different provinces, let the sentence of the canon prevail, which pronounces that those persons who have been cast out by one bishop are not to be received again into communion by any others. Inquiry should, however, be made whether they have been excommunicated through the petty jealousy or contentiousness, or other such-like bitterness, of the bishop. And in order that this inquiry may be conveniently made, it is decreed to be proper that synods should be assembled twice every year in every province, that all the bishops of the province being assembled together, such questions may be examined into, that so those who have confessedly offended against the bishop may appear to be with reason excommunicated by all the bishops, until it shall seem fit to their general assembly to pronounce a more lenient sentence upon them. And of these synods one is to be held before Lent,

---

[2] Those under instruction in preparation for full admission into the church.
[3] I Tim. 3:6.
[4] Matt. 18:16.

that all petty jealousy being removed, a pure gift may be offered to God. The other in the season of autumn.

Let the ancient customs hold good which are in Egypt and Libya and Pentapolis, according to which the Bishop of Alexandria has authority over all these places. For this is also customary to the Bishop of Rome. In like manner in Antioch and in the other provinces, the privileges are to be preserved to the Churches. But this is clearly to be understood, that, if any one be made a bishop without the consent of the Metropolitan, the great Synod declares that he shall not be a bishop. If, however, two or three bishops shall from private contention oppose the common choice of all the others, it being a reasonable one and made according to the ecclesiastical canons, let the choice of the majority hold good.

Since a custom and ancient tradition has held good, that the Bishop of Aelia[5] should be honoured, let him have his proper honour, saving to the Metropolis (i.e., Caesarea) the honour peculiar to it.

Concerning those who have formerly called themselves Cathari, i.e., Novatianists,[6] but who come over to the Catholic and Apostolic Church, the holy Synod has decreed that they, having received imposition of hands, shall so remain in the clergy. It is right, however, that they should in the first instance make profession in writing that they will agree to and follow the decrees of the Catholic and Apostolic Church; in particular, that they will communicate with those persons who have been twice married and with those who, having lapsed in persecution, have had a certain period of penitence assigned to them and a time for reconciliation fixed; and, generally, that they will follow in all things the decrees of the Catholic Church. Wherever, therefore, whether in villages or cities, all who have been ordained are found to be of this party only, they shall continue in the clergy in the same rank in which they are found. But if any of these come to a place where there is already a bishop or presbyter of the Catholic Church, it is clear that the bishop of the Church is to have the episcopal dignity, and he who had the name of a bishop amongst those who are called Cathari, shall have the rank of a presbyter, unless it shall seem fit to the bishop to allow him to partake of the honour of the name. If the bishop is not pleased to do so, he shall assign him the place of a Chorepiscopus[7] or Presbyter, that he may indeed altogether appear to be in the clergy, but that there may not be two bishops in the city.

If any have been promoted to be presbyters without inquiry, or if upon examination they have confessed their sins, and, notwithstanding their having confessed, any man has in opposition to the canon laid hands upon them, the canon does not admit persons so ordained. For the Church vindicates only irreproachable characters.

If any who have lapsed have been ordained in ignorance, or even if those

---

[5] The Gentile city which the Emperor Hadrian founded on the site of Jerusalem.

[6] Rigorist schismatics who did not believe that Christians who had lapsed under persecution should be readmitted to the Church.

[7] At this time, the bishop of a country district, having only limited powers.

who ordained them were aware of the fact, this does not prejudice the Ecclesiastical Canon; for upon the circumstances being made known, they are deposed.

Concerning those who have fallen away without necessity, or without the spoiling of their goods, or without being in danger, or any other such reason, as happened under the tyranny of Licinius, the Synod has decreed that although they are undeserving of any kindness, they shall nevertheless be dealt with mercifully. As many, therefore, as shall truly repent, shall continue three years amongst the hearers[8] as believers (i.e., as having been already baptized), and seven amongst the prostrators, and for two years they shall communicate with the people in prayer without the offering.

Those who have been called by grace, and have at first displayed their ardour, but afterwards have run like *dogs to their own vomit*[9] (insomuch that some have spent money, and by means of gifts have acquired again their military station), must continue amongst the prostrators for ten years, after having been for three years amongst the hearers. In all such cases, however, it is proper to examine into the purpose and nature of their repentance; for as many as manifest their conversion in deed, and not in appearance only, by their fear, and tears, and patience and good works, these having completed the prescribed time as hearers, may properly communicate in the prayers, and the bishop may be allowed to determine yet more favourably respecting them. But those who hear their sentence with indifference, and think the form of entering into the Church sufficient for their conversion, must complete the whole time.

Concerning those who are likely to depart,[10] the old and canonical law is still to be observed that if any one is about to depart, he must not be deprived of the perfect and most necessary provision for his journey. If, however, after having been given over, and having received the Communion, he is again restored to health, let him continue amongst those who communicate in prayers only. But generally, and as regards every one who is likely to die, and who desires to partake of the Eucharist, the Bishop, after examination, shall impart it to him.

Concerning those who are catechumens, and who have lapsed, the holy and great Synod has decreed that they shall be only three years amongst the hearers and after that shall pray with the catechumens.

On account of the great disturbance and disputes which have occurred, it seems right that the custom which has been admitted in some places contrary to the canon should by all means be done away; and that no bishop, presbyter or deacon should remove from one city to another. But if any person,

---

[8] Penitents set apart from the rest of the congregation by special robes and close-cut hair.

[9] Prov. 26:11. The clause refers to those civil servants and soldiers who gave up their professions to avoid having to sacrifice, but then had second thoughts and used bribery to obtain them again.

[10] To die.

after the decision of the holy and great Synod, shall attempt any such thing or shall lend himself to any such practice, that arrangement shall be totally annulled, and he shall be restored to the church in which he was ordained bishop or presbyter.

If any persons recklessly and not having the fear of God before their eyes, nor regarding the canons of the Church, whether they be presbyters or deacons, or any others who are enrolled in the list of the clergy, shall remove from their own Church, they ought by no means to be received into any other, but they must be constrained to return to their own parish, or if they continue they must be without communion. And if any bishop shall dare to usurp what belongs to another, and to ordain in his church any such person without the consent of the proper bishop from whom he has seceded, let the ordination be void.

Since many persons of the ecclesiastical order, being led away by covetousness, and a desire of filthy lucre, have forgotten the Holy Scripture which says, *he gave not his money to usury*,[11] and in lending require their twelve per cent,[12] the holy and great Synod considers it right that if any one after this decision shall be found receiving money by actual arrangement, or going about the business in any other way, as by requiring the whole and a half,[13] or using any other device whatsoever for filthy lucre's sake, shall be deposed from the clergy, and struck out of the list.

It has come to the knowledge of the holy Synod that in certain places and cities, the deacons give the Eucharist to the presbyters, whereas neither canon nor custom allows that they who have no authority to offer should give the Body of Christ to those who do offer. It has also been made known that now some of the deacons receive the Eucharist even before the bishops. Let all such practices be done away, and let the deacons keep within their proper bounds, knowing that they are the ministers of the bishop and inferior to the presbyters. Let them, therefore, receive the Eucharist, according to their order, after the presbyters, either the bishop or presbyter administering it to them. Further, the deacons are not to be allowed to sit among the presbyters; for this is done contrary to the canon and due order. But if any one even after this decision will not obey, let him be put out of the diaconate.

Concerning the Paulianists who have come over to the Catholic Church, the decision is that they must by all means be baptized again.[14] But if any of them have in time past been enrolled amongst the clergy, if they appear to be blameless and without reproach, after they have been rebaptized, let them be ordained by the bishop of the Catholic Church. If, however, upon examination, they are found to be unfit, they must be deposed. In like manner, as regards the deaconesses, and, in short, any who have been enrolled amongst the

[11] Ps. 15:5.

[12] The normal Roman rate.

[13] The practice of requiring a 50 percent bonus on repayment of a loan.

[14] This unusual decision was no doubt taken because the Paulianists, or followers of Paul of Samosata, denied the Trinity, and their baptisms would therefore be invalid.

clergy, the same form shall be observed. And we took note of those deaconesses who are enrolled as far as concerns dress, since they have not any imposition of hands, so that they are altogether to be reckoned amongst the laity.

Since there are some persons who kneel on the Lord's Day and in the days of Pentecost; in order that all things may be observed in like manner in every parish, the holy Synod has decreed that all should at those times offer up their prayers to God standing.

8. JULIAN THE APOSTATE: ON PAGANISM AND CHRISTIANITY[1]

The Emperor Julian (reigned 361-363) was brought up as a Christian, but he had small reason to admire the morality of a Christian state. When Constantine died in 337, nearly all his relatives were murdered in order to simplify the succession. His three sons were spared to inherit the throne, and two nephews, one of whom was Julian, on account of their tender age. Julian's youth was spent largely in exile, because his imperial cousin Constantius (reigned 337-361) wished to banish danger before it materialized. In his solitude Julian read the Greek classics and found stronger spiritual excitement in them than in Christianity. Eventually he was allowed to study, and his conversion was completed by the pagan philosophers of Greece and Asia Minor. He went to Athens and probably became an initiate of the Eleusinian mysteries; he himself tells us that when he was twenty he also embraced Mithraism. He venerated the Great Mother and was strongly influenced by Neo-Platonism. After he became sole emperor in 361 he restored pagan worship and attempted to propagate a syncretic and emotional pagan theology. At the same time he tried to establish a pagan church which would rival the Christians in organization and good works. Death in the Persian wars cut short his plans.

Julian's letter to the pagan high priest of Galatia provides interesting evidence regarding the weaknesses of paganism and the corresponding strengths of Christianity: the clerical discipline and social dynamism of the latter were alien to the old faith. His rescript on education sets forth his attitude towards the Christian religion, for which he was fond of using the words *atheism* and *insanity*. Christians were to be given no opportunity to become martyrs, but at the same time they were not to be allowed to pervert the minds of the young by teaching in the schools and casting scorn on the ancient legends of paganism. If Julian had ruled longer, his policies might have had considerable effect; the pagan element in the Roman Empire was still very strong. His early death made his reign only

[1] Reprinted by permission of the publishers from the LOEB CLASSICAL LIBRARY, W. C. Wright, editor and translator, *The Works of the Emperor Julian*, Cambridge, Mass.: Harvard University Press, 1923. Vol. III, pp. 67-73, 117-123.

an interlude, but his name was long cherished by defenders of the religious heritage of the pagan past.

LETTER 22: JULIAN TO ARSACIUS, HIGH-PRIEST OF GALATIA (c. 362)

The Hellenic religion[2] does not yet prosper as I desire, and it is the fault of those who profess it; for the worship of the gods is on a splendid and magnificent scale, surpassing every prayer and every hope. May Adrasteia[3] pardon my words, for indeed no one, a little while ago, would have ventured even to pray for a change of such a sort or so complete within so short a time. Why, then, do we think that this is enough, why do we not observe that it is their benevolence to strangers, their care for the graves of the dead and the pretended holiness of their lives that have done most to increase atheism?[4] I believe that we ought really and truly to practise every one of these virtues. And it is not enough for you alone to practise them, but so must all the priests in Galatia, without exception. Either shame or persuade them into righteousness or else remove them from their priestly office, if they do not, together with their wives, children, and servants, attend the worship of the gods but allow their servants or sons or wives to show impiety towards the gods and honour atheism more than piety. In the second place, admonish them that no priest may enter a theatre or drink in a tavern or control any craft or trade that is base and not respectable. Honour those who obey you, but those who disobey, expel from office. In every city establish frequent hostels in order that strangers may profit by our benevolence; I do not mean for our own people only, but for others also who are in need of money. I have but now made a plan by which you may be well provided for this; for I have given directions that 30,000 modii[5] of corn shall be assigned every year for the whole of Galatia, and 60,000 pints of wine. I order that one-fifth of this be used for the poor who serve the priests, and the remainder be distributed by us to strangers and beggars. For it is disgraceful that, when no Jew ever has to beg, and the impious Galilaeans support not only their own poor but ours as well, all men see that our people lack aid from us. Teach those of the Hellenic faith to contribute to public service of this sort, and the Hellenic villages to offer their first fruits to the gods; and accustom those who love the Hellenic religion to these good works by teaching them that this was our practice of old. At any rate Homer makes Eumaeus say: "Stranger, it is not lawful for me, not even though a baser man than you should come, to dishonour a stranger. For from Zeus come

---

[2] Julian's paganism was more Greek and Near-Eastern than Roman.
[3] Nemesis.
[4] Christianity.
[5] A measure equivalent to slightly more than two gallons.

all strangers and beggars. And a gift, though small, is precious."[6] Then let us not, by allowing others to outdo us in good works, disgrace by such remissness, or rather, utterly abandon, the reverence due to the gods. If I hear that you are carrying out these orders I shall be filled with joy.

As for the government officials, do not interview them often at their homes, but write to them frequently. And when they enter the city no priest must go to meet them, but only meet them within the vestibule when they visit the temples of the gods. Let no soldier march before them into the temple, but any who will may follow them; for the moment that one of them passes over the threshold of the sacred precinct he becomes a private citizen. For you yourself, as you are aware, have authority over what is within, since this is the bidding of the divine ordinance. Those who obey it are in very truth god-fearing, while those who oppose it with arrogance are vainglorious and empty-headed.

I am ready to assist Pessinus[7] if her people succeed in winning the favour of the Mother of the Gods. But, if they neglect her, they are not only not free from blame, but, not to speak harshly, let them beware of reaping my enmity also. "For it is not lawful for me to cherish or to pity men who are the enemies of the immortal gods." Therefore persuade them, if they claim my patronage, that the whole community must become suppliants of the Mother of the Gods.

LETTER 36: RESCRIPT ON CHRISTIAN TEACHERS (362)

I hold that a proper education results, not in laboriously acquired symmetry of phrases and language, but in a healthy condition of mind, I mean a mind that has understanding and true opinions about things good and evil, honourable and base. Therefore, when a man thinks one thing and teaches his pupils another, in my opinion he fails to educate exactly in proportion as he fails to be an honest man. And if the divergence between a man's convictions and his utterances is merely in trivial matters, that can be tolerated somehow, though it is wrong. But if in matters of the greatest importance a man has certain opinions and teaches the contrary, what is that but the conduct of hucksters, and not honest but thoroughly dissolute men in that they praise most highly the things that they believe to be most worthless, thus cheating and enticing by their praises those to whom they desire to transfer their worthless wares. Now all who profess to teach anything whatever ought to be men of upright character, and ought not to harbour in their souls opinions irreconcilable with what they publicly profess; and, above all, I believe it is necessary that those who associate with the young and teach them rhetoric should be of that upright character; for they expound the writings of the ancients, whether they be rhetoricians or grammarians, and still more if they are

[6] Odyssey XIV, 56.

[7] A city in Galatia which contained a famous temple dedicated to the Great Mother.

sophists. For these claim to teach, in addition to other things, not only the use of words, but morals also, and they assert that political philosophy is their peculiar field. Let us leave aside, for the moment, the question whether this is true or not. But while I applaud them for aspiring to such high pretensions, I should applaud them still more if they did not utter falsehoods and convict themselves of thinking one thing and teaching their pupils another. What! Was it not the gods who revealed all their learning to Homer, Hesiod, Demosthenes, Herodotus, Thucydides, Isocrates and Lysias?[8] Did not these men think that they were consecrated, some to Hermes, others to the Muses?[9] I think it is absurd that men who expound the works of these writers should dishonour the gods whom they used to honour. Yet, though I think this absurd, I do not say that they ought to change their opinions and then instruct the young. But I give them this choice: either not to teach what they do not think admirable, or, if they wish to teach, let them first really persuade their pupils that neither Homer nor Hesiod nor any of these writers whom they expound and have declared to be guilty of impiety, folly and error in regard to the gods, is such as they declare. For since they make a livelihood and receive pay from the works of those writers, they thereby confess that they are most shamefully greedy of gain, and that, for the sake of a few drachmae, they would put up with anything. It is true that, until now, there were many excuses for not attending the temples, and the terror that threatened on all sides absolved men for concealing the truest beliefs about the gods.[10] But since the gods have granted us liberty, it seems to me absurd that men should teach what they do not believe to be sound. But if they believe that those whose interpreters they are and for whom they sit, so to speak, in the seat of the prophets, were wise men, let them be the first to emulate their piety towards the gods. If, however, they think that those writers were in error with respect to the most honoured gods, then let them betake themselves to the churches of the Galilaeans to expound Matthew and Luke, since you Galilaeans are obeying them when you ordain that men shall refrain from temple-worship. For my part, I wish that your ears and your tongues might be "born anew," as you would say, as regards these things[11] in which may I ever have part, and all who think and act as is pleasing to me.

For religious and secular teachers let there be a general ordinance to this effect: Any youth who wishes to attend the schools is not excluded; nor indeed would it be reasonable to shut out from the best way boys who are still too ignorant to know which way to turn, and to overawe them into being led against their will to the beliefs of their ancestors. Though indeed it might be proper to cure these, even against their will, as one cures the insane, except that we concede indulgence to all for this sort of disease.[12] For we ought, I think, to teach, but not punish, the demented.

---

[8] Isocrates and Lysias were famous Greek orators.
[9] Some to rhetoric, others to the poets.
[10] A reference to Christian hostility to pagan worship.
[11] The pagan myths and mysteries.
[12] I.e., the insanity of Christian belief.

9. THE THEODOSIAN CODE: JEWS AND PAGANS[1]

It was in general the rule of Christian authorities from patristic to late medieval times that the Jewish religion was to be tolerated, that Jews were to be treated fairly, and that they were not to be subjected to forcible conversion. They were, however, always set apart by more or less severe civil disabilities, as in the rather mild provision of the Theodosian Code that they were to be excluded from the imperial service. More violent persecution came only in later centuries and was usually, though not always, initiated by the Christian populace rather than by church or state.

Very different was the attitude of the Christian emperors towards the pagans. Constantine the Great had tolerated them, while at the same time extending special privileges to Christians. His prohibitions of divination, sacrifice, and the repair of temples were more theoretical than practical. Constantine's son Constantius also prohibited sacrifice and ordered temples to be closed, but in many areas these edicts seem not to have been executed. The pagan interlude of Julian's reign and the relative neutrality of the Christian emperors Valentinian and Valens followed. It was not until the accession of Gratian (reigned 375-383) and of Theodosius (reigned 379-395) that the attack on paganism began in earnest. After the crushing in 394 of a rebellion by Arbogastes, a Frankish general friendly to the old religion, the complete triumph of Christianity was assured. Excerpts are given below from the legislation of Constantius, Theodosius, and the latter's sons, Arcadius and Honorius, against the pagans. By 423 Theodosius the Younger could say, "We believe that they are no more."

LAWS CONCERNING THE JEWS (412-418)

THE SAME AUGUSTUSES TO PHILIPPUS, PRAETORIAN PREFECT OF ILLYRICUM.

No person shall be trampled upon when he is innocent, on the ground that he is a Jew, nor shall any religion cause any person to be exposed to contumely. Their synagogues and habitations shall not be burned indiscriminately, nor shall they be injured wrongfully without any reason, since, moreover, even if any person should be implicated in crimes, nevertheless, the vigor of Our courts and the protection of public law appear to have been

[1] Reprinted from *The Theodosian Code and Novels*, Book XVI, Titles 8 and 10, ed. and trans. by C. Pharr, by permission of Princeton University Press. Pp. 469-470, 472-475. Copyright 1952 by Princeton University Press.

established in Our midst for the purpose that no person should have the power to seek his own revenge.

But just as it is Our will that the foregoing provision shall be made for the persons of the Jews, so We decree that the Jews also shall be admonished that they perchance shall not become insolent and, elated by their own security, commit any rash act in disrespect of the Christian religion.

Given on the eighth day before the ides of August at Constantinople in the year of the ninth consulship of Honorius Augustus and the fifth consulship of Theodosius Augustus.—August 6, 412; 418; 420.

. . . . . .

THE SAME AUGUSTUSES TO PALLADIUS, PRAETORIAN PREFECT.

Those persons who live in the Jewish superstition shall hereafter be barred from seeking entrance to the imperial service. To those persons who have undertaken the oaths of enlistment in the imperial service as members of the secret service or as palatines We grant the right to complete such service and to end it within the statutory periods, ignoring the fact rather than favoring it. But the regulation which We wish to be relaxed for a few at present shall not be permitted in the future.

We decree, however, that those persons who are bound to the perversity of this race and who are proved to have sought armed imperial service shall unquestionably be released from their cincture of office, and they shall not be protected by the patronage of their earlier merits.

Indeed, We do not prohibit Jews instructed in liberal studies from acting as advocates, and We permit them to enjoy the honor of the compulsory public service of decurions, which they obtain through the prerogative of birth and splendor of family.

Since the aforesaid privileges ought to suffice them, they must not consider the prohibition of imperial service as a mark of infamy.

Given on the sixth day before the ides of March at Ravenna in the year of the twelfth consulship of Honorius Augustus and the eighth consulship of Theodosius Augustus.—March 10, 418.

LAWS AGAINST THE PAGANS (341-408)

EMPEROR CONSTANTIUS AUGUSTUS TO MADALIANUS, VICE PRAETORIAN PREFECT.

Superstition shall cease: the madness of sacrifices shall be abolished. For if any man in violation of the law of the sainted Emperor, Our father, and in violation of this command of Our Clemency, should dare to perform sacrifices, he shall suffer the infliction of a suitable punishment and the effect of an immediate sentence.

Received in the year of the consulship of Marcellinus and Probinus.—
341.

THE SAME AUGUSTUSES TO CATULLINUS, PREFECT OF THE CITY.

Although all superstitions must be completely eradicated, nevertheless, it is Our will that the buildings of the temples situated outside the walls shall remain untouched and uninjured. For since certain plays or spectacles of the circus or contests derive their origin from some of these temples, such structures shall not be torn down, since from them is provided the regular performance of long established amusements for the Roman people.

Given on the kalends of November in the year of the fourth consulship of Constantius Augustus and the third consulship of Constans Augustus.—
November 1, 346; 342.

THE SAME AUGUSTUSES TO TAURUS, PRAETORIAN PREFECT.

It is Our pleasure that the temples shall be immediately closed in all places and in all cities, and access to them forbidden, so as to deny to all abandoned men the opportunity to commit sin. It is also Our will that all men shall abstain from sacrifices. But if perchance any man should perpetrate any such criminality, he shall be struck down with the avenging sword. We also decree that the property of a man thus executed shall be vindicated to the fisc. The governors of the provinces shall be similarly punished if they should neglect to avenge such crimes.

Given on the kalends of December in the year of the fourth consulship of Constantius Augustus and the third consulship of Constans Augustus.—
December 1, 346; 354; 356.

EMPERORS THEODOSIUS, ARCADIUS, AND HONORIUS AUGUSTUSES TO RUFINUS, PRAETORIAN PREFECT

No person at all, of any class or order whatsoever of men or of dignities, whether he occupies a position of power or has completed such honors, whether he is powerful by the lot of birth or is humble in lineage, legal status and fortune, shall sacrifice an innocent victim to senseless images in any place at all or in any city. He shall not, by more secret wickedness, venerate his lar with fire, his genius with wine, his penates with fragrant odors; he shall not burn lights to them, place incense before them, or suspend wreaths for them.

But if any man should dare to immolate a victim for the purpose of sacrifice, or to consult the quivering entrails, according to the example of a person guilty of high treason he shall be reported by an accusation which is permitted to all persons, and he shall receive the appropriate sentence, even though he has inquired nothing contrary to, or with reference to, the welfare of the Emperors. For it is sufficient to constitute an enormous crime that any person should wish to break down the very laws of nature, to investigate forbidden matters, to disclose hidden secrets, to attempt interdicted practices, to seek to know the end of another's life, to promise the hope of another person's death.

But if any person should venerate, by placing incense before them, images made by the work of mortals and destined to suffer the ravages of time, and if, in a ridiculous manner, he should suddenly fear the effigies which he himself has formed, or should bind a tree with fillets, or should erect an altar of turf that he has dug up, or should attempt to honor vain images with the offering of a gift, which even though it is humble, still is a complete outrage against religion, such person, as one guilty of the violation of religion, shall be punished by the forfeiture of that house or landholding in which it is proved that he served a pagan superstition. For We decree that all places shall be annexed to Our fisc, if it is proved that they have reeked with the vapor of incense, provided, however, that such places are proved to have belonged to such incense burners.

But if any person should attempt to perform any such kind of sacrifice in public temples or shrines, or in the buildings or fields of others, and if it is proved that such places were usurped without the knowledge of the owner, the offender shall be compelled to pay twenty-five pounds of gold as a fine. If any person should connive at such a crime, he shall be held subject to the same penalty as that of the person who performed the sacrifice.

It is Our will that this regulation shall be so enforced by the judges, as well as by the defenders and decurions of the several cities, that the information learned by the defenders and decurions shall be immediately reported to the courts, and the crimes so reported shall be punished by the judges. Moreover, if the defenders and decurions should suppose that any such crime should be concealed through favoritism or overlooked through carelessness, they shall be subjected to judicial indignation. If the judges should be advised of such crimes and should defer punishment through connivance, they shall be fined thirty pounds of gold; their office staffs also shall be subjected to an equal penalty.

Given on the sixth day before the ides of November at Constantinople in the year of the second consulship of Arcadius Augustus and the consulship of Rufinus.—November 8, 392.

EMPERORS ARCADIUS, HONORIUS, AND THEODOSIUS AUGUSTUSES TO CURTIUS, PRAETORIAN PREFECT.

(After other matters.) Their income from taxes in kind shall be taken away from the temples and shall assist the annonarian account for the benefit of the expenses of Our most devoted soldiers.

If any images stand even now in the temples and shrines, and if they have received, or do now receive, the worship of the pagans anywhere, they shall be torn from their foundations, since We recognize that this regulation has been very often decreed by repeated sanctions.

The buildings themselves of the temples which are situated in cities or towns or outside the towns shall be vindicated to public use. Altars shall be destroyed in all places, and all temples situated on Our landholdings shall be transferred to suitable uses. The proprietors shall be compelled to destroy them.

It shall not be permitted at all to hold convivial banquets in honor of sacrilegious rites in such funereal places or to celebrate any solemn ceremony. We grant to bishops also of such places the right to use ecclesiastical power to prohibit such practices. Moreover, We constrain the judges by a penalty of twenty pounds of gold, and their office staffs by an equal sum, if they should neglect the enforcement of these regulations by their connivance.

Given on the seventeenth day before the kalends of December at Rome in the year of the consulship of Bassus and Philippus.—November 15, 408; 407.

10.   ST. AMBROSE: BISHOP *v.* EMPEROR[1]

St. Ambrose (c. 339-397), Bishop of Milan, considered (along with St. Jerome, St. Augustine, and St. Gregory the Great) to be one of the four traditional Doctors or Fathers of the Latin Church, was perhaps the most powerful ecclesiastic of the fourth century. He secured the removal of the pagan altar of Victory from the building that housed the Roman Senate. He was also a leader in the fight against the Arian heretics. The tone of independence he adopted towards the secular power was remarkable for his time and very different from the uncritical attitude of Eusebius. His close relationship with the Emperor Theodosius (reigned 379-395) was troubled by two major disputes, referred to in three of his letters (40, 41, and 51), extracts from which are given below. The first was addressed to Theodosius soon after the Christian burning of the Jewish synagogue at Callinicum[2] in 388 caused the Emperor to order the bishop and clergy of that city to rebuild it at their own expense. Ambrose's protest reveals his conviction that Christians should be treated with special indulgence by a Christian emperor. The second, from Ambrose to his sister, tells of the sermon that the Bishop preached in the Emperor's presence against his alleged support of the Jews. The

---

[1] Ambrose, *Letters* 40, 41, 51, trans. by H. de Romestein, *A Select Library of Nicene and Post-Nicene Fathers of the Christian Church*, Series II, ed. by P. Schaff and H. Wace (reprinted Grand Rapids, Mich., Wm. B. Eerdmans Publishing Company, 1955), X, pp. 444-445, 450, 451, 452.

[2] Ar-Rakka on the Euphrates River.

third is a letter of stern yet tactful reproof directed to Theodosius because of the massacre in 390 of several thousand inhabitants of Thessalonica, in revenge for a riot in which the imperial commandant of the city had been killed. The resolute Ambrose forced Theodosius to do public penance for his crime.

LETTER 40: AMBROSE TO THEODOSIUS (DECEMBER, 388)

. . . It is a serious matter to endanger your salvation for the Jews. When Gideon had slain the sacred calf, the heathen said, The gods will themselves avenge the injury done to them.[3] Who is to avenge the Synagogue? Christ, Whom they slew, Whom they denied? Will God the Father avenge those who do not receive the Father, since they have not received the Son? Who is to avenge the heresy of the Valentinians?[4] How can your piety avenge them, seeing it has commanded them to be excluded, and denied them permission to meet together? If I set before you Josiah as a king approved of God, will you condemn that in them which was approved in him?[5]

But at any rate if too little confidence is placed in me, command the presence of those bishops whom you think fit, let it be discussed, O Emperor, what ought to be done without injury to the faith. If you consult your officers concerning pecuniary causes, how much more just is it that you should consult the priests of God in the cause of religion.

Let your Clemency consider from how many plotters, how many spies the Church suffers. If they come upon a slight crack, they plant a dart in it. I speak after the manner of men, but God is feared more than men, Who is rightly set before even emperors. If any one thinks it right that deference should be paid to a friend, a parent, or a neighbour, I am right in judging that deference should be paid to God, and that He should be preferred to all. Consult, O Emperor, your own advantage, or suffer me to consult mine.

What shall I answer hereafter, if it be discovered that, by authority given from this place, Christians have been slain by the sword, or by clubs, or thongs knotted with lead? How shall I explain such a fact? How shall I excuse it to those bishops, who now mourn bitterly because some, who have discharged the office of the priesthood for thirty and many more years, or other ministers of the Church, are withdrawn from their sacred office, and set to discharge municipal duties? For if they who war for you serve for a stated time of service, how much more ought you to consider those who war for God. How, I say, shall I excuse this to the bishops, who make complaint concerning the clergy, and write that the Churches are wasted by a serious attack upon them?

[3] Judges 6:25-32.
[4] Followers of Valentinian, a second century Gnostic. Earlier in the letter Ambrose refers to the burning of one of their shrines by monks.
[5] II Kings 23:3-8, II Chron. 34:2-7.

I was desirous that this should come to the knowledge of your Clemency. You will, when it pleases you, vouchsafe to consider and give order according to your will, but exclude and cast out that which troubles me, and troubles me rightly. You do yourself whatever you order to be done, even if he, your officer, do not do it. I much prefer that you should be merciful, than that he should not do what he has been ordered.

You have those[6] for whom you ought yet to invite and to merit the mercy of the Lord in regard to the Roman Empire; you have those for whom you hope even more than for yourself; let the grace of God for them, let their salvation appeal to you in these words of mine. I fear that you may commit your cause to the judgment of others. Everything is still unprejudiced before you. On this point I pledge myself to our God for you, do not fear your oath. Is it possible that that should displease God which is amended for His honour? You need not alter anything in that letter, whether it be sent or is not yet sent. Order another to be written, which shall be full of faith, full of piety. For you it is possible to change for the better, for me it is not possible to hide the truth.

You forgave the Antiochians the insult offered to you;[7] you have recalled the daughters of your enemy[8] and given them to be brought up by a relative; you sent sums of money to the mother of your enemy from your own treasury. This so great piety, this so great faith towards God, will be darkened by this deed. Do not you, then, I entreat, who spared enemies in arms, and preserved your adversaries, think that Christians ought to be punished with such eagerness.

And now, O Emperor, I beg you not to disdain to hear me who am in fear both for yourself and for myself, for it is the voice of a Saint which says: "Wherefore was I made to see the misery of my people?" that I should commit an offence against God. I, indeed, have done what could be done consistently with honour to you, that you might rather listen to me in the palace, lest, if it were necessary, you should listen to me in the Church.

LETTER 41: AMBROSE TO HIS SISTER MARCELLINA (DECEMBER, 388)

The sermon with which Ambrose threatened Theodosius at the end of *Letter 40* proved necessary. After reproducing it for his sister, the Bishop described the Emperor's reaction:

[6] A reference to the Emperor's children, Honorius and Arcadius.

[7] In 387 the mob of Antioch had rioted in protest against new taxation and had smashed the statues of the Emperor and Empress. After his anger had cooled, Theodosius granted amnesty to the city.

[8] The rebel Maximus, who seized power in the West in 383 and was defeated and killed in 388.

When I came down from the pulpit, he said to me: "You spoke about me." I replied: "I dealt with matters intended for your benefit." Then he said: "I had indeed decided too harshly about the repairing of the synagogue by the bishop, but that has been rectified. The monks commit many crimes." Then Timasius the general began to be over-vehement against the monks, and I answered him: "With the Emperor I deal as is fitting, because I know that he has the fear of God, but with you, who speaks so roughly, one must deal otherwise."

Then, after standing for some time, I said to the Emperor: "Let me offer for you without anxiety, set my mind at ease." As he continued sitting and nodded, but did not give an open promise, and I remained standing, he said that he would amend the edict. I went on at once to say that he must end the whole investigation, lest the Count should use the opportunity of the investigation to do any injury to the Christians. He promised that it should be so. I said to him, "I act on your promise," and repeated, "I act on your promise." "Act," he said, "on my promise." And so I went to the altar, whither I should not have gone unless he had given me a distinct promise. And indeed so great was the grace attending the offering, that I felt myself that that favour granted by the Emperor was very acceptable to our God, and that the divine presence was not wanting. And so everything was done as I wished.

LETTER 51: AMBROSE TO THEODOSIUS (SEPTEMBER, 390)

. . . Listen, august Emperor. I cannot deny that you have a zeal for the faith; I do confess that you have the fear of God. But you have a natural vehemence, which, if any one endeavours to soothe, you quickly turn to mercy; if any one stirs it up, you rouse it so much more that you can scarcely restrain it. Would that if no one soothe it, at least no one may inflame it! To yourself I willingly entrust it, you restrain yourself, and overcome your natural vehemence by the love of piety.

This vehemence of yours I preferred to commend privately to your own consideration, rather than possibly raise it by any action of mine in public. And so I have preferred to be somewhat wanting in duty rather than in humility, and that others should rather think me wanting in priestly authority than that you should find me lacking in most loving reverence, that having restrained your vehemence your power of deciding on your counsel should not be weakened. I excuse myself by bodily sickness, which was in truth severe, and scarcely to be lightened but by great care. Yet I would rather have died than not wait two or three days for your arrival. But it was not possible for me to do so.

There was that done in the city of the Thessalonians of which no similar record exists, which I was not able to prevent happening; which, indeed, I had before said would be most atrocious when I so often petitioned against it, and that which you yourself show by revoking it too late you consider to be grave, this I could not extenuate when done. When it was first heard of, a synod had met because of the arrival of the Gallican Bishops. There was not one who did not lament it, not one who thought lightly of it; your being in fellowship with Ambrose was no excuse for your deed. Blame for what had been done would have been heaped more and more on me, had no one said that your reconciliation to our God was necessary.

Are you ashamed, O Emperor, to do that which the royal prophet David, the forefather of Christ, according to the flesh, did? To him it was told how the rich man who had many flocks seized and killed the poor man's one lamb, because of the arrival of his guest, and recognizing that he himself was being condemned in the tale, for that he himself had done it, he said: "I have sinned against the Lord."[9] Bear it, then, without impatience, O Emperor, if it be said to you: "You have done that which was spoken of to King David by the prophet. For if you listen obediently to this, and say: "I have sinned against the Lord," if you repeat those words of the royal prophet: "O come let us worship and fall down before Him, and mourn before the Lord our God, Who made us," it shall be said to you also: "Since thou repentest, the Lord putteth away thy sin, and thou shalt not die."

.   .   .   .   .

I have written this, not in order to confound you, but that the examples of these kings may stir you up to put away this sin from your kingdom, for you will do it away by humbling your soul before God. You are a man, and it has come upon you, conquer it. Sin is not done away but by tears and penitence. Neither angel can do it, nor archangel. The Lord Himself, Who alone can say, "I am with you," if we have sinned, does not forgive any but those who repent.

I urge, I beg, I exhort, I warn, for it is a grief to me, that you who were an example of unusual piety, who were conspicuous for clemency, who would not suffer single offenders to be put in peril, should not mourn that so many have perished. Though you have waged battle most successfully, though in other matters, too, you are worthy of praise, yet piety was ever the crown of your actions. The devil envied that which was your most excellent possession. Conquer him whilst you still possess that wherewith you may conquer. Do not add another sin to your sin by a course of action which has injured many.

I, indeed, though a debtor to your kindness, for which I cannot be ungrateful, that kindness which has surpassed that of many emperors, and has been equalled by one only; I, I say, have no cause for a charge of contumacy against you, but have cause for fear; I dare not offer the sacrifice if you intend

[9] II Samuel 12:1-13.

to be present. Is that which is not allowed after shedding the blood of one innocent person, allowed after shedding the blood of many? I do not think so.

Lastly, I am writing with my own hand that which you alone may read. As I hope that the Lord will deliver me from all troubles. I have been warned, not by man, nor through man, but plainly by Himself that this is forbidden me. For when I was anxious, in the very night in which I was preparing to set out, you appeared to me in a dream to have come into the Church, and I was not permitted to offer the sacrifice. I pass over other things, which I could have avoided, but I bore them for love of you, as I believe. May the Lord cause all things to pass peaceably. Our God gives warnings in many ways, by heavenly signs, by the precepts of the prophets; by the visions even of sinners He wills that we should understand, that we should entreat Him to take away all disturbances, to preserve peace for you emperors, that the faith and peace of the Church, whose advantage it is that emperors should be Christians and devout, may continue.

11. ST. AUGUSTINE: DEFINITION OF A TRUE COMMONWEALTH (*AFTER 410*)[1]

St. Augustine (354-430), Bishop of Hippo and the most influential theologian of the Latin Church before St. Thomas Aquinas, shaped to a large extent the thought of the medieval period. Born at Tagaste in northern Africa, son of a Christian mother and a pagan father, he was given elementary Christian instruction as a child but was not baptized. He received a normal Roman education and was sent to Carthage to study rhetoric. Later he taught this subject in Rome and Milan. Shocked by some of the stories in the Old Testament and scornful of the unpolished Latin of the pre-Vulgate Biblical translation, he abandoned Christianity first for Manicheanism, then for skepticism, and then for Neo-Platonism. After this long spiritual odyssey, he was ultimately re-converted to Christianity, partly as a result of the sermons of Bishop Ambrose of Milan. Augustine later became Bishop of Hippo and one of the leading ecclesiastics in the African Church. He fought the two most dangerous heresies of the day, Donatism and Pelagianism, both through public debates and through the writing of a multitude of controversial tracts. Against the former he emphasized the validity of sacramental orders, independent of the personal worthiness of the cleric. Against the latter he emphasized the overriding importance of divine grace as opposed to human free

[1] St. Augustine, *The City of God*, V, 24; XIX, 21-26; trans. by M. Dods, *A Select Library of the Nicene and Post-Nicene Fathers of the Christian Church*, Series I, ed. P. Schaff (reprinted Grand Rapids, Mich., Wm. B. Eerdmans Publishing Company, 1956), II, 104-105, 414-415, 418.

choice. His theory of the predestination of souls to heaven by the unsearchable *fiat* of God was later appropriated and developed by Protestant reformers like Calvin. At the same time he had a strong sense of the Church as a visible society guided by a hierarchy of bishops who were the successors of Christ.

St. Augustine's two most famous works were the *Confessions,* which related his spiritual wanderings and eventual conversion, and the *City of God,* which set forth a theology of history based on the opposition between two cities, that of God (including good angels, saints, and true Christians) and that of man (containing the Devil, bad angels, and unregenerate sinners). Augustine painted a glowing portrait of the virtues of a truly Christian Emperor, but he disapproved of any life or society not directed towards salvation, as is shown by the following extracts from the *City of God.* The work was begun shortly after 410 to demonstrate both to pagans and Christians that the sack of Rome by Alaric the Visigoth had nothing to do with the success of the true religion and could not discredit it, since the latter promised not a temporal but an eternal reward.

For neither do we say that certain Christian emperors were therefore happy because they ruled a long time, or, dying a peaceful death, left their sons to succeed them in the empire, or subdued the enemies of the republic, or were able both to guard against and to suppress the attempt of hostile citizens rising against them. These and other gifts or comforts of this sorrowful life even certain worshippers of demons have merited to receive, who do not belong to the kingdom of God to which these belong; and this is to be traced to the mercy of God, who would not have those who believe in Him desire such things as the highest good. But we say that they are happy if they rule justly; if they are not lifted up amid the praises of those who pay them sublime honors, and the obsequiousness of those who salute them with an excessive humility, but remember that they are men; if they make their power the handmaid of His majesty by using it for the greatest possible extension of His worship; if they fear, love, worship God; if more than their own they love that kingdom in which they are not afraid to have partners; if they are slow to punish, ready to pardon; if they apply that punishment as necessary to government and defence of the republic, and not in order to gratify their own enmity; if they grant pardon, not that iniquity may go unpunished, but with the hope that the transgressor may amend his ways; if they compensate with the lenity of mercy and the liberality of benevolence for whatever severity they may be compelled to decree; if their luxury is as much restrained as it might have been unrestrained; if they prefer to govern depraved desires rather than any nation whatever; and if they do all these things, not through ardent desire of empty glory, but through love of eternal felicity, not neglecting to offer to the true God, who is their God, for their sins, the sacrifices of humility, contrition, and prayer. Such Christian emperors, we say, are happy in the present time by hope, and are destined to be so in the enjoyment of the reality itself, when that which we wait for shall have arrived.

. . . . .

This, then, is the place where I should fulfill the promise I gave in the second book of this work,[2] and explain, as briefly and clearly as possible, that if we are to accept the definitions laid down by Scipio in Cicero's *De Republica*, there never was a Roman republic; for he briefly defines a republic as the weal of the people. And if this definition be true, there never was a Roman republic, for the people's weal was never attained among the Romans. For the people, according to his definition, is an assemblage associated by a common acknowledgment of right and by a community of interests. And what he means by a common acknowledgment of right he explains at large, showing that a republic cannot be administered without justice. Where, therefore, there is no true justice there can be no right. For that which is done by right is justly done, and what is unjustly done cannot be done by right. For the unjust inventions of men are neither to be considered nor spoken of as rights; for even they themselves say that right is that which flows from the fountain of justice, and deny the definition which is commonly given by those who misconceive the matter, that right is that which is useful to the stronger party. Thus, where there is not true justice there can be no assemblage of men associated by a common acknowledgment of right, and therefore there can be no people, as defined by Scipio or Cicero; and if no people, then no weal of the people, but only of some promiscuous multitude unworthy of the name of people. Consequently, if the republic is the weal of the people, and there is no people if it be not associated by a common acknowledgment of right, and if there is no right where there is no justice, then most certainly it follows that there is no republic where there is no justice. Further, justice is that virtue which gives every one his due. Where, then, is the justice of man, when he deserts the true God and yields himself to impure demons? Is this to give every one his due? Or is he who keeps back a piece of ground from the purchaser, and gives it to a man who has no right to it, unjust, while he who keeps back himself from the God who made him, and serves wicked spirits, is just?

This same book, *De Republica*, advocates the cause of justice against injustice with great force and keenness. The pleading for injustice against justice was first heard, and it was asserted that without injustice a republic could neither increase nor even subsist, for it was laid down as an absolutely unassailable position that it is unjust for some men to rule and some to serve; and yet the imperial city to which the republic belongs cannot rule her provinces without having recourse to this injustice. It was replied in behalf of justice, that this ruling of the provinces is just, because servitude may be advantageous

[2] In Book II, chapter 21.

to the provincials, and is so when rightly administered,—that is to say, when lawless men are prevented from doing harm. And further, as they became worse and worse so long as they were free, they will improve by subjection. To confirm this reasoning, there is added an eminent example drawn from nature: for "why," it is asked, "does God rule man, the soul the body, the reason the passions and other vicious parts of the soul?" This example leaves no doubt that, to some, servitude is useful; and, indeed, to serve God is useful to all. And it is when the soul serves God that it exercises a right control over the body; and in the soul itself the reason must be subject to God if it is to govern as it ought the passions and other vices. Hence, when a man does not serve God, what justice can we ascribe to him, since in this case his soul cannot exercise a just control over the body, nor his reason over his vices? And if there is no justice in such an individual, certainly there can be none in a community composed of such persons. Here, therefore, there is not that common acknowledgment of right which makes an assemblage of men a people whose affairs we call a republic. And why need I speak of the advantageousness, the common participation in which, according to the definition, makes a people? For although, if you choose to regard the matter attentively, you will see that there is nothing advantageous to those who live godlessly, as every one lives who does not serve God but demons, whose wickedness you may measure by their desire to receive the worship of men though they are most impure spirits, yet what I have said of the common acknowledgment of right is enough to demonstrate that, according to the above definition, there can be no people, and therefore no republic, where there is no justice. For if they assert that in their republic the Romans did not serve unclean spirits, but good and holy gods, must we therefore again reply to this evasion, though already we have said enough, and more than enough, to expose it? He must be an uncommonly stupid, or a shamelessly contentious person, who has read through the foregoing books to this point, and can yet question whether the Romans served wicked and impure demons. But, not to speak of their character, it is written in the law of the true God, "He that sacrificeth unto any god save unto the Lord only, he shall be utterly destroyed." He, therefore, who uttered so menacing a commandment decreed that no worship should be given either to good or bad gods.

But it may be replied, Who is this God, or what proof is there that He alone is worthy to receive sacrifice from the Romans? One must be very blind to be still asking who this God is. He is the God whose prophets predicted the things we see accomplished. He is the God from whom Abraham received the assurance, "In thy seed shall all nations be blessed." That this was fulfilled in Christ, who according to the flesh sprang from that seed, is recognized, whether they will or no, even by those who have continued to be the enemies of this name. He is the God whose divine Spirit spake by the men whose predictions I cited in the preceding book, and which are fulfilled in the Church which has extended over all the world. This is the God whom Varro, the most learned of the Romans,[3] supposed to be Jupiter, though he knows not what he says; yet I think it right to note the circumstance that a man of such learning was unable to suppose that this God had no existence or was contemptible, but believed Him to be the same as the supreme God. In fine, He is the God whom Porphyry, the most learned of the philosophers, though the bitterest enemy of the Christians, confesses to be a great God, even according to the oracles of those whom he esteems gods.

. . . . .

But if we discard this definition of a people, and, assuming another, say that a people is an assemblage of reasonable beings bound together by a common agreement as to the objects of their love, then, in order to discover the character of any people, we have only to observe what they love. Yet whatever it loves, if only it is an assemblage of reasonable beings and not of beasts, and is bound together by an agreement as to the objects of love, it is reasonably called a people; and it will be a superior people in proportion as it is bound together by higher interests, inferior in proportion as it is bound together by lower. According to this definition of ours, the Roman people is a people, and its weal is without doubt a commonwealth or republic. But what its tastes were in its early and subsequent days, and how it declined into sanguinary seditions and then to social and civil wars, and so burst asunder or rotted off the bond of concord in which the health of a people consists, history shows, and in the preceding books I have related at large. And yet I would not on this account say either that it was not a people, or that its administration was not a republic, so long as there remains an assemblage of reasonable beings bound together by a common agreement as to the objects of love. But what I say of this people and of this republic I must be understood to think and say of the Athenians or any Greek state, of the Egyptians, of the early Assyrian Babylon, and of every other nation, great or small, which had a public government. For, in general, the city of the ungodly, which did not obey the command of God that it should offer no sacrifice save to Him alone, and which, therefore, could not give to the soul its proper command over the body, nor to the reason its just authority over the vices, is void of true justice.

For though the soul may seem to rule the body admirably, and the reason the vices, if the soul and reason do not themselves obey God, as God has commanded them to serve Him, they have no proper authority over the body and the vices. For what kind of mistress of the body and the vices can that mind be which is ignorant of the true God, and which, instead of being subject to His authority, is prostituted to the corrupting influences of the most vicious demons? It is for this reason that the virtues which it seems to itself

---

[3] Called "the most learned of Romans" by the great rhetorician Quintilian, Varro (116-27 B.C.) wrote over 600 volumes on a wide variety of subjects, most of which are lost.

to possess, and by which it restrains the body and the vices that it may obtain and keep what it desires, are rather vices than virtues so long as there is no reference to God in the matter. For although some suppose that virtues which have a reference only to themselves, and are desired only on their own account, are yet true and genuine virtues, the fact is that even then they are inflated with pride, and are therefore to be reckoned vices rather than virtues. For as that which gives life to the flesh is not derived from flesh, but is above it, so that which gives blessed life to man is not derived from man, but is something above him; and what I say of man is true of every celestial power and virtue whatsoever.

Wherefore, as the life of the flesh is the soul, so the blessed life of man is God, of whom the sacred writings of the Hebrews say, "Blessed is the people whose God is the Lord." Miserable, therefore, is the people which is alienated from God. Yet even this people has a peace of its own which is not to be lightly esteemed, though, indeed, it shall not in the end enjoy it, because it makes no good use of it before the end. But it is our interest that it enjoy this peace meanwhile in this life; for as long as the two cities are commingled, we also enjoy the peace of Babylon. For from Babylon the people of God is so freed that it meanwhile sojourns in its company. And therefore the apostle also admonished the Church to pray for kings and those in authority, assigning as the reason, "that we may live a quiet and tranquil life in all godliness and love." And the prophet Jeremiah, when predicting the captivity that was to befall the ancient people of God, and giving them the divine command to go obediently to Babylonia, and thus serve their God, counselled them also to pray for Babylonia, saying, "In the peace thereof shall ye have peace,"—the temporal peace which the good and the wicked together enjoy.

12. CLAIMS FOR THE PRIMACY OF THE BISHOP OF ROME[1]

It was only very gradually that the Bishop of Rome secured general acceptance for his claims to spiritual and legal supremacy over the Church. These claims

[1] Of the following selections St. Jerome's letter and Valentinian III's edict are taken from Documents Illustrating Papal Authority, A.D. 96-454, ed. E. Giles (London, S.P.C.K., 1952), pp. 148-150, 286-287; Pope Leo I's sermon (trans. by C. L. Feltoe) from A Select Library of Nicene and Post-Nicene Fathers of the Christian Church, Series II (reprinted Grand Rapids, Mich., Wm. B. Eerdmans Publishing Company, 1955), XII, pp. 116-118.

were based on Christ's words to the apostle Simon: "Thou art Peter (*petrus*), and upon this rock (*petram*) will I build my church, and the gates of Hell shall not prevail against it. And I will give unto thee the keys of the kingdom of heaven. And whatsoever thou shalt bind on earth, shall be bound in heaven; and whatsoever thou shalt loose on earth, shall be loosed also in heaven." They could also be connected with Christ's famous commission to Peter, "Feed my sheep." But centuries passed before it was appropriate to invoke such statements as a justification of particular and acknowledged prerogatives. From very early times the see of Rome had a special authority, for it was regarded not only as the ancient imperial capital but also as the city which had witnessed the martyrdoms of Peter and of Paul. Ecclesiastical jurisdiction over it seems first to have been exercised by a board of presbyters, which was later supplanted, as in many other ecclesiastical centers, by a bishop who had quasi-monarchical authority. But because of the unique prestige of his see, the Bishop of Rome was not merely ruler in his own diocese. He was also accounted *primus inter pares,* or "first among equals," by his fellow bishops. His decision on disputed questions came to be regarded as a touchstone of orthodoxy. This view was expressed very vigorously by St. Jerome (c. 342-420), a great scholar and ascetic who used his vast learning to make a new translation of Scripture into Latin (the Vulgate, still the standard Roman Catholic Bible), and who served as the secretary of Pope Damasus (reigned 366-384). His influential letter to Damasus, written in 375, asserted the Pope's right to be the supreme arbiter of Christian doctrine.

A further and extremely important step was taken by the Emperor Valentinian III (reigned 425-455) in the year 445. He recognized the papal claim to possess legal preeminence and appellate jurisdiction over other bishops. The contemporary Pope Leo I (reigned 440-461) preached at approximately the same time a sermon affirming and elucidating the Petrine basis of the Roman primacy.

ST. JEROME: *LETTER 15:* TO POPE DAMASUS I (375)

Since the East, dashed against itself by the accustomed fury of its peoples, is tearing piecemeal the undivided tunic of Christ, woven from the top throughout, and foxes are destroying the vine of Christ, so that among the broken cisterns which have no water it is hard to locate the sealed fountain and the enclosed garden, I have considered that I ought to consult the chair of Peter, and the faith praised by the mouth of the apostle, asking now food for my soul, from the place whence I received the garment of Christ. Neither the vast expanse of ocean, nor all the breadth of land which separates us could preclude me from seeking the precious pearl. "Wherever the body is, there will the eagles be gathered together." Now that evil children have squandered their patrimony, you alone keep your heritage intact. There the fertile earth reproduces a hundredfold the purity of the Lord's seed. Here the corn, cast into the furrows, degenerates into darnel or wild oats. It is now in the West that the sun of justice rises; whilst in the East Lucifer who fell has set his seat above the stars. "Ye are the light of the world." "Ye are the salt of the earth." Ye are vessels of gold and silver. Here the vessels of clay or wood await the iron rod and eternal fire.

Yet though your greatness terrifies me, your kindness attracts me. From the priest I ask the salvation of the victim; from the shepherd, the safety of the sheep. Away with envy! The canvassing of the Roman height recedes. I speak with the successor of the fisherman, with the disciple of the cross. Following none in the first place but Christ, I am in communion with your beatitude, that is with the chair of Peter. On that rock I know the Church is built. Whoever shall eat the Lamb outside this house is profane. If any be not with Noah in the ark, he shall perish in the flood. And because for my sins I have migrated to this solitude, where Syria borders on the barbarians, and I cannot always at this great distance ask for the Holy One of the Lord from your holiness, therefore I follow here your colleagues the Egyptian confessors; and under these great ships, my little vessel lies hid. Vitalis I know not, Meletius I reject; I ignore Paulinus.[2] Whoso gathereth not with thee scattereth, that is, he who is not of Christ is anti-Christ.

Now, alas, after the creed of Nicaea, after the decree of Alexandria joined to the West, the new expression of three hypostases[3] is required of me, a Roman, by that progeny of Arius, the Campenses![4] What new Paul, doctor of the nations, has taught this? . . .

Decide, I beseech, if you please, and I will not fear to acknowledge three hypostases. If you order it, let a new creed be compiled after the Nicene, and the orthodox will confess in like words with the Arians. . . . Well might Ursinus[5] be joined to your beatitude, Auxentius[6] to Ambrose. Far be this from the faith of Rome. May the devout hearts of the people drink no such sacrilege. Let us be satisfied to say one substance, three persons subsisting, perfect, equal, coeternal. Let us drop three hypostases, if you please, and hold one. It is no use using different words in the same sense. . . . But if you think right that, with explanations, we should say three hypostases, we do not refuse. . . .

Wherefore I beseech your holiness, by the crucified Saviour of the world, that you will write and authorize me to say or refuse the hypostases. . . . Likewise inform me with whom I ought to communicate at Antioch; for the Campenses are joined to the heretical Tarsenes, and desire nothing but to preach three hypostases in the old sense, as if supported by the authority of your communion.

[2] Three rival claimants to the see of Antioch. Meletius (or more correctly Melitius) was eventually recognized as its patriarch.

[3] Latin theologians misunderstood, and therefore condemned, the Eastern use of this Greek word to signify the three persons joined together in the Trinity.

[4] *Campenses* is a nickname for the followers of Melitius, who after his exile were forced to meet outside the city in the *campi* or fields.

[5] Antipope.

[6] Arian predecessor of Ambrose as Bishop of Milan.

VALENTINIAN III: EDICT *CERTUM EST* (8 JULY 445)

THE EMPERORS THEODOSIUS AND VALENTINIAN TO AETIUS,[7] MASTER OF THE MILITARY AND PATRICIAN.

It is certain that for us the only defence lies in the favour of the God of heaven; and to deserve it our first care is to support the Christian faith and its venerable religion. Inasmuch then as the primacy of the apostolic see is assured, by the merit of S. Peter, who is chief of the episcopal order, by the rank of the city of Rome, and also by the authority of a sacred synod, let no one presume to attempt any illicit act contrary to the authority of that see. For then at length will the peace of the churches be maintained everywhere, if the whole body acknowledges its ruler. Hitherto these customs have been observed without fail; but Hilary of Arles,[8] as we are informed by the trustworthy report of that venerable man Leo, Pope of Rome, has with contumacious daring ventured upon certain unlawful proceedings; and therefore the churches beyond the Alps have been invaded by abominable disorders, of which a recent example particularly bears witness. For Hilary who is called Bishop of Arles, without consulting the pontiff of the church of the city of Rome, has in solitary rashness usurped his jurisdiction by the ordination of bishops. He has removed some without authority, and indecently ordained others who are unwelcome and repugnant to the citizens. Since these were not readily received by those who had not chosen them, he has collected to himself an armed band and in hostility has either prepared a barrier of walls for a blockade or embarked on aggression. Thus he has led into war those who prayed for peace to the haven of rest. Such men have been admitted contrary to the dignity of the empire and contrary to the reverence due to the apostolic see; and after investigation they have been dispersed by the order of that pious man the Pope of the city. The sentence applies to Hilary and to those whom he has wickedly ordained. This same sentence would have been valid through the Gauls without imperial sanction; for what is not allowed in the Church to the authority of so great a pontiff? Hilary is allowed still to be called a bishop, only by the kindness of the gentle president; and our just command is, that it is not lawful either for him or for anyone else to mix church affairs with arms or to obstruct the orders of the Roman overseer. By such deeds of daring, confidence in, and respect for, our empire is broken down. Not only then do we put away so great a crime; but in order that not even the least disturbance may arise amongst the churches, nor the discipline

---

[7] Aetius (d. 454), "master of both services" (the infantry and the cavalry) and a great general in wars against the barbarians (especially the Visigoths, Burgundians, and Huns), was the most powerful man in the West.

[8] St. Hilary (403-449) was Archbishop of Arles. One of the bishops he tried to remove seems to have been outside his province.

of religion appear in any instance to be weakened, we decree by this eternal law that it shall not be lawful for the bishops of Gaul or of the other provinces, contrary to ancient custom, to do aught without the authority of the venerable Pope of the eternal city. And whatever the authority of the apostolic see has sanctioned, or may sanction, shall be the law for all; so that if any bishop summoned to trial before the pontiff of Rome shall neglect to come, he shall be compelled to appear by the governor of that province. Those things which our divine parents conferred on the Roman church are to be upheld in every way. Wherefore your illustrious and eminent magnificence is to cause what is enacted above to be observed in virtue of this present edict and law. . . .

POPE LEO I: *SERMON III* (c. 450)

As often as GOD's mercy deigns to bring round the day of His gifts to us, there is, dearly-beloved, just and reasonable cause for rejoicing, if only our appointment to the office be referred to the praise of Him who gave it. For though this recognition of GOD may well be found in all His priests, yet I take it to be peculiarly binding on me, who, regarding my own utter insignificance and the greatness of the office undertaken, ought myself also to utter that exclamation of the Prophet, "LORD, I heard Thy speech and was afraid: I considered Thy works and was dismayed." For what is so unwonted and so dismaying as labour to the frail, exaltation to the humble, dignity to the undeserving? And yet we do not despair nor lose heart, because we put our trust not in ourselves but in Him who works in us. And hence also we have sung with harmonious voice the psalm of David, dearly beloved, not in our own praise, but to the glory of Christ the LORD. For it is He of whom it is prophetically written, "Thou art a priest for ever after the order of Melchizedeck," that is, not after the order of Aaron, whose priesthood descending along his own line of offspring was a temporal ministry, and ceased with the law of the Old Testament, but after the order of Melchizedeck, in whom was prefigured the eternal High Priest. And no reference is made to his parentage because in him it is understood that He was portrayed, whose generation cannot be declared. And finally, now that the mystery of this Divine priesthood has descended to human agency, it runs not by the line of birth, nor is that which flesh and blood created; chosen, but without regard to the privilege of paternity and succession by inheritance, those men are received by the Church as its rulers whom the Holy Ghost prepares: so that in the people of GOD's adoption, the whole body of which is priestly and royal, it is not the prerogative of earthly origin which obtains the unction, but the condescension of Divine grace which creates the bishop.

Although, therefore, dearly beloved, we be found both weak and slothful in fulfilling the duties of our office, because, whatever devoted and vigorous action we desire to do, we are hindered by the frailty of our very condition; yet having the unceasing propitiation of the Almighty and perpetual Priest, who being like us and yet equal with the Father, brought down His Godhead even to things human, and raised His Manhood even to things Divine, we worthily and piously rejoice over His dispensation, whereby, though He has delegated the care of His sheep to many shepherds, yet He has not Himself abandoned the guardianship of His beloved flock. And from His overruling and eternal protection we have received the support of the Apostles' aid also, which assuredly does not cease from its operation: and the strength of the foundation, on which the whole superstructure of the Church is reared, is not weakened by the weight of the temple that rests upon it. For the solidity of that faith which was praised in the chief of the Apostles is perpetual: and as that remains which Peter believed in Christ, so that remains which Christ instituted in Peter. For when, as has been read in the Gospel lesson, the LORD had asked the disciples whom they believed Him to be amid the various opinions that were held, and the blessed Peter had replied, saying, "Thou art the Christ, the Son of the living GOD," the LORD said, "Blessed art thou, Simon Bar-Jona, because flesh and blood hath not revealed it to thee, but My Father, which is in heaven. And I say to thee, that thou art Peter, and upon this rock will I build My church, and the gates of Hades shall not prevail against it. And I will give unto thee the keys of the kingdom of heaven. And whatsoever thou shalt bind on earth, shall be bound in heaven; and whatsoever thou shalt loose on earth, shall be loosed also in heaven."

The dispensation of Truth therefore abides, and the blessed Peter persevering in the strength of the Rock, which he has received, has not abandoned the helm of the Church, which he undertook. For he was ordained before the rest in such a way that from his being called the Rock, from his being pronounced the Foundation, from his being constituted the Doorkeeper of the kingdom of heaven, from his being set as the Umpire to bind and to loose, whose judgments shall retain their validity in heaven, from all these mystical titles we might know the nature of his association with Christ. And still to-day he more fully and effectually performs what is entrusted to him, and carries out every part of his duty and charge in Him and with Him, through Whom he has been glorified. And so if anything is rightly done and rightly decreed by us, if anything is won from the mercy of GOD by our daily supplications, it is of his work and merits whose power lives and whose authority prevails in his See. For this, dearly-beloved, was gained by that confession, which, inspired in the Apostle's heart by GOD the Father, transcended all the uncertainty of human opinions, and was endued with the firmness of a rock, which no assaults could shake. For throughout the Church Peter daily says, "Thou art the Christ, the Son of the living GOD," and every tongue which confesses the LORD, accepts the instruction his voice conveys. This Faith conquers the devil, and breaks the bonds of his prisoners. It uproots us from this earth and plants us in heaven, and the gates of Hades cannot prevail against it. For with such solidity is it endued by GOD that the depravity of heretics cannot mar it nor the unbelief of the heathen overcome it.

And so, dearly beloved, with reasonable obedience we celebrate to-day's festival by such methods, that in my humble person he may be recognized and honoured, in whom abides the care of all the shepherds, together with the charge of the sheep commended to him, and whose dignity is not abated even in so unworthy an heir. And hence the presence of my venerable brothers and fellow-priests, so much desired and valued by me, will be the more sacred and precious, if they will transfer the chief honour of this service in which they have deigned to take part to him whom they know to be not only the patron of this see, but also the primate of all bishops. When therefore we utter our exhortations in your ears, holy brethren, believe that he is speaking whose representative we are: because it is his warning that we give, nothing else but his teaching that we preach, beseeching you to "gird up the loins of your mind" and lead a chaste and sober life in the fear of GOD, and not to let your mind forget his supremacy and consent to the lusts of the flesh. Short and fleeting are the joys of this world's pleasures which endeavour to turn aside from the path of life those who are called to eternity. The faithful and religious spirit, therefore, must desire the things which are heavenly, and being eager for the Divine promises, lift itself to the love of the incorruptible Good and the hope of the true Light. But be sure, dearly-beloved, that your labour, whereby you resist vices and fight against carnal desires, is pleasing and precious in GOD's sight, and in GOD's mercy will profit not only yourselves but me also, because the zealous pastor makes his boast of the progress of the LORD's flock. "For ye are my crown and joy," as the Apostle says; if your faith, which from the beginning of the Gospel has been preached in all the world, has continued in love and holiness. For though the whole Church, which is in all the world, ought to abound in all virtues, yet you especially, above all people, it becomes to excel in deeds of piety, because founded as you are on the very citadel of the Apostolic Rock, not only has our LORD Jesus Christ redeemed you in common with all men, but the blessed Apostle Peter has instructed you far beyond all men. Through the same Christ our LORD.

13. THE DONATION OF CONSTANTINE
(c. 750 - c. 800)[1]

One cannot say with certainty when this most famous of all forgeries was made or what precise historical circumstances led to its composition. Different scholars still propose various dates for its appearance and various explanations of its immediate purpose. Obviously it was intended to furnish a documentary basis

[1] From *Select Historical Documents of the Middle Ages,* trans. and ed. by E. F. Henderson (London: G. Bell & Sons Ltd., 1896), pp. 319-329.

for papal territorial and jurisdictional claims in Italy. Probably at least a first draft of it was made shortly after the middle of the eighth century in order to assist Pope Stephen II in his negotiations with the Frankish Mayor of the Palace, Pepin the Short. The Pope crossed the Alps to anoint the latter as king in 754, thereby enabling the Carolingian family, to which Pepin belonged, to supplant the old Merovingian royal line which had become decadent and powerless and to become in law as well as in fact rulers of the Franks. In return, Pepin seems to have promised to give to the Pope those lands in Italy which the Lombards had taken from Byzantium. The promise was fulfilled in 756. Constantine's alleged gift made it possible to interpret Pepin's grant not as a benefaction but as a restoration. Until the Renaissance the Donation was generally, though not universally, accepted as genuine, and it was sometimes used as an argument for asserting the temporal as well as the spiritual supremacy of the Pope over the monarchs of the West.

In the name of the holy and indivisible Trinity, the Father, namely, and the Son and the Holy Spirit. The emperor Caesar Flavius Constantine in Christ Jesus, the Lord God our Saviour, one of that same holy Trinity—faithful, merciful, supreme, beneficent, Alamannic, Gothic, Sarmatic, Germanic, Britannic, Hunic,[2] pious, fortunate, victor and triumpher, always august: to the most holy and blessed father of fathers Sylvester, bishop of the city of Rome and pope, and to all his successors the pontiffs who are about to sit upon the chair of St. Peter until the end of time—also to all the most reverend and of God beloved catholic bishops, subjected by this our imperial decree throughout the whole world to this same holy Roman church, who have been established now and in all previous times—grace, peace, charity, rejoicing, longsuffering, mercy, be with you all from God the Father almighty and from Jesus Christ his Son and from the Holy Ghost.

Our most gracious serenity desires, in clear discourse, through the page of this our imperial decree, to bring to the knowledge of all the people in the whole world what things our Saviour and Redeemer the Lord Jesus Christ, the Son of the most High Father, has most wonderfully seen fit to bring about through his holy apostles Peter and Paul and by the intervention of our father Sylvester, the highest pontiff and the universal pope. First, indeed, putting forth, with the inmost confession of our heart, for the purpose of instructing the mind of all of you, our creed which we have learned from the aforesaid most blessed father and our confessor, Sylvester the universal pontiff; and then at length announcing the mercy of God which has been poured upon us.

For we wish you to know, as we have signified through our former imperial decree, that we have gone away from the worship of idols, from mute and deaf images made by hand, from devilish contrivances and from all the pomps of Satan; and have arrived at the pure faith of the Christians, which is the true light and everlasting life. Believing, according to what he—that same

---

[2] These titles refer to imperial victories over the barbarians.

one, our revered supreme father and teacher, the pontiff Sylvester—has taught us, in God the Father, the almighty maker of Heaven and earth, of all things visible and invisible; and in Jesus Christ, his only Son, our Lord God, through whom all things are created; and in the Holy Spirit, the Lord and vivifier of the whole creature. We confess these, the Father and the Son and the Holy Spirit, in such way that, in the perfect Trinity, there shall also be a fulness of divinity and a unity of power. The Father is God, the Son is God, and the Holy Spirit is God; and these three are one in Jesus Christ.

There are therefore three forms but one power. For God, wise in all previous time, gave forth from himself the word through which all future ages were to be born; and when, by that sole word of His wisdom, He formed the whole creation from nothing, He was with it, arranging all things in His mysterious secret place.

Therefore, the virtues of the Heavens and all the material part of the earth having been perfected, by the wise nod of His wisdom first creating man of the clay of the earth in His own image and likeness, He placed him in a paradise of delight. Him the ancient serpent and envious enemy, the devil, through the most bitter taste of the forbidden tree, made an exile from these joys; and, he being expelled, did not cease in many ways to cast his poisonous darts; in order that, turning the human race from the way of truth to the worship of idols, he might persuade it, namely, to worship the creature and not the creator; so that, through them (the idols), he might cause those whom he might be able to entrap in his snares to be burned with him in eternal punishment. But our Lord, pitying His creature, sending ahead His holy prophets, announcing through them the light of the future life—the coming, that is, of His Son our Lord and Saviour Jesus Christ—sent that same only begotten Son and Word of wisdom: He descending from Heaven on account of our salvation, being born of the Holy Spirit and of the Virgin Mary,—the word was made flesh and dwelt among us. He did not cease to be what He had been, but began to be what He had not been, perfect God and perfect man: as God, performing miracles; as man, sustaining human sufferings. We so learned Him to be very man and very God by the preaching of our father Sylvester, the supreme pontiff, that we can in no wise doubt that He was very God and very man. And, having chosen twelve apostles, He shone with miracles before them and an innumerable multitude of people. We confess that this same Lord Jesus Christ fulfilled the law and the prophets; that He suffered, was crucified, on the third day arose from the dead according to the Scriptures; was received into Heaven, and sitteth on the right hand of the Father. Whence He shall come to judge the quick and the dead, whose kingdom shall have no end. For this is our orthodox creed, placed before us by our most blessed father Sylvester, the supreme pontiff. We exhort, therefore, all people, and all the different nations, to hold, cherish and preach this faith; and, in the name of the Holy Trinity, to obtain the grace of baptism; and, with devout heart, to adore the Lord Jesus Christ our Saviour, who, with the Father and the Holy Spirit, lives and reigns through infinite ages; whom Sylvester our father, the universal pontiff, preaches.

For He himself, our Lord God, having pity on me a sinner, sent His holy apostles to visit us, and caused the light of His splendour to shine upon us. And do ye rejoice that I, having been withdrawn from the shadow, have come to the true light and to the knowledge of truth. For, at a time when a mighty and filthy leprosy had invaded all the flesh of my body, and the care was administered of many physicians who came together, nor by that of any one of them did I achieve health: there came hither the priests of the Capitol, saying to me that a font should be made on the Capitol, and that I should fill this with the blood of innocent infants; and that, if I bathed in it while it was warm, I might be cleansed. And very many innocent infants having been brought together according to their words, when the sacrilegious priests of the pagans wished them to be slaughtered and the font to be filled with their blood: Our Serenity perceiving the tears of the mothers, I straightway abhorred the deed. And, pitying them, I ordered their own sons to be restored to them; and, giving them vehicles and gifts, sent them off rejoicing to their own.

That day having passed therefore—the silence of night having come upon us—when the time of sleep had arrived, the apostles St. Peter and Paul appear, saying to me:

Since thou hast placed a term to thy vices, and hast abhorred the pouring forth of innocent blood, we are sent by Christ the Lord our God, to give to thee a plan for recovering thy health. Hear, therefore, our warning, and do what we indicate to thee. Sylvester—the bishop of the city of Rome—on Mount Serapte, fleeing thy persecutions, cherishes the darkness with his clergy in the caverns of the rocks. This one, when thou shalt have led him to thyself, will himself show thee a pool of piety; in which, when he shall have dipped thee for the third time, all that strength of the leprosy will desert thee. And, when this shall have been done, make this return to thy Saviour, that by thy order through the whole world the churches may be restored. Purify thyself, moreover, in this way, that, leaving all the superstition of idols, thou do adore and cherish the living and true God—who is alone and true—and that thou attain to the doing of His will.

Rising, therefore, from sleep, straightway I did according to that which I had been advised to do by the holy apostles; and, having summoned that excellent and benignant father and our enlightener—Sylvester the universal pope—I told him all the words that had been taught me by the holy apostles; and asked him who were those gods Peter and Paul. But he said that they were not really called gods, but apostles of our Saviour the Lord God Jesus Christ. And again we began to ask that same most blessed pope whether he had some express image of those apostles; so that, from their likeness, we might learn that they were those whom revelation had shown to us. Then that same venerable father ordered the images of those same apostles to be shown by his deacon. And, when I had looked at them, and recognized, represented in those images, the countenances of those whom I had seen in my dream: with a great noise, before all my satraps,[3] I confessed that they were those whom I had seen in my dream.

Hereupon that same most blessed Sylvester our father, bishop of the city of Rome, imposed upon us a time of penance—within our Lateran palace, in the chapel, in a hair garment,—so that I might obtain pardon from our Lord God Jesus Christ our Saviour by vigils, fasts, and tears and prayers, for all things that had been impiously done and unjustly ordered by me. Then through the imposition of the hands of the clergy, I came to the bishop himself; and there, renouncing the pomps of Satan and his works, and all idols made by hands, of my own will before all the people I confessed: that I believed in God the Father almighty, maker of Heaven and earth, and of all things visible and invisible; and in Jesus Christ, His only Son our Lord, who was born of the Holy Spirit and of the Virgin Mary. And, the font having been blessed, the wave of salvation purified me there with a triple immersion. For there I, being placed at the bottom of the font, saw with my own eyes a hand from Heaven touching me; whence rising, clean, know that I was cleansed from all the squalor of leprosy. And, I being raised from the venerable font—putting on white raiment, he administered to me the sign of the seven-fold holy Spirit, the unction of the holy oil; and he traced the sign of the holy cross on my brow, saying: God seals thee with the seal of His faith in the name of the Father and the Son and the Holy Spirit, to signalize thy faith. All the clergy replied: "Amen." The bishop added, "peace be with thee."

And so, on the first day after receiving the mystery of the holy baptism, and after the cure of my body from the squalor of the leprosy, I recognized that there was no other God save the Father and the Son and the Holy Spirit; whom the most blessed Sylvester the pope doth preach; a trinity in one, a unity in three. For all the gods of the nations, whom I have worshipped up to this time, are proved to be demons; works made by the hand of men; inasmuch as that same venerable father told to us most clearly how much power in Heaven and on earth He, our Saviour, conferred on his apostle St. Peter, when finding him faithful after questioning him He said: "Thou art Peter, and upon this rock (*petram*) shall I build My Church, and the gates of hell shall not prevail against it." Give heed ye powerful, and incline the ear of your hearts to that which the good Lord and Master added to His disciple, saying: "and I will give thee the keys of the kingdom of Heaven; and whatever thou shalt bind on earth shall be bound also in Heaven, and whatever thou shalt loose on earth shall be loosed also in Heaven." This is very wonderful and glorious, to bind and loose on earth and to have it bound and loosed in Heaven.

And when, the blessed Sylvester preaching them, I perceived these things, and learned that by the kindness of St. Peter himself I had been entirely re-

[3] There were, of course, no such officials in the Roman Empire.

stored to health: I—together with all our satraps and the whole senate and the nobles and all the Roman people, who are subject to the glory of our rule —considered it advisable that, as on earth he (Peter) is seen to have been constituted vicar of the Son of God, so the pontiffs, who are the representatives of that same chief of the apostles, should obtain from us and our empire the power of a supremacy greater than the earthly clemency of our imperial serenity is seen to have had conceded to it,—we choosing that same prince of the apostles, or his vicars, to be our constant intercessors with God. And, to the extent of our earthly imperial power, we decree that his holy Roman church shall be honoured with veneration; and that, more than our empire and earthly throne, the most sacred seat of St. Peter shall be gloriously exalted; we giving to it the imperial power, and dignity of glory, and vigour and honour.

And we ordain and decree that he shall have the supremacy as well over the four chief seats Antioch, Alexandria, Constantinople[4] and Jerusalem, as also over all the churches of God in the whole world. And he who for the time being shall be pontiff of that holy Roman church shall be more exalted than, and chief over, all the priests of the whole world; and, according to his judgment, everything which is to be provided for the service of God or the stability of the faith of the Christians is to be administered. It is indeed just, that there the holy law should have the seat of its rule where the founder of holy laws, our Saviour, told St. Peter to take the chair of the apostleship; where also, sustaining the cross, he blissfully took the cup of death and appeared as imitator of his Lord and Master; and that there the people should bend their necks at the confession of Christ's name, where their teacher, St. Paul the apostle, extending his neck for Christ, was crowned with martyrdom. There, until the end, let them seek a teacher, where the holy body of the teacher lies; and there, prone and humiliated, let them perform the service of the heavenly king, God our Saviour Jesus Christ, where the proud were accustomed to serve under the rule of an earthly king.

Meanwhile we wish all the people, of all the races and nations throughout the whole world, to know: that we have constructed within our Lateran palace, to the same Saviour our Lord God Jesus Christ, a church with a baptistry from the foundations. And know that we have carried on our own shoulders from its foundations, twelve baskets weighted with earth, according to the number of the holy apostles. Which holy church we command to be spoken of, cherished, venerated and preached of, as the head and summit of all the churches in the whole world—as we have commanded through our other imperial decrees. We have also constructed the churches of St. Peter and St. Paul, chiefs of the apostles, which we have enriched with gold and silver; where also, placing their most sacred bodies with great honour, we have constructed their caskets of electrum, against which no force of the elements prevails. And we have placed a cross of purest gold and precious gems on each

[4] At the time of the fictional date of the Donation, Constantinople was not yet founded.

of their caskets, and fastened them with golden keys. And on these churches for the endowing of divine services we have conferred estates, and have enriched them with different objects; and, through our sacred imperial decrees, we have granted them our gift of land in the East as well as in the West; and even on the northern and southern coast;—namely in Judea, Greece, Asia, Thrace, Africa and Italy and the various islands: under this condition indeed, that all shall be administered by the hand of our most blessed father the pontiff Sylvester and his successors.

For let all the people and the nations of the races in the whole world rejoice with us; we exhorting all of you to give unbounded thanks, together with us, to our Lord and Saviour Jesus Christ. For He is God in Heaven above and on earth below, who, visiting us through His holy apostles, made us worthy to receive the holy sacrament of baptism and health of body. In return for which, to those same holy apostles, my masters, St. Peter and St. Paul; and, through them, also to St. Sylvester, our father,—the chief pontiff and universal pope of the city of Rome,—and to all the pontiffs his successors, who until the end of the world shall be about to sit in the seat of St. Peter: we concede and, by this present, do confer, our imperial Lateran palace, which is preferred to, and ranks above, all the palaces in the whole world; then a diadem, that is, the crown of our head, and at the same time the tiara; and, also, the shoulder band,—that is, the collar that usually surrounds our imperial neck; and also the purple mantle, and crimson tunic, and all the imperial raiment; and the same rank as those presiding over the imperial cavalry; conferring also the imperial sceptres, and, at the same time, the spears and standards; also the banners and different imperial ornaments, and all the advantage of our high imperial position, and the glory of our power.

And we decree, as to those most reverend men, the clergy who serve, in different orders, that same holy Roman church, that they shall have the same advantage, distinction, power and excellence by the glory of which our most illustrious senate is adorned; that is, that they shall be made patricians and consuls,—we commanding that they shall also be decorated with the other imperial dignities. And even as the imperial soldiery, so, we decree, shall the clergy of the holy Roman church be adorned. And even as the imperial power is adorned by different offices—by the distinction, that is, of chamberlains, and door keepers, and all the guards,—so we wish the holy Roman church to be adorned. And, in order that the pontifical glory may shine forth more fully, we decree this also: that the clergy of this same holy Roman church may use saddle cloths of linen of the whitest colour; namely that their horses may be adorned and so be ridden, and that, as our senate uses shoes with goats' hair, so they may be distinguished by gleaming linen; in order that, as the celestial beings, so the terrestrial may be adorned to the glory of God. Above all things, moreover, we give permission to that same most holy one our father Sylvester, bishop of the city of Rome and pope, and to all the most blessed pontiffs who shall come after him and succeed him in all future times—for the honour and glory of Jesus Christ our Lord,—to receive into that great catholic and apostolic church of God, even into the number of the monastic clergy, any one from our senate, who, in free choice, of his own accord, may wish to become a cleric; no one at all presuming thereby to act in a haughty manner.

We also decreed this, that this same venerable one our father Sylvester, the supreme pontiff, and all the pontiffs his successors, might use and bear upon their heads—to the praise of God and for the honour of St. Peter—the diadem; that is, the crown which we have granted him from our own head, of purest gold and precious gems. But he, the most holy pope, did not at all allow that crown of gold to be used over the clerical crown which he wears to the glory of St. Peter; but we placed upon his most holy head, with our own hands, a tiara of gleaming splendour representing the glorious resurrection of our Lord. And, holding the bridle of his horse, out of reverence for St. Peter we performed for him the duty of groom; decreeing that all the pontiffs his successors, and they alone, may use that tiara in processions.

In imitation of our own power, in order that for that cause the supreme pontificate may not deteriorate, but may rather be adorned with power and glory even more than is the dignity of an earthly rule: behold we—giving over to the oft-mentioned most blessed pontiff, our father Sylvester the universal pope, as well our palace, as has been said, as also the city of Rome and all the provinces, districts and cities of Italy or of the western regions; and re-linquishing them, by our inviolable gift, to the power and sway of himself or the pontiffs his successors—do decree, by this our godlike charter and imperial constitution, that it shall be (so) arranged; and do concede that they (the palaces, provinces etc.) shall lawfully remain with the holy Roman church.

Wherefore we have perceived it to be fitting that our empire and the power of our kingdom should be transferred and changed to the regions of the East; and that, in the province of Byzantium, in a most fitting place, a city should be built in our name; and that our empire should there be established. For, where the supremacy of priests and the head of the Christian religion has been established by a heavenly ruler, it is not just that there an earthly ruler should have jurisdiction.

We decree, moreover, that all these things which, through this our im-perial charter and through other godlike commands, we have established and confirmed, shall remain uninjured and unshaken until the end of the world. Wherefore, before the living God, who commanded us to reign, and in the face of his terrible judgment, we conjure, through this our imperial decree, all the emperors our successors, and all our nobles, the satraps also and the most glorious senate, and all the people in the whole world now and in all times previously subject to our rule: that no one of them, in any way, allow himself to oppose or disregard, or in any way seize, these things which, by our imperial sanction, have been conceded to the holy Roman church and to all its pontiffs. If any one, moreover,—which we do not believe—prove a scorner or despiser in this matter, he shall be subject and bound over to eternal damnation; and shall feel that the holy chiefs of the apostles of God, Peter and Paul, will be opposed to him in the present and in the future life. And, being burned in the nethermost hell, he shall perish with the devil and all the impious.

The page, moreover, of this our imperial decree, we, confirming it with our own hands, did place above the venerable body of St. Peter chief of the apostles; and there, promising to that same apostle of God that we would preserve inviolably all its provisions, and would leave in our commands to all the emperors our successors to preserve them, we did hand it over, to be enduringly and happily possessed, to our most blessed father Sylvester the supreme pontiff and universal pope, and, through him, to all the pontiffs his successors —God our Lord and our Saviour Jesus Christ consenting.

And the imperial subscription: May the Divinity preserve you for many years, oh most holy and blessed fathers.

Given at Rome on the third day before the Kalends of April, our master the august Flavius Constantine, for the fourth time, and Galligano, most illustrious men, being consuls.

II

THE BARBARIANS

The irruption of the barbarian tribes into the Roman Empire diluted and altered but did not blot out Roman civilization. Both numerically and culturally inferior to the inhabitants of the lands they overran, they were dazzled by the ancient glory of Rome and often wished to become not the destroyers but merely the new possessors of her authority. Their more intimate contacts with Roman culture, however, came mainly through the intermediary of the already romanized Christian Church. The evangelical zeal of the Irish and Benedictine monks formed the spearhead of her efforts to tame and convert the invaders. When Roman armed resistance failed, her pacific legions moved forward to win a religious and cultural, and therefore final, victory.

1. AMMIANUS MARCELLINUS: A ROMAN DEFEAT (378)[1]

Ammianus Marcellinus (c. 330 - c. 400) was the last great Roman and pagan historian. He wrote a continuation of the history of Tacitus in thirty-one books, of which the last half survived. A soldier who became acquainted with Julian the Apostate (reigned 361-363) in Gaul and who accompanied him on his ill-fated

[1] Reprinted by permission of the publishers of the LOEB CLASSICAL LIBRARY. Translated by John C. Rolfe, *Ammianus Marcellinus,* Volumes I and III, Cambridge, Mass.: Harvard University Press (1935, 1939). I, pp. 279-295; III, 463-483.

Persian expedition, he had a remarkable knowledge of fourth-century army life. The selection below deals with the defeat and death of the Emperor Valens (reigned 364-378) at Hadrianople in 378 at the hands of the Visigoths.

In those same days Valens was troubled for two reasons: first, by the news that the Lentienses had been defeated; secondly, because Sebastianus[2] wrote from time to time exaggerating his exploits. He therefore marched forth from Melanthias,[3] being eager to do some glorious deed to equal his young nephew,[4] whose valiant exploits consumed him with envy. He had under his command a force made up of varying elements, but one neither contemptible, nor unwarlike; for he had joined with them also a large number of veterans, among whom were other officers of high rank and Trajanus, shortly before a commander-in-chief, whom he had recalled to active service. And since it was learned from careful reconnoitring that the enemy were planning with strong guards to block the roads over which the necessary supplies were being brought, he tried competently to frustrate this attempt by quickly sending an infantry troop of bowmen and a squadron of cavalry, in order to secure the advantages of the narrow passes, which were near by. During the next three days, when the barbarians, advancing at a slow pace and through unfrequented places, since they feared a sally, were fifteen miles distant from the city,[5] and were making for the station of Nice,[6] through some mistake or other the emperor was assured by his skirmishers that all that part of the enemy's horde which they had seen consisted of only ten thousand men, and carried away by a kind of rash ardour, he determined to attack them at once.

Accordingly, advancing in square formation, he came to the vicinity of a suburb of Hadrianopolis, where he made a strong rampart of stakes, surrounded by a moat, and impatiently waited for Gratian; there he received Richomeres, general of the household troops, sent in advance by Gratian with a letter, in which he said that he himself also would soon be there. Since the contents besought him to wait a while for the partner in his dangers, and not rashly to expose himself alone to serious perils, Valens called a council of various of his higher officers and considered what ought to be done. And while some, influenced by Sebastianus, urged him to give battle at once, the man called Victor, a commander of cavalry, a Sarmatian by birth, but foresighted and careful, with the support of many others recommended that his imperial colleague be awaited, so that, strengthened by the addition of the Gallic army, he might the more easily crush the fiery over-confidence of the

2 Commander of infantry in the East.
3 Town fifteen miles west of Constantinople.
4 Gratian (reigned 367-383), Emperor in the West.
5 Constantinople.
6 Nike, in Thrace.

barbarians. However, the fatal insistence of the emperor prevailed, supported by the flattering opinion of some of his courtiers, who urged him to make all haste in order that Gratian might not have a share in the victory which (as they represented) was already all but won.

While the necessary preparations for the decisive battle were going on, a Christian presbyter (to use their own term), who had been sent by Fritigern[7] as an envoy, in company with some humble folk came to the emperor's camp. He was courteously received and presented a letter from the same chieftain, openly requesting that to him and his people, whom the rapid forays of savage races had made exiles from their native lands, Thrace only should be granted as a habitation, with all its flocks and crops; and they promised lasting peace if this request were granted. Besides this the aforesaid Christian, apparently a confidant and trusted friend of Fritigern, presented also a private letter of the same king, who, all too skilled in craft and in various forms of deception, informed Valens, pretending that he hoped soon to be his friend and ally, that he could not tame the savagery of his people, or entice them to adopt conditions favourable to the Roman state, unless the emperor should from time to time show them near at hand his army ready for battle, and through the fear aroused by the imperial name check their destructive eagerness for war. But as to the envoys, their sincerity was doubted, and they left without accomplishing their purpose.

But on the dawn of that day which is numbered in the calendar as the fifth before the Ides of August[8] the army began its march with extreme haste, leaving all its baggage and packs near the walls of Hadrianopolis with a suitable guard of legions; for the treasury, and the insignia of imperial dignity besides, with the prefect and the emperor's council, were kept within the circuit of the walls. So after hastening a long distance over rough ground, while the hot day was advancing towards noon, finally at the eighth hour[9] they saw the wagons of the enemy, which, as the report of the scouts had declared, were arranged in the form of a perfect circle. And while the barbarian soldiers, according to their custom, uttered savage and dismal howls, the Roman leaders so drew up their line of battle that the cavalry on the right wing were first pushed forward, while the greater part of the infantry waited in reserve. But the left wing of the horsemen (which was formed with the greatest difficulty, since very many of them were still scattered along the roads) was hastening to the spot at swift pace. And while that same wing was being extended, still without interruption, the barbarians were terrified by the awful din, the hiss of whirring arrows and the menacing clash of shields; and since a part of their forces under Alatheus and Saphrax was far away and, though sent for, had not yet returned, they sent envoys to beg for

[7] Leader of the Visigoths.
[8] 9 August.
[9] 2 p.m.

peace. The emperor scorned these because of their low origin, demanding for the execution of a lasting treaty that suitable chieftains be sent; meanwhile the enemy purposely delayed, in order that during the pretended truce their cavalry might return, who, they hoped, would soon make their appearance; also that our soldiers might be exposed to the fiery summer heat and exhausted by their dry throats, while the broad plains gleamed with fires, which the enemy were feeding with wood and dry fuel, for this same purpose. To that evil was added another deadly one, namely, that men and beasts were tormented by severe hunger.

Meanwhile Fritigern, shrewd to foresee the future and fearing the uncertainty of war, on his own initiative sent one of his common soldiers as a herald, requesting that picked men of noble rank be sent to him at once as hostages and saying that he himself would fearlessly meet the threats of his soldiers and do what was necessary. The proposal of the dreaded leader was welcome and approved, and the tribune Aequitius, then marshal of the court and a relative of Valens, with the general consent was chosen to go speedily as a surety. When he objected, on the ground that he had once been captured by the enemy but had escaped from Dibaltum, and therefore feared their unreasonable anger, Richomeres voluntarily offered his own services and gladly promised to go, thinking this also to be a fine act and worthy of a brave man. And soon he was on his way [bringing] proofs of his rank and birth. . . . As he was on his way to the enemy's rampart, the archers and the targeteers, then under the command of one Bacurius of Hiberia and Cassio, had rushed forward too eagerly in hot attack, and were already engaged with their adversaries; and as their charge had been untimely, so their retreat was cowardly; and thus they gave an unfavourable omen to the beginning of the battle.

This unseasonable proceeding not only thwarted the prompt action of Richomeres, who was not allowed to go at all, but also the Gothic cavalry, returning with Alatheus and Saphrax, combined with a band of the Halani, dashed out as a thunderbolt does near high mountains, and threw into confusion all those whom they could find in the way of their swift onslaught, and quickly slew them.

On every side armour and weapons clashed, and Bellona, raging with more than usual madness for the destruction of the Romans, sounded her lamentable war-trumpets; our soldiers who were giving way rallied, exchanging many encouraging shouts, but the battle, spreading like flames, filled their hearts with terror, as numbers of them were pierced by strokes of whirling spears and arrows. Then the lines dashed together like beaked ships, pushing each other back and forth in turn, and tossed about by alternate movements, like waves at sea.

And because the left wing, which had made its way as far as the very wagons, and would have gone farther if it had had any support, being deserted by the rest of the cavalry, was hard pressed by the enemy's numbers, it was crushed, and overwhelmed, as if by the downfall of a mighty rampart.

The foot-soldiers thus stood unprotected, and their companies were so crowded together that hardly anyone could pull out his sword or draw back his arm. Because of clouds of dust the heavens could no longer be seen, and echoed with frightful cries. Hence the arrows whirling death from every side always found their mark with fatal effect, since they could not be seen beforehand nor guarded against. But when the barbarians, pouring forth in huge hordes, trampled down horse and man, and in the press of ranks no room for retreat could be gained anywhere, and the increased crowding left no opportunity for escape, our soldiers also, with a contempt of death which was their last feeling, received their deathblows, yet struck down their assailants; and on both sides the strokes of axes split helmet and breastplate. Here one might see a barbarian filled with lofty courage, his cheeks contracted in a hiss, hamstrung or with right hand severed, or pierced through the side, on the very verge of death threateningly casting about his fierce glance; and by the fall of the combatants on both sides the plains were covered with the bodies of the slain strewn over the ground, while the groans of the dying and of those who had suffered deep wounds caused a most fearful sound, as they were heard. In this great tumult and confusion the infantry, exhausted by their efforts and the danger, deprived alike of strength and power for planning anything, their lances for the most part broken by constant clashing, content to fight with drawn swords, plunged into the dense masses of the foe, regardless of their lives, seeing all around that every loophole of escape was lost. The ground covered with streams of blood whirled their slippery foothold from under them, so they could only strain every nerve to sell their lives dearly; and they opposed the onrushing foe with such great resolution that some fell by the weapons of their own comrades. Finally, when the whole scene was discoloured with the hue of dark blood, and wherever men turned their eyes heaps of slain met them, they trod upon the bodies of the dead without mercy. Now the sun had risen higher, and when it had finished its course through Leo, and was passing into the house of the heavenly Virgo, scorched the Romans, who were more and more exhausted by hunger and worn out by thirst, as well as distressed by the heavy burden of their armour. Finally our line was broken by the onrushing weight of the barbarians, and since that was the only resort in their last extremity, they took to their heels in disorder as best they could.

While all scattered in flight over unknown paths, the emperor, hedged about by dire terrors, and slowly treading over heaps of corpses, took refuge with the lancers and the *mattiarii*, who, so long as the vast numbers of the enemy could be sustained, had stood unshaken with bodies firmly planted. On seeing him Trajanus cried that all hope was gone, unless the emperor, abandoned by his body-guard, should at least be protected by his foreign auxiliaries. On hearing this the general called Victor hastened to bring quickly to the emperor's aid the Batavi, who had been posted not far off as a reserve force; but when he could find none of them, he retired and went away. And in the same way Richomeres and Saturninus made their escape from danger.

And so the barbarians, their eyes blazing with frenzy, were pursuing our men, in whose veins the blood was chilled with numb horror: some fell without knowing who struck them down, others were buried beneath the mere weight of their pursuers, and some were slain by the sword of a comrade; for though they often rallied, there was no ground given, nor did anyone spare those who retreated. Besides all this, the roads were blocked by many who lay mortally wounded, lamenting the torment of their wounds; and with them also mounds of fallen horses filled the plains with corpses. To these ever irreparable losses, so costly to the Roman state, a night without the bright light of the moon put an end.

At the first coming of darkness the emperor, amid the common soldiers as was supposed (for no one asserted that he had seen him or been with him), fell mortally wounded by an arrow, and presently breathed his last breath; and he was never afterwards found anywhere. For since a few of the foe remained for a long time in the neighbourhood for the purpose of robbing the dead, no one of the fugitives or of the natives ventured to approach the spot. The Caesar Decius, we are told, met a similar fate; for when he was fiercely fighting with the barbarians and his horse, whose excitement he could not restrain, stumbled and threw him, he fell into a marsh, from which he could not get out, nor could his body be found. Others say that Valens did not give up the ghost at once, but with his bodyguard and a few eunuchs was taken to a peasant's cottage near by, well fortified in its second storey; and while he was being treated by unskilful hands, he was surrounded by the enemy, who did not know who he was, but was saved from the shame of captivity. For while the pursuers were trying to break open the bolted doors, they were assailed with arrows from a balcony of the house; and fearing through the inevitable delay to lose the opportunity for pillage, they piled bundles of straw and firewood about the house, set fire to them, and burned it men and all. From it one of the bodyguard leaped through a window, but was taken by the enemy; when he told them what had happened, he filled them with sorrow at being cheated of great glory, in not having taken the ruler of the Roman empire alive. This same young man, having later escaped and returned secretly to our army, gave this account of what had occurred. When Spain had been recovered after a similar disaster, the second of the Scipios, we are told, was burned with a tower in which he had taken refuge and which the enemy had set on fire. This much, at any rate, is certain, that neither Scipio nor Valens had the fortune of burial which is death's final honour.

Amid this manifold loss of distinguished men, the deaths of Trajanus and Sebastianus stood out. With them fell thirty-five tribunes, without special assignments, and leaders of bodies of troops as well as Valerianus and Aequitius, the one having charge of the stables, the other, of the Palace. Among these also Potentius lost his life in the first flower of his youth; he was tribune of the *promoti*,[10] respected by all good men and honoured both for his own services and those of his father Ursicinus, formerly a commander-in-chief.

[10] Soldiers given a special rank for their good service.

Certain it is that barely a third part of our army escaped. The annals record no such massacre of a battle except the one at Cannae, although the Romans more than once, deceived by trickery due to an adverse breeze of Fortune, yielded for a time to ill-success in their wars, and although the storied dirges of the Greeks have mourned over many a contest.

2. PRISCUS: AN EMBASSY TO THE HUNS (448)[1]

The Roman historian Priscus accompanied the ambassador Maximin on an embassy from the Emperor Theodosius II to Attila in 448. He wrote an account of his mission which does much to dissipate the impression obtained from some contemporary historians of the utter savagery and primitiveness of the Huns.

When Attila entered the village he was met by girls advancing in rows, under thin white canopies of linen, which were held up by the outside women who stood under them, and were so large that seven or more girls walked beneath each. There were many lines of damsels thus canopied, and they sang Scythian songs. When he came near the house of Onegesius,[2] which lay on his way, the wife of Onegesius issued from the door, with a number of servants, bearing meat and wine, and saluted him and begged him to partake of her hospitality. This is the highest honour that can be shown among the Scythians. To gratify the wife of his friend, he ate, just as he sat on his horse, his attendants raising the tray to his saddlebow; and having tasted the wine, he went on to the palace, which was higher than the other houses and built on an elevated site. But we remained in the house of Onegesius, at his invitation, for he had returned from his expedition with Attila's son. His wife and kinsfolk entertained us to dinner, for he had no leisure himself, as he had to relate to Attila the result of his expedition, and explain the accident which had happened to the young prince, who had slipped and broken his right arm. After dinner we left the house of Onegesius, and took up our quarters nearer the palace, so that Maximin might be at a convenient distance for visiting Attila or holding intercourse with his court. The next morning, at dawn of

---

[1] J. B. Bury, *History of the Later Roman Empire* (London, Macmillan and Company Ltd., 1923), I, 283-288, by permission of Macmillan and Company Ltd. and St. Martin's Press, Inc.

[2] One of Attila's chieftains.

day, Maximin sent me to Onegesius, with presents offered by himself as well
as those which the Emperor had sent, and I was to find out whether he would
have an interview with Maximin and at what time. When I arrived at the
house, along with the attendants who carried the gifts, I found the doors
closed, and had to wait until some one should come out and announce our
arrival. As I waited and walked up and down in front of the enclosure which
surrounded the house, a man, whom from his Scythian dress I took for a
barbarian, came up and addressed me in Greek, with the word Χαῖρε, "Hail!"
I was surprised at a Scythian speaking Greek. For the subjects of the Huns,
swept together from various lands, speak, besides their own barbarous tongues,
either Hunnic or Gothic, or—as many as have commercial dealings with the
western Romans—Latin; but none of them easily speak Greek, except captives
from the Thracian or Illyrian sea-coast; and these last are easily known to any
stranger by their torn garments and the squalor of their heads, as men who
have met with a reverse. This man, on the contrary, resembled a well-to-do
Scythian, being well dressed, and having his hair cut in a circle after Scythian
fashion. Having returned his salutation, I asked him who he was and whence
he had come into a foreign land and adopted Scythian life. When he asked
me why I wanted to know, I told him that his Hellenic speech had prompted
my curiosity. Then he smiled and said that he was born a Greek and had gone
as a merchant to Viminacium, on the Danube, where he had stayed a long
time, and married a very rich wife. But the city fell a prey to the barbarians,
and he was stript of his prosperity, and on account of his riches was allotted
to Onegesius in the division of the spoil, as it was the custom among the
Scythians for the chiefs to reserve for themselves the rich prisoners. Having
fought bravely against the Romans and the Acatiri, he had paid the spoils he
won to his master, and so obtained freedom. He then married a barbarian
wife and had children, and had the privilege of eating at the table of
Onegesius.

   He considered his new life among the Scythians better than his old life
among the Romans, and the reasons he gave were as follows: "After war the
Scythians live in inactivity, enjoying what they have got, and not at all, or
very little, harassed. The Romans, on the other hand, are in the first place
very liable to perish in war, as they have to rest their hopes of safety on others,
and are not allowed, on account of their *tyrants,* to use arms. And those who
use them are injured by the cowardice of their generals, who cannot support
the conduct of war. But the condition of the subjects in time of peace is far
more grievous than the evils of war, for the exaction of the taxes is very severe,
and unprincipled men inflict injuries on others, because the laws are practically not valid against all classes. A transgressor who belongs to the wealthy
classes is not punished for his injustice, while a poor man, who does not
understand business, undergoes the legal penalty, that is if he does not depart
this life before the trial, so long is the course of lawsuits protracted, and so
much money is expended on them. The climax of the misery is to have to

pay in order to obtain justice. For no one will give a court to the injured man unless he pay a sum of money to the judge and the judge's clerks."

In reply to this attack on the Empire, I asked him to be good enough to listen with patience to the other side of the question. "The creators of the Roman republic," I said, "who were wise and good men, in order to prevent things from being done at haphazard, made one class of men guardians of the laws, and appointed another class to the profession of arms, who were to have no other object than to be always ready for battle, and to go forth to war without dread, as though to their ordinary exercise, having by practice ex-hausted all their fear beforehand. Others again were assigned to attend to the cultivation of the ground, to support both themselves and those who fight in their defence, by contributing the military corn-supply. . . . To those who protect the interests of the litigants a sum of money is paid by the latter, just as a payment is made by the farmers to the soldiers. Is it not fair to support him who assists and requite him for his kindness? The support of the horse benefits the horseman. . . . Those who spend money on a suit and lose it in the end cannot fairly put it down to anything but the injustice of their case. And as to the long time spent on lawsuits, that is due to concern for justice, that judges may not fail in passing correct judgments, by having to give sen-tence offhand; it is better that they should reflect, and conclude the case more tardily, than that by judging in a hurry they should both injure man and transgress against the Deity, the institutor of justice. . . . The Romans treat their servants better than the king of the Scythians treats his subjects. They deal with them as fathers or teachers, admonishing them to abstain from evil and follow the lines of conduct which they have esteemed honourable; they reprove them for their errors like their own children. They are not allowed, like the Scythians, to inflict death on them. They have numerous ways of conferring freedom; they can manumit not only during life, but also by their wills, and the testamentary wishes of a Roman in regard to his property are law."

My interlocutor shed tears, and confessed that the laws and constitution of the Romans were fair, but deplored that the governors, not possessing the spirit of former generations, were ruining the State. . . .

The next day I entered the enclosure of Attila's palace, bearing gifts to his wife, whose name was Kreka. She had three sons, of whom the eldest governed the Acatiri and the other nations who dwell in Pontic Scythia. Within the enclosure were numerous buildings, some of carved boards beau-tifully fitted together, others of straight, fastened on round wooden blocks which rose to a moderate height from the ground. Attila's wife lived here, and, having been admitted by the barbarians at the door, I found her reclin-ing on a soft couch. The floor of the room was covered with woollen mats for walking on. A number of servants stood round her, and maids sitting on the floor in front of her embroidered with colours linen cloths intended to be placed over the Scythian dress for ornament. Having approached, saluted, and presented the gifts, I went out, and walked to another house, where Attila was, and waited for Onegesius, who, as I knew, was with Attila. I stood in the middle of a great crowd—the guards of Attila and his attendants knew me, and so no one hindered me. I saw a number of people advancing, and a great commotion and noise, Attila's egress being expected. And he came forth from the house with a dignified gait, looking round on this side and on that. He was accompanied by Onegesius, and stood in front of the house; and many persons who had lawsuits with one another came up and received his judgment. Then he returned into the house, and received ambassadors of barbarous peoples. . . .

When we returned to our tent the father of Orestes came with an invitation from Attila for both of us to a banquet at three o'clock. When the hour arrived we went to the palace, along with the embassy from the western Romans, and stood on the threshold of the hall in the presence of Attila. The cup-bearers gave us a cup, according to the national custom, that we might pray before we sat down. Having tasted the cup, we proceeded to take our seats; all the chairs were ranged along the walls of the room on either side. Attila sat in the middle on a couch; a second couch was set behind him, and from it steps led up to his bed, which was covered with linen sheets and wrought coverlets for ornament, such as Greeks and Romans use to deck bridal beds. The places on the right of Attila were held chief in honour, those on the left, where we sat, were only second. Berichus, a noble among the Scythians, sat on our side, but had the precedence of us. Onegesius sat on a chair on the right of Attila's couch, and over against Onegesius on a chair sat two of Attila's sons; his eldest son sat on his couch, not near him, but at the extreme end, with his eyes fixed on the ground, in shy respect for his father. When all were arranged, a cup-bearer came and handed Attila a wooden cup of wine. He took it, and saluted the first in precedence, who, honoured by the salutation, stood up, and might not sit down until the king, having tasted or drained the wine, returned the cup to the attendant. All the guests then honoured Attila in the same way, saluting him, and then tasting the cups; but he did not stand up. Each of us had a special cup-bearer, who would come forward in order to present the wine, when the cup-bearer of Attila retired. When the second in precedence and those next to him had been honoured in like manner, Attila toasted us in the same way according to the order of the seats. When this ceremony was over the cup-bearers retired, and tables, large enough for three or four, or even more, to sit at, were placed next the table of Attila, so that each could take of the food on the dishes without leaving his seat. The attendant of Attila first entered with a dish full of meat, and behind him came the other attendants with bread and viands, which they laid on the tables. A luxurious meal, served on silver plate, had been made ready for us and the barbarian guests, but Attila ate nothing but meat on a wooden trencher. In everything else, too, he showed himself temperate; his cup was of wood, while to the guests were given goblets of gold and silver. His dress, too, was quite simple, affecting only to be clean. The sword he carried at his side, the latchets of his Scythian shoes, the bridle of his horse were not adorned, like those of the other Scythians, with gold or gems or anything costly. When the viands of the first course had been consumed we all stood up, and did not resume our seats until each one, in the order before observed, drank to the health of Attila in the goblet of wine presented to him. We then sat down, and a second dish was placed on each table with eatables of another kind. After this course the same ceremony was observed as after the first. When evening fell torches were lit, and two barbarians coming forward in front of Attila sang songs they had composed, celebrating his victories and deeds of valour in war. And of the guests, as they looked at the singers, some were pleased with the verses, others reminded of wars were excited in their souls, while yet others, whose bodies were feeble with age and their spirits compelled to rest, shed tears. After the songs a Scythian, whose mind was deranged, appeared, and by uttering outlandish and senseless words forced the company to laugh. After him Zerkon, the Moorish dwarf, entered. He had been sent by Attila as a gift to Aetius, and Edecon had persuaded him to come to Attila in order to recover his wife, whom he had left behind him in Scythia; the lady was a Scythian whom he had obtained in marriage through the influence of his patron Bleda. He did not succeed in recovering her, for Attila was angry with him for returning. On the occasion of the banquet he made his appearance, and threw all except Attila into fits of unquenchable laughter by his appearance, his dress, his voice, and his words, which were a confused jumble of Latin, Hunnic, and Gothic. Attila, however, remained immovable and of unchanging countenance, nor by word or act did he betray anything approaching to a smile of merriment except at the entry of Ernas, his youngest son, whom he pulled by the cheek, and gazed on with a calm look of satisfaction. I was surprised that he made so much of this son, and neglected his other children; but a barbarian who sat beside me and knew Latin, bidding me not reveal what he told, gave me to understand that prophets had forewarned Attila that his race would fall, but would be restored by this boy. When the night had advanced we retired from the banquet, not wishing to assist further at the potations.

3. GREGORY OF TOURS: CLOVIS (*c. 591*)[1]

Bishop Gregory of Tours (*c.* 540-594) wrote a most valuable (if somewhat credulous and ungrammatical) history of the Franks down to the year 591. A pious churchman of ancient and aristocratic Gallo-Roman stock, he devoted much of his work, as might be expected, to the condemning of Merovingian crimes, particularly

[1] From Gregory of Tours, *History of the Franks,* trans. by O. M. Dalton, 1927, by permission of the Clarendon Press, Oxford. II, pp. 65-70, 74-81.

those of Chilperic I of Neustria (561-584) and his wicked queen Fredegund. He was a supporter, however, of King Guntram of Burgundy (561-592) and saw the necessity for an alliance between king and church in order to control local anarchy. His account of the career of Clovis I (reigned 481-511) is certainly embellished by legend, but there is no reason to doubt its substantial accuracy. Gregory had every reason to be prejudiced in favor of the first Christian ruler of the Franks; this makes his portrait of a ruthless and faithless conqueror all the more convincing.

After this, Childeric died,[2] and Clovis his son reigned in his stead. In the fifth year of his reign, Syagrius, king of the Romans, son of Aegidius, had his residence in the city of Soissons, which had before been the home of the above-mentioned Aegidius. Clovis marched against him, with his relation Ragnachar, himself also a king, and called upon him to fix a field of battle. Syagrius did not seek delay nor did he fear to stand his ground. And so when the battle was joined between them, Syagrius, seeing his army crushed, turned to flight and escaped as fast as he could to Alaric at Toulouse.[3] But Clovis sent to Alaric calling upon him to surrender the fugitive, else he must look to be himself invaded for giving him refuge. Then Alaric, lest he should incur the wrath of the Franks for his sake, was afraid, after the craven habit of the Goths, and handed him over to the messengers in bonds. When Clovis received him prisoner, he ordered him to be imprisoned; had him put to the sword in secret, while he took possession of his kingdom.

At this time many churches were plundered by the troops of Clovis, because he was yet fast held in pagan errors. Thus it happened that a ewer of great size and beauty had been taken, with other ornaments used in the service of the church. But the bishop of that church sent messengers to the king, asking that if no other of the sacred vessels might be restored, his church might at least receive back this ewer. When the king heard this he said to the envoy: "Follow us to Soissons, for there all the booty is to be divided, and if the lot gives me the vessel, I will fulfil the desire of the bishop." When they were at Soissons and all the spoil was laid out in open view, the king said: "I ask you, most valiant warriors, not to refuse to cede me that vessel" (he meant the ewer of which I have spoken) "over and above my share." After this speech all the men of sense replied: "All that is before our eyes, most glorious king, is thine; we ourselves are submitted to thy power. Do now that which seemeth good to thee, for none is so strong as to say thee nay." At these words a soldier of a vain, jealous, and unstable temper raised his axe and smote the ewer, crying with a loud voice: "Naught shalt thou receive of this but that which thine own lot giveth thee." While all stood astounded at this act, the king suppressed his resentment at the wrong under a show of patient mildness; he then took the ewer and restored it to the bishop's envoy. But the wound re-

---

[2] In 490.
[3] Alaric II, d. 507 in the Battle of Vouillé.

mained hidden in his heart. After the lapse of a year, he commanded the whole army to assemble with full equipment, and to exhibit their arms in their brightness on the field of Mars.[4] The king went round inspecting them all; but when he came to the man who struck the ewer he said: "None hath appeared with his arms so ill-kept as thou; neither thy lance, nor thy sword, nor thy axe is fit for use." He then seized the axe, and threw it on the ground. As the man bent down a little to take it up, the king swung his own axe high and cleft his skull, saying as he did it, "Thus didst thou treat the ewer at Soissons." The man lying dead, he dismissed the rest, having put great fear of him into their hearts by his act. Clovis waged many wars and won many victories. For in the tenth year of his reign he invaded the Thuringians and subjected them to his rule.

At that time the king of the Burgundians was Gundloc, of the race of the royal persecutor Athanaric whom I have before mentioned. He had four sons, Gundobad, Godigisel, Chilperic, and Gundomar. Gundobad put his brother Chilperic to the sword, and drowned his wife by tying a stone to her neck. Her two daughters he condemned to exile, the elder of whom, Chrona, had adopted the habit of a nun, while the younger was called Clotild. It happened that Clovis used often to send envoys into Burgundy, and they discovered the young Clotild. Observing her grace and understanding, and learning that she was of the blood royal, they spoke of these things to King Clovis, who straightway sent an embassy to Gundobad, asking her in marriage. Gundobad was afraid to refuse, and handed her over to the men, who received her, and with all speed brought her before the king. At sight of her he greatly rejoiced and was united to her in wedlock, having already by a concubine one son named Theuderic.

Of Queen Clotild the king had a firstborn son whom the mother wished to be baptized; she therefore persistently urged Clovis to permit it, saying: "The gods whom ye worship are naught; they cannot aid either themselves or others, seeing that they are images carved of wood or stone, or metal. Moreover the names which ye have given them are the names of men and not of gods. Saturn was a man, fabled to have escaped by flight from his son to avoid being thrust from his kingdom; Jupiter also, the lewdest practiser of all debaucheries and of unnatural vice, the abuser of the women of his own family, who could not even abstain from intercourse with his own sister, as she herself admitted in the words 'sister and spouse of Jove.' What power had Mars and Mercury? They may have been endowed with magical arts; they never had the power of the divine name. But ye should rather serve Him, who at His word created out of nothing the heaven and earth, the sea and all therein; who made the sun to shine and adorned the heaven with stars; who filled the waters with fish, the earth with animals, the air with birds; at whose nod the lands are made fair with fruits, the trees with apples, the vines

[4] In the spring of each year the early Franks customarily held a solemn military review.

with grapes; by whose hand the race of man was created; by whose largess every creature was made to render homage and service to the man whom he created." Though the queen ever argued thus, the king's mind was nowise moved towards belief, but he replied: "It is by command of our gods that all things are created and come forth; it is manifest that thy god availeth in nothing; nay more, he is not even proven to belong to the race of gods." But the queen, true to her faith, presented her son for baptism; she ordered the church to be adorned with hangings and curtains, that the king, whom no preaching could influence, might by this ceremony be persuaded to belief. The boy was baptized and named Ingomer, but died while yet clothed in the white raiment of his regeneration.[5] Thereupon the king was moved to bitter wrath, nor was he slow to reproach the queen, saying: "If the child had been dedicated in the name of my gods, surely he would have survived, but now, baptized in the name of thy God, he could not live a day." The queen replied: "I render thanks to Almighty God, Creator of all things, who hath not judged me all unworthy, and deigneth to take into His kingdom this child born of my womb. My mind is untouched by grief at this event, since I know that they which be called from this world in the white robes of baptism shall be nurtured in the sight of God." Afterwards she bore another son, who was baptized with the name of Chlodomer. When he too began to ail, the king said: "It cannot but befall that this infant like his brother shall straightway die, being baptized in the name of thy Christ." But the mother prayed, and God ordained that the child should recover.

Now the queen without ceasing urged the king to confess the true God, and forsake his idols; but in no wise could she move him to this belief, until at length he made war upon a time against the Alamanni, when he was driven of necessity to confess what of his free will he had denied.[6] It befell that when the two hosts joined battle there was grievous slaughter, and the army of Clovis was being swept to utter ruin. When the king saw this he lifted up his eyes to heaven; and knew compunction in his heart, and, moved to tears, cried aloud: "Jesus Christ, Thou that art proclaimed by Clotild Son of the living God, Thou that art said to give aid to those in stress, and to grant victory to those that hope in Thee, I entreat from a devout heart the glory of Thy succour. If Thou grant me victory over these enemies, and experience confirm that power which the people dedicated to Thy name claimeth to have proved, then will I also believe on Thee and be baptized in Thy name. I have called upon mine own gods, but here is proof that they have withdrawn themselves from helping me; wherefore I believe that they have no power, since they come not to the succour of their servants. Thee do I now invoke, on Thee am I fain to believe, if but I may be plucked out of the hands of mine adversaries." And as he said this, lo, the Alamanni turned their backs, and began

---

[5] A reference to the custom of wearing white robes during the period immediately after baptism.

[6] In 496.

to flee. And when they saw that their king was slain, they yielded themselves to Clovis, saying: "No longer, we entreat thee, let the people perish; we are now thy men." Then the king put an end to the war, and having admonished the people, returned in peace, relating to the queen how he had called upon the name of Christ and had been found worthy to obtain the victory. This happened in the fifteenth year of his reign.

Then the queen commanded the holy Remigius, bishop of Reims, to be summoned secretly, entreating him to impart the word of salvation to the king. The bishop, calling the king to him in privity, began to instil into him faith in the true God, Maker of heaven and earth, and urged him to forsake his idols, which were unable to help either himself or others. But Clovis replied: "I myself, most holy father, will gladly hearken to thee; but one thing yet remaineth. The people that followeth me will not suffer it that I forsake their gods; yet will I go, and reason with them according to thy word." But when he came before the assembled people, or ever he opened his mouth, the divine power had gone forth before him, and all the people cried with one voice: "O gracious king, we drive forth our gods that perish, and are ready to follow that immortal God whom Remigius preacheth." News of this was brought to the bishop, who was filled with great joy, and commanded the font to be prepared. The streets were overshadowed with coloured hangings, the churches adorned with white hangings, the baptistery was set in order, smoke of incense spread in clouds, perfumed tapers gleamed, the whole church about the place of baptism was filled with the divine fragrance. And now the king first demanded to be baptized by the bishop. Like a new Constantine, he moved forward to the water, to blot out the former leprosy, to wash away in this new stream the foul stains borne from old days. As he entered to be baptized the saint of God spoke these words with eloquent lips: "Meekly bow thy proud head, Sicamber;[7] adore that which thou hast burned, burn that which thou hast adored." For the holy Remigius, the bishop, was of excellent learning, and above all skilled in the art of rhetoric, and so exemplary in holiness that his miracles were equal to those of the holy Silvester; there is preserved to us a book of his life, in which it is related how he raised a man from the dead. The king therefore, confessing Almighty God, three in one, was baptized in the name of the Father, the Son, and the Holy Ghost, and anointed with holy chrism, with the sign of the Cross of Christ. Of his army were baptized more than three thousand; and his sister Albofled, who not long after was taken to the Lord, was likewise baptized. And when the king was sorrowing for her death, the holy Remigius sent him a letter of consolation, beginning after this fashion: "The cause of thy sadness doth afflict me with a great affliction, for that thy sister of fair memory hath passed away. But this shall console us, that she hath in such wise left the world as that we should rather lift up our eyes to her than mourn her." And another of his sisters was con-

---

[7] The Franks liked to identify themselves with the Sicambrians, an ancient barbarian tribe.

verted, by name Lanthechild, who had fallen into the heresy of the Arians; she also received the holy chrism, having confessed the Son and the Holy Ghost equal to the Father. . . .

Now when Alaric, king of the Goths, beheld the manner in which King Clovis kept steadily subduing his neighbours in war, he sent envoys to him with this message: "If it please thee, O my brother, I am minded that we two meet by God's grace." Clovis did not refuse, but came to him. They met on an island in the Loire near the village of Amboise in the territory of the city of Tours. There they conversed, ate and drank together, swore mutual friendship, and parted in peace. Many people in Gaul at this time ardently desired to live under the dominion of the Franks.

This was the reason why Quintianus, bishop of Rodez, incurred hatred and was driven from the city. Men said to him: "It is because thou desirest the Franks to become masters and possess this land."[8] A few days afterwards there was a quarrel between him and the citizens. Those of the Gothic nation dwelling in the town were suspicious of him, and the citizens accused him of wishing to bring them under the Frankish rule. They took counsel together, and planned to put him to the sword. But the man of God was warned, and rising in the night with the most faithful of his attendants, left Rodez and came to Clermont. There he was kindly received by the holy bishop Eufrasius, successor to Aprunculus of Dijon, who kept him with him, and bestowed on him houses, lands, and vineyards, saying: "The riches of this church suffice to support us both; only let the brotherly love preached by the blessed apostle continue among the priests of God." The bishop of Lyons also presented him with possessions of his church in Auvergne. The remaining history of the holy Quintianus, both the treachery which he endured, and the works which the Lord deigned to perform by his hands, is written in the book containing his life.

Now King Clovis said to his men: "It irketh me sore that these Arians hold a part of Gaul. Let us go forth, then, and with God's aid bring the land under our own sway." This speech finding favour with all, he assembled his army, and marched on Poitiers, where King Alaric then happened to be. Part of the troops had to traverse the territory of Tours, and out of reverence for the blessed Martin[9] the king issued an edict that none should take anything from that region but water and hay. Now a certain soldier, finding some hay belonging to a poor man, said: "Was it not the king's order that we should take grass and nothing besides? Well, this is grass, and if we take it we shall not transgress his bidding." So he took the hay from the poor man by force, taking advantage of his own strength. The matter came to the ears of the king, who straightway cut the man down with his own sword, saying: "Where shall be our hope of victory, if we offend the blessed Martin?" And the army was content to take nothing more from this region. Moreover the king sent mes-

[8] Clovis was preferred by the clergy because he was orthodox; the Goths were Arian heretics.

[9] A patron saint of France, bishop of Tours in the late fourth century, evangelizer of the pagan countryside, largely responsible for the rapid spread of monasticism in Gaul.

sengers to the church of the saint, with these words: "Go now, and haply ye shall bring some good auspice of victory from that sacred house." He entrusted them with offerings to be set in the holy place, saying: "If Thou, O Lord, art my helper, and if Thou hast determined to deliver into my hands this un-believing people, ever set against Thee, deign of Thy favour to give me a sign at the going in to the basilica of the blessed Martin, that I may know that Thou wilt deign to show Thy servant Thy favour." His men, setting forth on their journey, reached Tours according to the king's command. And as they were entering the church, the precentor chanced to lead this antiphon: "Thou hast girded me, O Lord, with strength unto the battle; Thou hast subdued under me those that rose up against me. Thou hast also made mine enemies turn their backs upon me, and Thou hast destroyed them that hate me." The messengers, hearing these words chanted, gave thanks to God, and vowing gifts to the blessed confessor, joyfully returned with their news to the king. But when Clovis had reached the Vienne with his army he was wholly at a loss where to cross the stream, for it was swollen by heavy rains. That night he besought the Lord that He would show him where he might pass, and lo! at dawn a hind of wondrous size entered the river at God's bidding, and where she forded the host saw that it could cross. When the king came to the neighbourhood of Poitiers, but was abiding at some distance in his tents, he saw a fiery beacon issue from the church of the holy Hilary and come over above his head; it signified that aided by the light of the blessed confessor Hilary he might more surely overcome the host of those heretics against whom the saint himself had so often done battle for the faith. He adjured the whole army to despoil no man, either there or upon the way, and to rob none of his goods.

In those days the abbot Maxentius, a man laudable in holiness, lived rec-luse for the fear of God in his monastery in the territory of Poitiers. I give no particular name to the monastery, since to our own day the place is always known as the cell of the holy Maxentius. Now when the monks beheld a dense body of soldiers drawing near the monastery, they besought the abbot to come forth out of his cell for their encouragement. He delayed to come. Then, stricken with panic, they opened the cell door and brought him out, whereupon he went forth fearlessly to meet the enemy as if to ask peace of them. One of their number unsheathed his sword to strike the abbot on the head, when lo! he found his hand held rigid at the level of his ear, while the sword fell backwards; he then fell at the feet of the holy man, and besought his pardon. When the rest saw what was done, they returned to the army in great dread, fearing that they might all perish. But the blessed confessor rubbed the man's arm with consecrated oil, and making the sign of the Cross, restored him to health; thus by his protection the monastery remained un-harmed. He performed many other miracles, which whoso seeks diligently will find as he reads the history of the abbot's Life. This took place in the twenty-fifth year of Clovis.

In the mean time King Clovis encountered Alaric, king of the Goths, on

the field of Vouillé at the tenth milestone out of Poitiers. Part of the combatants fought with missiles from a distance, another part hand to hand. But
when, as their habit is, the Goths turned to fly, King Clovis by God's aid
obtained the victory. He had with him as an ally Chloderic, son of Sigibert
the Lame. This Sigibert, in the fight at Zülpich against the Alamanni, was
wounded in the knee so that he limped. When the Goths were put to flight,
and the king had slain Alaric, two of the enemy suddenly came up and struck
at him with their spears on each side; the cuirass which he wore and the
speed of his horse preserved him from death. There perished on this field a
great number of the people of Auvergne who had come with Apollinaris,[10] and
the chief men of senatorial family fell. From this battle Amalaric, son of
Alaric, fled into Spain and ruled with prudence his father's kingdom. Clovis
sent his own son Theuderic through Albi and Rodez to Clermont. Traversing
these cities he subdued beneath his father's sway the whole country from the
Gothic to the Burgundian frontier. Alaric had reigned twenty-two years.
Clovis, after wintering in Bordeaux, carried off all Alaric's treasures from
Toulouse and came to Angoulême. And the Lord showed him such favour
that the walls fell down of themselves before his eyes; he drove out the Goths
and subjected the city to his own rule. Then, his victory being complete, he
returned to Tours and made many offerings to the holy shrine of the holy
Martin.

Clovis received letters from the emperor Anastasius[11] conferring the con-
sulate[12] and in the church of the blessed Martin he was vested in the purple
tunic, and in a mantle, and set the diadem upon his head. Then, mounting
his horse, he showered with his own hand in the generosity of his heart pieces
of gold and silver among the people all along the road between the gate of
the atrium of the holy Martin's church, and the church of the city. From that
day he was hailed as consul or Augustus.[13] He left Tours and came to Paris,
where he established the seat of his government. There he was joined by
Theuderic.

After the death of Eustochius, bishop of Tours, Licinius was consecrated
as eighth bishop after Martin. In his time was waged the war which I have
above described, and it was in his time that King Clovis came to Tours. He is
said to have been in the East, to have visited the holy places, and to have even
entered Jerusalem; it is related that he often saw the places of the Passion and
Resurrection of our Lord, of which we read in the Gospels.

While Clovis was sojourning at Paris, he sent secretly to the son of Sigibert,[14] saying: "Thy father is grown old, and is lame of one foot. If he were

[10] Son of Sidonius Apollinaris (c. 432 - c. 480), Bishop of Auvergne, poet and letter
writer.

[11] Byzantine Emperor, 491-518.

[12] Barbarian kings gained prestige from Roman titles, however unrelated they were
to political reality.

[13] Clovis was certainly not given the title *Augustus* because this was reserved for
the Emperor.

[14] King of the Ripuarian Franks.

to die, his kingdom would fall to thee of right, together with our friendship."
The prince, seduced through his ambition, plotted his father's death. One day
Sigibert left Cologne and crossed the Rhine, to walk in the forest of Buchau.
He was enjoying a midday repose in his tent when his son compassed his
death by sending assassins against him, intending so to get possession of the
kingdom. But by the judgement of God he fell himself into the pit which
he had treacherously digged for his father. He sent messengers to King Clovis
announcing his father's death in these terms: "My father hath perished, and
his kingdom and treasures are in my power. Come to me, and right gladly
will I hand over to thee whatever things may please thee from his treasure."
Clovis answered: "I thank thee for thy goodwill, and request of thee that thou
show all to my envoys; but thou shalt keep the whole." On the arrival of the
envoys, the prince displayed his father's treasure, and while they were inspecting its various contents, said to them: "In this coffer my father used to amass
pieces of gold." They answered: "Plunge in thy hand to the bottom, to make
sure of all." He did so; but as he was stooping, one of them raised his two-
edged axe and buried it in his brain; so was his guilt towards his father requited on himself. When Clovis heard that Sigibert was slain, and his son
also, he came to Cologne and called all the people together, addressing them
in these words: "Hear ye what hath befallen. While I was sailing the Scheldt,
Chloderic, son of my cousin, was harassing his father, and telling him that I
desired his death. When his father fled through the forest of Buchau, he set
bandits upon him, delivering him over to death. But he in his turn hath
perished, stricken I know not by whom, while he was showing his father's
treasure. To all these deeds I was in no wise privy; for I could not bear to shed
the blood of my kindred, holding it an impious deed. But since things have so
fallen out, I offer you this counsel, which take, if it seemeth good to you:
turn ye to me, and live under my protection." At these words the clash of
shields vied with their applause; they raised Clovis upon a shield, and recognized him as their king. Thus he became possessed of the kingdom of Sigibert
and of his treasures, and submitted the people also to his dominion. For daily
the Lord laid his enemies low under his hand, and increased his kingdom, because he walked before Him with an upright heart, and did that which was
pleasing in His sight.

After this he marched against King Chararic.[15] For during his war with
Syagrius, this Chararic, summoned to his aid, stood aloof, joining neither side,
but awaiting the issue in order to ally himself with the victor, for which cause
Clovis marched against him full of wrath. And he cunningly circumvented
him and took him, together with his son; he then bound them, and cut off
their hair, commanding that Chararic should be ordained priest, and his son
deacon. Chararic lamented his humiliation and wept; but they say that his
son replied: "These branches have been cut from a green tree, nor are they
all withered, but shall soon shoot forth, and grow again. May he who has done
these things as swiftly perish!" This saying reached the ears of Clovis, who

[15] King of the Salian Franks.

thought that they threatened to let their hair grow again and compass his death. He therefore ordered both of their heads to be cut off. After their death, he took possession of their kingdom, together with their treasure and their people.

There was at that time in Cambrai a king named Ragnachar, whose wantonness was so unbridled that he hardly spared his own near kindred. He had as counsellor a certain Farron, defiled by the same foul taint, in regard to whom it was alleged that when any one brought the king a gift of food or a present, or any other kind of thing, the king would say that the gift was sufficient for him and his Farron. On this account the hearts of the Franks were swollen with the utmost indignation. Thereupon Clovis presented armlets and baldrics of spurious gold to the *leudes*[16] of Ragnachar in order that they might call him in against their lord; the supposed gold was only copper, cunningly gilded. When he had set his army on foot against him, Ragnachar kept sending out scouts to bring in intelligence. These men were asked on their return in what strength the enemy was. They answered: "Abundant force for thee and for thy Farron." But Clovis came, and drew up his battle array. And when Ragnachar saw his army vanquished, he made ready to escape in flight, but he was caught by his own men, and brought before Clovis with his arms bound behind his back; so likewise was Ricchar his brother. Clovis said to him: "Why hast thou disgraced our race by suffering thyself to be bound? It had been better for thee to die"; he then raised his axe and buried it in his head. Afterwards he turned to his brother, and said: "If thou hadst stood by thy brother, he would not have been thus bound," and slew him in the same way with a blow of his axe. After their death, their betrayers for the first time discovered that the gold which Clovis had given them was false. But when they remonstrated with the king, men say that he replied: "This is the kind of gold deserved by the man who of set mind lureth his lord to his death"; adding that they ought to be content to have escaped with their lives, not expiating the betrayal of their lords by a death amid torments. When they heard this, they chose to sue for grace, declaring that it sufficed them if they were judged worthy to live. The two kings of whom I have spoken were kinsmen of Clovis. Their brother, Rignomer, was slain at Le Mans by his command, and the kingdom and treasures of all three passed into his possession. He caused many other kings to be slain and the near relatives whom he suspected of usurping his kingdom; in this way he extended his dominion over all Gaul. Upon a day when he had assembled his own people, he is said to have spoken as follows of the kinsmen whom he had destroyed: "Woe unto me who remain as a traveller among strangers, and have none of my kin to help me in the evil day." But he did not thus allude to their death out of grief, but craftily, to see if he could bring to light some new relative to kill.

After these events Clovis died at Paris,[17] and was buried in the church

[16] Sworn companions and followers.
[17] In 506.

of the Holy Apostles[18] which he had himself built, with Clotild his queen. It was the fifth year after the battle of Vouillé that he passed away. And all the days of his reign were thirty years, and of his own age forty-five. From the passing of the holy Martin to the passing of Clovis, which was in the eleventh year of the episcopate of Licinius, bishop of Tours, there are counted one hundred and twelve years. After the death of her lord, Queen Clotild came to Tours, and, save for rare visits to Paris, here she remained all the days of her life, distinguished for her great modesty and kindliness.

4. POPE GREGORY I: ST. BENEDICT (593-594)[1]

St. Benedict of Nursia (*c.* 480 - *c.* 547) is justly regarded as the father of western monasticism. His rule, which he said was written "for beginners," exerted a very important influence on the religious life of the Middle Ages. St. Benedict enjoined his monks to follow poverty, chastity, and obedience, to respect the commands of their abbot as if they were those of Christ, and to cherish a lifelong allegiance to their particular monastic house. He did not deny the merits of extreme asceticism as practiced by the solitary hermit, especially popular in the East, but his legislation, more suitable to the practical temper of the West, was directed towards those who preferred the moderate cenobitic way and who wished to submit themselves to the discipline of a monastic society. His followers, including both laymen and clerics, were expected to work as well as to pray. The multitude of religious houses that observed his Rule became oases of economic and cultural activity in addition to serving as fortresses of religious devotion and missionary zeal.

St. Benedict's biographer St. Gregory the Great (reigned 590-604) was one of the most remarkable of early medieval popes. His achievements included the defense of Rome against the Lombards, the conversion of England, and the writing of many famous works of mystical and practical theology. He was always a vigorous supporter of monasticism, in which he found an extremely useful instrument for the furtherance of his policies.

There was a man of saintly life; blessed Benedict was his name, and he was blessed also with God's grace. Even in boyhood he showed mature understanding, for he kept his heart detached from every pleasure with a strength of character far beyond his years. While still living in the world, free to enjoy

---

[18] Later Sainte Geneviève.

[1] St. Gregory the Great, *Dialogues,* trans. by Odo John Zimmerman, O.S.B., from *The Fathers of the Church,* Vol. 39 (New York, 1959), pp. 55-60, 79-81, 107-108, reprinted by permission of the Catholic University of America Press.

its earthly advantages, he saw how barren it was with its attractions and turned from it without regret.

He was born in the district of Norcia of distinguished parents, who sent him to Rome for a liberal education. But when he saw many of his fellow students falling headlong into vice, he stepped back from the threshold of the world in which he had just set foot. For he was afraid that if he acquired any of its learning he, too, would later plunge, body and soul, into the dread abyss. In his desire to please God alone, he turned his back on further studies, gave up home and inheritance and resolved to embrace the religious life. He took this step, well aware of his ignorance, yet wise, uneducated though he was.

I was unable to learn about all his miraculous deeds. But the few that I am going to relate I know from the lips of four of his own disciples: Constantine, the holy man who succeeded him as abbot; Valentinian, for many years superior of the monastery at the Lateran; Simplicius, Benedict's second successor; and Honoratus, who is still abbot of the monastery where the man of God first lived.[2]

When Benedict abandoned his studies to go into solitude, he was accompanied only by his nurse, who loved him dearly. As they were passing through Affile, a number of devout men invited them to stay there and provided them with lodging near the Church of St. Peter. One day, after asking her neighbors to lend her a tray for cleaning wheat, the nurse happened to leave it on the edge of the table and when she came back found it had slipped off and broken in two. The poor woman burst into tears; she had only borrowed this tray and now it was ruined. Benedict, who had always been a devout and thoughtful boy, felt sorry for his nurse when he saw her weeping. Quietly picking up both the pieces, he knelt down by himself and prayed earnestly to God, even to the point of tears. No sooner had he finished his prayer than he noticed that the two pieces were joined together again, without even a mark to show where the tray had been broken. Hurrying back at once, he cheerfully reassured his nurse and handed her the tray in perfect condition.

News of the miracle spread to all the country around Affile and stirred up so much admiration among the people that they hung the tray at the entrance of their church. Ever since then it has been a reminder to all of the great holiness Benedict had acquired at the very outset of his monastic life. The tray remained there many years for everyone to see, and it is still hanging over the doorway of the church in these days of Lombard rule. Benedict, however, preferred to suffer ill-treatment from the world rather than enjoy its praises. He wanted to spend himself laboring for God, not to be honored by the applause of men. So he stole away secretly from his nurse and fled to a lonely wilderness about thirty-five miles from Rome called Subiaco. A stream of cold, clear water running through the region broadens out at this point to form a lake, then flows off and continues on its course. On his way there

[2] At Subiaco, in central Italy.

Benedict met a monk named Romanus, who asked him where he was going. After discovering the young man's purpose, Romanus kept it secret and even helped him carry it out by clothing him with the monastic habit and supplying his needs as well as he could.

At Subiaco, Benedict made his home in a narrow cave and for three years remained concealed there, unknown to anyone except the monk Romanus, who lived in a monastery close by under the rule of Abbot Deodatus. With fatherly concern this monk regularly set aside as much bread as he could from his own portion; then from time to time, unnoticed by his abbot, he left the monastery long enough to take the bread to Benedict. There was no path leading from the monastery down to his cave because of a cliff that rose directly over it. To reach him Romanus had to tie the bread to the end of a long rope and lower it over the cliff. A little bell attached to the rope let Benedict know when the bread was there, and he would come out to get it. The ancient Enemy of mankind grew envious of the kindness shown by the older monk in supplying Benedict with food, and one day, as the bread was being lowered, he threw a stone at the bell and broke it. In spite of this, Romanus kept on with his faithful service.

At length the time came when almighty God wished to grant him rest from his toil and reveal Benedict's virtuous life to others. Like a shining lamp his example was to be set on a lampstand to give light to everyone in God's house. The Lord therefore appeared in a vision to a priest some distance away, who had just prepared his Easter dinner. "How can you prepare these delicacies for yourself," He asked, "while my servant is out there in the wilds suffering from hunger?"

Rising at once, the priest wrapped up the food and set out to find the man of God that very day. He searched for him along the rough mountainsides, in the valleys, and through the caverns, until he found him hidden in the cave. They said a prayer of thanksgiving together and then sat down to talk about the spiritual life. After a while the priest suggested that they take their meal. "Today is the great feast of Easter," he added.

"It must be a great feast to have brought me this kind visit," the man of God replied, not realizing after his long separation from men that it was Easter Sunday.

"Today is really Easter," the priest insisted, "the feast of our Lord's Resurrection. On such a solemn occasion you should not be fasting. Besides, I was sent here by almighty God so that both of us could share in His gifts."

After that they said grace and began their meal. When it was over they conversed some more and then the priest went back to his church.

At about the same time some shepherds also discovered Benedict's hiding place. When they first looked through the thickets and caught sight of him clothed in rough skins, they mistook him for some wild animal. Soon, however, they recognized in him a servant of God, and many of them gave up their sinful ways for a life of holiness. As a result, his name became known to all the people in that locality and great numbers visited his cave, supplying him with the food he needed and receiving from his lips in return spiritual food for their souls.

One day, while the saint was alone, the Tempter came in the form of a little blackbird, which began to flutter in front of his face. It kept so close that he could easily have caught it in his hand. Instead, he made the sign of the cross and the bird flew away. The moment it left, he was seized with an unusually violent temptation. The evil spirit recalled to his mind a woman he had once seen, and before he realized it his emotions were carrying him away. Almost overcome in the struggle, he was on the point of abandoning the lonely wilderness, when suddenly with the help of God's grace he came to himself.

He then noticed a thick patch of nettles and briers next to him. Throwing his garment aside he flung himself into the sharp thorns and stinging nettles. There he rolled and tossed until his whole body was in pain and covered with blood. Yet, once he had conquered pleasure through suffering, his torn and bleeding skin served to drain the poison of temptation from his body. Before long, the pain that was burning his whole body had put out the fires of evil in his heart. It was by exchanging these two fires that he gained the victory over sin. So complete was his triumph that from then on, as he later told his disciples, he never experienced another temptation of this kind.

Soon after, many forsook the world to place themselves under his guidance, for now that he was free from these temptations he was ready to instruct others in the practice of virtue. That is why Moses commanded the Levites to begin their service when they were twenty-five years old or more and to become guardians of the sacred vessels only at the age of fifty.

. . . . .

. . . Once while the Goths[3] were still in power, Totila their king happened to be marching in the direction of Benedict's monastery.[4] When still some distance away, he halted with his troops and sent a messenger ahead to announce his coming, for he had heard that the man of God possessed the gift of prophecy. As soon as he received word that he would be welcomed, the crafty king decided to put the saint's prophetic powers to a test. He had Riggo, his sword-bearer, fitted out with royal robes and riding boots and directed him to go in this disguise to the man of God. Vul, Ruderic and Blidin, three men from his own bodyguard, were to march at his side as if he really were king of the Goths. To supplement these marks of kingship, Totila also provided him with a swordbearer and other attendants.

As Riggo entered the monastery grounds in his kingly robes and with all his attendants, Benedict caught sight of him and as soon as the company came

[3] The Ostrogoths.
[4] Probably in 543.

within hearing called out from where he sat. "Son, lay aside the robes you are wearing," he said. "Lay them aside. They do not belong to you." Aghast at seeing what a great man he had tried to mock, Riggo sank to the ground, and with him all the members of his company. Even after they had risen to their feet they did not dare approach the saint, but hurried back in alarm to tell their king how quickly they had been detected.

King Totila then went to the monastery in person. The moment he noticed the man of God sitting at a distance, he was afraid to come any closer and fell down prostrate where he was. Two or three times Benedict asked him to rise. When Totila still hesitated to do so in his presence, the servant of Christ walked over to him and with his own hands helped him from the ground. Then he rebuked the king for his crimes and briefly foretold everything that was going to happen to him. "You are the cause of many evils," he said. "You have caused many in the past. Put an end now to your wickedness. You will enter Rome and cross the sea. You have nine more years to rule, and in the tenth year you will die."

Terrified at these words, the king asked for a blessing and went away. From that time on he was less cruel. Not long after, he went to Rome and then crossed over to Sicily. In the tenth year of his reign he lost his kingdom and his life as almighty God had decreed.

There is also a story about the bishop of Canosa, who made regular visits to the abbey and stood high in Benedict's esteem because of his saintly life. Once while they were discussing Totila's invasion and the downfall of Rome,[5] the bishop said, "The city will be destroyed by this king and left without a single inhabitant."

"No," Benedict assured him, "Rome will not be destroyed by the barbarians. It will be shaken by tempests and lightnings, hurricanes and earthquakes, until finally it lies buried in its own ruins."

The meaning of this prophecy is perfectly clear to us now. We have watched the walls of Rome crumble and have seen its homes in ruins, its churches destroyed by violent storms, and its dilapidated buildings surrounded by their own debris.

. . . . .

I should like to tell you much more about this saintly abbot, but I am purposely passing over some of his miraculous deeds in my eagerness to take up those of others. There is one more point, however, I want to call to your attention. With all the renown he gained by his numerous miracles, the holy man was no less outstanding for the wisdom of his teaching. He wrote a Rule for Monks that is remarkable for its discretion and its clarity of language. Anyone who wishes to know more about his life and character can discover in his Rule exactly what he was like as abbot, for his life could not have differed from his teaching.

[5] Captured by Totila in 546.

In the year that was to be his last, the man of God foretold the day of his holy death to a number of his disciples. In mentioning it to some who were with him in the monastery, he bound them to strict secrecy. Some others, however, who were stationed elsewhere he only informed of the special sign they would receive at the time of his death.

Six days before he died he gave orders for his tomb to be opened. Almost immediately he was seized with a violent fever that rapidly wasted his remaining strength. Each day his condition grew worse until finally, on the sixth day, he had his disciples carry him into the chapel, where he received the Body and Blood of our Lord to gain strength for his approaching end. Then, supporting his weakened body on the arms of his brethren, he stood with his hands raised to heaven and as he prayed breathed his last.

That day two monks, one of them at the monastery, the other some distance away, received the very same revelation. They both saw a magnificent road covered with rich carpeting and glittering with thousands of lights. From his monastery it stretched eastward in a straight line until it reached up into heaven. And there in the brightness stood a man of majestic appearance, who asked them, "Do you know who passed this way?"

"No," they replied.

"This," he told them, "is the road taken by blessed Benedict, the Lord's beloved, when he went to heaven."

Thus, while the brethren who were with Benedict witnessed his death, those who were absent knew about it through the sign he had promised them. His body was laid to rest in the Chapel of St. John the Baptist, which he had built to replace the altar of Apollo.

5. IRISH MONASTIC EVANGELISM[1]

St. Columban came to Gaul while Gregory of Tours was still alive, but represents an altogether more ascetic view of Christianity than his contemporary. With St. Columba of Iona, Columban is the most illustrious representative of Irish monastic evangelism, which for a time had hardly a rival in missionary fervor and success. Leaving Bangor in Ireland about 590, he came to Gaul and set up two monasteries at Annegray and Luxeuil. Though at first received kindly, he antagonized the Frankish bishops by his independence and introduction of Irish usages. He also

[1] Jonas, *Life of St. Columban,* trans. by D. C. Munro, *Translations and Reprints from the Original Sources of European History,* Series I, Vol. II, No. 7 (Philadelphia, University of Pennsylvania Press, 1902), pp. 18-24; St. Columban, *Boat-Song,* trans. by C. T. Davis from *Sancti Columbani Opera,* ed. by G. S. M. Walker (Dublin, Institute for Advanced Studies, 1957), pp. 190-192.

enraged King Theuderich (reigned 595-613) by his open denunciation of that monarch's refusal to put away his concubines. Exiled in 610, Columban spent some time preaching among the heathen Alamanni around Lake Constance and then settled in northern Italy, where he founded the great house and center of learning, Bobbio, in 612.

Jonas, his biographer, came to Bobbio in 618 and was soon asked by Abbot Bertulf to write the saint's life. Since Jonas could use both documents and firsthand oral accounts, his biography is unusually reliable.

Columban's *Boat-Song* combines Virgilian allusions with a fresh and direct style which conveys well the mixture of adventurous wanderlust and austere religiosity that characterized the missionaries of Ireland.

JONAS: FROM *LIFE OF ST. COLUMBAN* (c. 620)

The fame of Columban had already penetrated into all parts of Gaul and Germany, and everyone was praising the venerable man. Theuderich too came often to him and humbly begged his prayers. For Theuderich had succeeded to the kingdom in the following manner: Sigibert had been murdered in the royal estate of Vitry, which is not far from Arras, at the instigation of his brother Chilperich, who was then living in Tournay and was being hunted to death by Sigibert. After the death of the latter, through the influence of his wife Brunhilda, the kingdom passed to his son Childebert (II). When the latter died in his youth,[2] he was succeeded by his two sons, Theudebert and Theuderich, who ruled together with their grandmother Brunhilda. Austrasia went to Theudebert, Burgundy to Theuderich, who thought that he was fortunate in having St. Columban in his kingdom.

As he very often visited Columban, the holy man began to reprove him because he sinned with concubines, and did not satisfy himself with the comforts of a lawful wife, in order to beget royal children from an honored queen, and not bastards by his concubines. After this reproof from Columban, the king promised to abstain from such sinful conduct. But the old serpent came to his grandmother Brunhilda, who was a second Jezebel, and aroused her pride against the holy man, because she saw that Theuderich was obedient to him. For she feared that her power and honor would be lessened if, after the expulsion of the concubines, a queen should rule the court.

St. Columban happened one day to go to Brunhilda, who was then on the estate of Brocariaca.[3] As she saw him enter the court, she led to him the illegitimate sons of Theuderich. When St. Columban saw her, he asked what she wanted of him. Brunhilda answered, "These are the king's sons; give them thy blessing." He replied, "Know that these boys will never bear the royal sceptre, for they were begotten in sin." Enraged, she told the boys to go. When after this Columban left the court, a loud cracking noise was heard, the whole

[2] A.D. 596.
[3] Near Autun. [Translator's notes.]

house trembled and everyone shook with fear. But that did not avail to check the wrath of the wretched woman.

From that time she began to persecute the neighboring monasteries. She issued an order that none of the monks should be allowed to leave the lands of the monasteries, no one should receive them into other houses or give them any aid. When Columban saw that at the court all were arrayed against him, he hastened to Spissia, where the king was then staying, in order to subdue such defiance by his warnings. When he reached that place, about sunset, and it was announced to the king that Columban was there but would not enter the palace, Theuderich said it would be better with due reverence to offer the needful services to the man of God, than to arouse the wrath of the Lord, by insulting His servant. Accordingly he ordered suitable food to be prepared in the royal kitchen and sent to the servant of God.

When the attendants came to Columban and, in accordance with the king's command, offered him food and drink prepared with royal magnificence, he asked what they meant by it. When they told him that it was sent by the king, he pushed it from him and said: "It is written, 'The Most High is not pleased with the offerings of the wicked. For it is not meet that the mouth of the servant of the Lord should be defiled by the food of him who shuts out the servant of God, not only from his own dwelling, but also from the dwellings of others.'" At these words all of the dishes broke into pieces, so that the wine and liquor ran out on the ground and the food was scattered here and there. Terrified, the servants announced this to the king. Full of anxiety, he, together with his grandmother, hastened to Columban early in the morning. Both begged him to forgive their past sins and promised amendment. With his fears quieted by this, Columban returned to his convent. But they failed to keep their promises, and very soon the persecutions were renewed with increased bitterness by the king, who continued in his former sinful course. Then Columban sent him a letter full of reproaches, and threatened him with the ban if he did not amend his conduct.

Now Brunhilda began again to incite the king against Columban in every way, urged all the nobles and others at court to do the same, and influenced the bishops to attack Columban's faith and to abolish his monastic rule. She succeeded so fully that the holy man was obliged to answer for his faith or leave the country. The king, incited by Brunhilda, went to Luxeuil and accused Columban of violating the customs of the country and of not allowing all Christians to enter the interior of the monastery. To these accusations Columban answered, for he was unterrified and full of courage, that it was not his custom to allow laymen to enter the dwelling of the servant of God, but he had prepared a suitable place where all who came would be received. The king replied: "If you wish to enjoy any longer the gifts of our grace and favor, everyone in the future must be allowed free entrance everywhere." Columban answered: "If you dare to violate the monastic rule in any particular, I will not accept any gift or aid from you in the future. But if you come here to destroy the monasteries of the servant of God and to undermine their discipline and regulations, I tell you that your kingdom will be destroyed together with all your royal family." This the king afterward found to be true. In his audacity, he had already stepped into the refectory; terrified by these words, he withdrew hastily.

But when Columban attacked him with bitter insults, Theuderich said: "You want me to honor you with the crown of martyrdom; do not believe that I am foolish enough to commit such a crime. But I will follow a wiser and more useful plan. Since you depart from the common customs, I will send you back to the home from which you came." At the same time the members of the court resolved unanimously that they would not put up with anyone who was unwilling to associate with everyone. But Columban said that he would not leave his monastery unless he was dragged out by force.

The king now withdrew, but left behind a nobleman named Baudulf. The latter drove the holy man out of his monastery and carried him to Besançon into banishment, until the king had determined what further action to take. While there Columban heard that the prison was full of condemned men awaiting the death penalty. The man of God hastened to them and, having entered the gate without opposition, he preached the word of God to the condemned. They promised him that if they were liberated they would amend their lives and would do penance for the crimes which they had committed. After this Columban commanded his attendant, whom we have mentioned above, to take in his hand the iron to which their feet were fettered, and to pull it. When the boy took hold of it and pulled, it broke into bits like the rotten trunk of a tree. Columban ordered the condemned to leave the prison now that their feet were free and, after preaching the Gospel to them, he washed their feet and dried them with a linen towel. Then he commanded them to go to the church and do penance for the crimes they had committed and to wash away their faults by their tears. They hastened thither and found the doors of the church fastened.

When the captain of the soldiers saw the fetters of the condemned broken by Columban, through the power of God, and that only the empty prison remained, he started, as though aroused from sleep, to follow the tracks of the condemned. The latter, seeing that the soldiers were coming after them and that the doors of the church were shut, hemmed in by the two-fold difficulty, reproached the man of God for having released them. But he, breathing anxiously, raised his face to heaven and prayed to the Lord that He would not permit those whom He had released from the iron by His strength, to be again delivered into the hands of the soldiers. Without delay, the goodness of the Creator opened the doors, which had been securely fastened, and disclosed a way of escape to those in peril. The condemned quickly entered the church. After their entrance the doors were shut without human hands, before the eyes of the soldiers, just as if a custodian with a key had quickly unlocked them and then locked them again. Columban arrived with his followers and the captain coming up at the same time with his soldiers, found the doors shut. They sought the janitor, Aspasius by name, to get the key. When he came with the key and tried to open the doors he said he had never found them more tightly closed. Nor did anyone, after that, dare to do any injury to the condemned, whom the divine grace had liberated.

As Columban now saw that he was not watched at all and that no one did him any injury (for all saw that he was strong in the strength of the Lord and therefore all refrained from injuring him, in order not to be associated in guilt), one Sunday he climbed to the top of the mountain. For the city is so situated that the houses are clustered together on the side of a steep mountain. Above, the lofty cliffs rise perpendicularly into the heavens. The mountain cut off on all sides by the river Dou, which surrounds it, leaves no path open for travelers. Columban waited till noon to see whether anyone would prevent his returning to his monastery. Then he took the road leading directly through the city.

When they heard of this, Brunhilda and Theuderich were embittered still more. They again ordered a band of soldiers to carry off the man of God by violence and to take him again to his former place of exile. Accordingly the soldiers went with their captain and wandered through the precincts of the monastery, seeking the man of God. He was then in the vestibule of the church reading a book. They came repeatedly and passed near him, so that some struck against him with their feet and touched his garments with their garments, but did not see him because their eyes were blinded. And it was a most beautiful sight. He, exulting, perceived that he was sought and was not found. While he saw them, they did not see him sitting in the midst of them. The captain came and, looking through the window, saw the man of God sitting joyfully amid them and reading. Perceiving the power of God, he said: "Why do you go wandering about the vestibule of the church and do not find him? Your hearts are wholly filled with the madness of insanity; for you will not be able to find him whom the divine power conceals. Leave this undertaking and we will hasten to announce to the king that you could not find him." By this it was clearly shown that the captain of the soldiers had not come willingly to do injury to the man of God, and therefore had merited to see him.

They told the king. He, impelled by the madness of his wretched purpose, sent Count Bertarius, with the men of his guard, to seek more diligently for Columban, and at the same time Baudulf whom he had formerly sent. They finding the holy man in the church praying and singing psalms with all the brethren, said to him: "Oh man of God, we beg you to obey the king's orders and our own, and to return to the place whence you came to this land." But Columban answered, "I do not think it would be pleasing to my Creator if I should go back to the home which I left because of my love for Christ." When they saw that Columban would not obey them they withdrew. But they left behind several men of rough disposition and character.

Those who remained urged the man of God to have pity on them, since they had been perfidiously left behind to perform such a task, and to think of their peril. If they did not violently eject him they would be in danger of death. But he, as he had very often asserted, said he would not withdraw unless he was compelled to by violence. The men impelled by fear, since they were in imminent peril in either event, clung to the robe which he wore; others upon their knees besought him not to impute to them the guilt of so great a crime, since they were not following their own wishes, but obeying the commands of the king.

He finally decided to yield, in order not to imperil others, and departed amid universal sorrow and grief. Escorts were furnished him who were not to leave his side until they had conducted him to the boundary of the kingdom at Nantes. Ragamund was their leader. All the brethren followed, as if it was a funeral; for grief filled the hearts of all. The father in anxiety for the loss of so many members, raised his eyes to heaven, and said, "Oh Creator of the world, prepare for us a place where Thy people may worship Thee." Then he comforted the brethren, telling them to put their trust in the Lord and to give great praise to omnipotent God. This was not an injury to him or his followers, but an opportunity to increase the number of monks. Those who wished to follow him and had courage to bear all his sufferings might come. The others who wanted to remain in the monastery should do so, knowing that God would quickly avenge their injuries. But since the monks did not want to be deprived of the guardianship of their shepherd all resolved to go. But the king's servants declared that only those would be allowed to follow him who were his countrymen or who had come to him from Brittany; the others, by the king's command, were to remain in that place. When the father perceived that his followers were violently torn from him, his grief and that of his followers was increased. But he prayed to the Lord, the Comforter of all men, to take those into His own keeping, whom the king's violence tore from him. Among these was Eustasius, the scholar and servant of Columban, who was afterward abbot in this very convent, of which his uncle, Mietius, bishop of Langres, had charge.

So, twenty years after he had come to this place the holy man departed and went by the way of Besançon and Autun to the fortress Cavalo. On the way the king's master of horse wanted to kill him with a lance. But the hand of God hindered it and lamed the man's hand, so that the lance fell on the ground at his feet and he himself seized by a supernatural power fell prone before Columban. The latter, however, cared for him till the next morning and then sent him home healed.

ST. COLUMBAN: *BOAT-SONG* (c. 600)

Cut in the forests, swept down the two-horned Rhine,
Our keel, tight-caulked, now floats upon the sea.
Heia, men! Let the echoes resound with our heia!
The wild gusts swell, the slashing torrents fall,
But manly strength has force to tame the storm.

Heia, men! Let the echoes resound with our heia!
To earnest effort, clouds and tempest yield;
Zeal and unceasing labor conquer all.
Heia, men! Let the echoes resound with our heia!
Endure and save yourselves for better things;
O you who have suffered worse, this too shall end.
Heia, men! Let the echoes resound with our heia!
So when the loathsome foe assaults our hearts,
Tempting and shaking the depths of our hearts with passion,
Let your souls, men, remembering Christ, cry heia!
In resolution fixed, scorn Satan's wiles.
By virtues armed, defend yourselves with valor.
Let your souls, men, remembering Christ, cry heia!
Firm faith and holy ardor conquer all.
The ancient fiend, defeated, breaks his arrows.
Let your souls, men, remembering Christ, cry heia!
The Source of Good and Being, the Highest Power,
Offers the warrior and gives the victor prizes.
Let your souls, men, remembering Christ, cry heia!

6. ST. BEDE: CONVERSION OF THE ENGLISH[1]

One of the greatest medieval historians and scholars, St. Bede (c. 673-735) provides in his *Ecclesiastical History* an indispensable account of the early years of the English Church. The following selections from it give a description of two crucial occasions: the initial landing in 597 of the monks sent by Pope Gregory I and their reception by King Ethelbert of Kent; and the Synod of Whitby in 663, scene of the decisive confrontation in Northumbria of missionaries who followed the customs of Ireland and missionaries who obeyed the centralizing discipline of Rome.

ST. AUGUSTINE'S MISSION (597)

Reassured by the encouragement of the blessed father Gregory, Augustine and his fellow-servants of Christ resumed their work in the word of God, and

[1] Bede, *A History of the English Church and People*, I, 25-27; III, 24, trans. by Leo Sherley-Price (Harmondsworth, Middlesex, Penguin Books Ltd., 1955), pp. 66-71, 182-188.

arrived in Britain. The King of Kent at this time was the powerful King Ethelbert, whose domains extended northwards to the river Humber, which forms the boundary between the north and south Angles. To the east of Kent lies the large island of Thanet, which by English reckoning is six hundred hides[2] in extent; it is separated from the mainland by a waterway about three furlongs broad called the Wantsum, which joins the sea at either end, and is fordable only in two places. It was here that God's servant Augustine landed with companions, who are said to have been forty in number. At the direction of blessed Pope Gregory, they had brought interpreters from among the Franks, and they sent these to Ethelbert, saying that they came from Rome bearing very glad news, which infallibly assured all who would receive it of eternal joy in heaven, and an everlasting kingdom with the living and true God. On receiving this message, the king ordered them to remain in the island where they had landed, and gave directions that they were to be provided with all necessaries until he should decide what action to take. For he had already heard of the Christian religion, having a Christian wife of the Frankish royal house named Bertha,[3] whom he had received from her parents on condition that she should have freedom to hold and practise her faith unhindered with Bishop Liudhard whom they had sent as her chaplain.

After some days, the king came to the island, and sitting down in the open air, summoned Augustine and his companions to an audience. But he took precautions that they should not approach him in a house, for he held an ancient superstition that if they were practisers of magical arts, they might have opportunity to deceive and master him. But the monks were endowed with power from God, not from the Devil, and approached the king carrying a silver cross as their standard, and the likeness of our Lord and Saviour painted on a board. First of all they offered prayer to God, singing a litany for the eternal salvation both of themselves and of those for whose sake they had come. And when, at the king's command, Augustine had sat down and preached the word of life to the king and his court, the king said: "Your words and promises are fair indeed, but they are new and strange to us, and I cannot accept them and abandon the age-old beliefs of the whole English nation. But since you have travelled far, and I can see that you are sincere in your desire to instruct us in what you believe to be true and excellent, we will not harm you. We will receive you hospitably, and take care to supply you with all that you need; nor will we forbid you to preach and win any people you can to your religion." The king then granted them a dwelling in the city of Canterbury, which was the chief city of all his realm, and in accordance with his promise, he allowed them provisions and did not withdraw their freedom to preach. Tradition says that as they approached the city, bearing the holy cross and the likeness of our great King and Lord Jesus Christ as was their custom, they sang in unison this litany : "We pray Thee, O Lord, in all

[2] A hide was a unit of land, supposedly the normal holding of a peasant.
[3] Daughter of Charibert, King of Paris.

Thy mercy, that Thy wrath and anger may be turned away from this city and from Thy holy house, for we are sinners. Alleluia."

As soon as they had occupied the house given to them they began to emulate the life of the apostles and the primitive Church. They were constantly at prayer; they fasted and kept vigils; they preached the word of life to whomsoever they could. They regarded worldly things as of little importance, and accepted only necessary food from those they taught. They practised what they preached, and were willing to endure any hardship, and even to die for the Faith which they proclaimed. A number of heathen, admiring the simplicity of their holy lives and the comfort of their heavenly message, believed and were baptized. On the east side of the city stood an old church, built in honour of Saint Martin during the Roman occupation of Britain, where the Christian queen went to pray. Here they first assembled to sing the psalms, to pray, to say Mass, to preach, and to baptize, until the king's own conversion to the Faith enabled them to preach openly, and to build and restore churches everywhere.

At length the king and others, edified by the pure lives of these holy men and their gracious promises, the truth of which they confirmed by many miracles, believed and were baptized. Thenceforward great numbers gathered each day to hear the word of God, forsaking their heathen rites, and entering the unity of Christ's holy Church as believers. While the king was pleased at their faith and conversion, he would not compel anyone to accept Christianity, for he had learned from his instructors and guides to salvation that the service of Christ must be accepted freely and not under compulsion; nevertheless, he showed greater favour to believers, because they were fellow-citizens of the kingdom of heaven. And it was not long before he granted his teachers a property of their own in his capital of Canterbury, and gave them possessions of various kinds to supply their wants.

Meanwhile God's servant Augustine visited Arles, and in accordance with the holy father Gregory's directions, was consecrated archbishop of the English nation by Etherius, archbishop of that city. On his return to Britain, he sent the priest Laurentius and the monk Peter to Rome to inform the blessed Pope Gregory that the English had accepted the Faith of Christ, and that he himself had been consecrated bishop.

SYNOD OF WHITBY (663)

When Bishop Aidan[4] departed this life, he was succeeded in the Bishopric by Finan, who had been consecrated and sent by the Scots. He built a church in the Isle of Lindisfarne, his see, constructing it not of stone, but of hewn oak thatched with reeds after the Scots manner. It was later dedicated

[4] Aidan, leader of a mission from Iona to Northumbria, founded a monastery at Lindisfarne which became the episcopal see of Northumbria. He died in 651.

by the most reverend Archbishop Theodore in honour of the blessed Apostle Peter. But Eadbert, a later Bishop of Lindisfarne, removed the thatch, and covered both roof and walls with sheets of lead.

About this time there arose a great and recurrent controversy on the observance of Easter,[5] those trained in Kent and Gaul maintaining that the Scottish observance was contrary to that of the universal Church. The most zealous protagonist of the true Easter was a Scot named Ronan, who had been trained in theology and law in Gaul and Italy. He disputed against Finan and convinced many, or at least persuaded them to make more careful enquiry into the truth. But he entirely failed to move Finan, a hot-tempered man whom reproof made more obstinate, and openly hostile to the truth. James, formerly the deacon of the venerable Archbishop Paulinus,[6] of whom I have spoken, kept the true and Catholic Easter with all whom he could persuade to adopt the right observance. Also Queen Eanfleda and her court, having as chaplain a Kentish priest named Romanus who followed the Catholic customs, observed the customs she had seen in Kent. It is said that the confusion in those days was such that Easter was kept twice in one year, so that when the King had ended Lent and was keeping Easter, the Queen and her attendants were still fasting and keeping Palm Sunday. During Aidan's lifetime these differences of Eastern observance were partially tolerated by everyone, for it was realized that although he was in loyalty bound to retain the customs of those who sent him, he nevertheless laboured diligently to cultivate the faith, piety, and love that marks out God's saints. He was therefore rightly loved by all, even by those who differed from his opinion on Easter, and was held in high respect not only by ordinary folk, but by Honorius of Canterbury and Felix of East Anglia.

On the death of Aidan's successor Finan,[7] and the succession of Colman the Scot to the bishopric, an even more serious controversy arose about Easter and the rules of Church discipline. This dispute began to trouble the minds and consciences of many people, who feared that they might have received the name of Christian in vain. The matter came to the notice of King Oswy and his son Alfred, and the former preferred the Scots teaching, having been instructed and baptized by the Scots, and having a complete grasp of their language. But Alfred, who had been instructed in the Faith by Wilfrid—a very learned man who had gone to Rome for his theological studies, and spent a long time at Lyons under Dalfin, Archbishop of Gaul, from whom he had received the tonsure—rightly regarded Wilfrid's teaching as superior to all the traditions of the Scots. He had therefore given him a monastery with forty hides of land at Inhrypum,[8] which he had given not long previously to the

---

[5] The controversy concerned the method of determining the date of Easter.

[6] Paulinus first brought Christianity to Northumbria, making a missionary journey from Kent and baptizing King Edwin in 627. But after his departure five years later the main work of christianizing the region was done by Aidan and the Celts.

[7] In 660.

[8] The famous monastery of Ripon.

adherents of the Scottish customs; but since, when offered the alternative, these preferred to give up the place rather than alter their customs, he then offered it to Wilfrid, whose life and teaching made him a worthy recipient. About this time, Agilbert, Bishop of the West Saxons, whom I have mentioned, had come to visit the province of Northumbria. He was a friend both of King Alfred and Abbot Wilfrid, and at the king's request he made Wilfrid a priest in his monastery. He also had with him a priest named Agatho. And when discussion arose on the questions of Easter, the tonsure,[9] and various other church matters, it was decided to hold a synod to put an end to this dispute at the monastery of Streanaeshalch, which means The Bay of the Beacon, then ruled by the Abbess Hilda, a woman devoted to God. Both kings, father and son, came to this synod, and so did Bishop Colman with his Scots clergy, and Bishop Agilbert with the priests Agatho and Wilfrid. James and Romanus supported the latter, while Abbess Hilda and her community, together with the venerable bishop Cedd,[10] supported the Scots. Cedd, who as already mentioned had long ago been ordained by the Scots, acted as a most careful interpreter for both parties at the council.

King Oswy opened by observing that all who served the One God should observe one rule of life, and since they all hoped for one kingdom in heaven, they should not differ in celebrating the sacraments of heaven. The synod now had the task of determining which was the truest tradition, and this should be loyally accepted by all. He then directed his own bishop Colman to speak first, and to explain his own customs and their origin. Then Colman said: "The Easter customs which I observe were taught me by my superiors, who sent me here as a bishop; and all our forefathers, men beloved of God, are known to have observed these customs. And lest anyone condemns or rejects them as wrong, it is recorded that they owe their origin to the blessed evangelist Saint John, the disciple especially loved by our Lord, and all the churches over which he presided." When he had concluded these and similar arguments, the king directed Agilbert to explain the origin and authority of his own customs. Agilbert replied: "May I request that my disciple the priest Wilfrid be allowed to speak in my place? For we are in full agreement with all those here present who support the traditions of our Church, and he can explain our position in the English language more competently than I can do through an interpreter." When Wilfrid had received the king's permission to speak, he said: "Our Easter customs are those that we have seen universally observed in Rome, where the blessed Apostles Peter and Paul lived, taught, suffered, and are buried. We have also seen the same customs generally observed throughout Italy and Gaul when we travelled through these countries for study and prayer. Furthermore, we have found them to be observed in many different countries and languages at the same time, in Africa, Asia, Egypt, Greece, and throughout the world wherever the Church of Christ has

9 The Irish style of tonsure differed from the Roman.
10 Bishop of East Anglia.

spread. The only people who are stupid enough to disagree with the whole world are these Scots and their obstinate adherents the Picts and Britons, who inhabit only a portion of these two islands in the remote ocean." In reply to this statement, Colman answered: "It is strange that you call our customs stupid when they rest on the authority of so great an Apostle, who was considered worthy to lean on our Lord's breast, and whose great wisdom is acknowledged throughout the world." Wilfrid replied: "Far be it from us to charge John with foolishness, for he literally observed the Law of Moses at a time when the Church was still greatly influenced by the synagogue, and the Apostles were not able immediately to abrogate the observances of the Law once given by God. It was for this reason that all converts to the Faith had to forsake idols, which are an invention of the Devil, lest they gave offence to believers who were Jews. For the same reason Paul circumcised Timothy, offered sacrifice in the Temple, and shaved his head at Corinth with Aquila and Priscilla, with the sole intention of avoiding offence to the Jews. For James said to Paul: 'You see, brother, how many thousands among the Jews have believed, and all of them zealously observe the Law.' But today, as the Gospel spreads throughout the world, it is unnecessary and undesirable for the faithful to be circumcised or to offer animals to God in sacrifice. John, following the customs of the Law, at first used to keep the Feast of Easter on the evening of the fourteenth day of the first month, whether it fell on the Sabbath or on any other day. But when Peter preached in Rome, remembering that it was on the day after the Sabbath that our Lord rose from the dead and gave the world the hope of resurrection, he realized that Easter should begin at moonrise on the evening of the tenth day of the full moon. This was in accordance with the Law, and was John's own practice. And if the Lord's Day, then called the day after the Sabbath, fell on the following day, John began to observe Easter the same evening, as we do today. But if the Lord's Day did not fall on the day following the fourteenth day of the moon, but on the sixteenth, seventeenth, or any other day up to the twenty-first, he waited until that day, and on the Sabbath evening preceding it he began the observance of the Easter Festival. This evangelical and apostolical tradition does not abrogate but fulfil the Law, which ordained that the Passover be kept between the eve of the fourteenth and twenty-first days of the moon of that month. And this is the custom of all the successors of blessed John in Asia since his death, and is also that of the world-wide Church. This is the true and only Easter to be observed by the faithful. It was not newly decreed by the Council of Nicaea, but reaffirmed by it, as Church history records. It is quite apparent to us, Colman, that you follow neither the example of John, as you imagine, nor that of Peter, whose tradition you deliberately contradict. Your keeping of Easter agrees neither with the Law nor the Gospel. For John, who kept Easter in accordance with the decrees of Moses, did not keep to the first day after the Sabbath; but this is not your practice, for you keep Easter only on the first day after the Sabbath. Peter kept Easter between the fifteenth and twenty-first days of the moon; you do not, for you keep it between the fourteenth and twentieth days of the moon. As a result, you often begin Easter on the evening of the thirteenth day, which is not mentioned in the Law. Nor did our Lord, the Author and Giver of the Gospel, eat the old Passover or institute the Sacrament of the New Testament to be celebrated by the Church in memory of His Passion on that day, but on the fourteenth. Furthermore, when you keep Easter, you expressly exclude the twenty-first day, which the Law of Moses particularly ordered to be observed. Therefore, I repeat, you conform neither to John nor Peter, the Law nor the Gospel, in your keeping of our greatest Festival."

Colman in reply said: "Do· you maintain that Anatolius,[11] a holy man highly spoken of in Church history, taught contrary to the Law and the Gospel, when he wrote that Easter should be kept between the fourteenth and twentieth days of the moon? Are we to believe that our most revered Father Columba[12] and his successors, men so dear to God, thought or acted contrary to Holy Scripture when they followed this custom? The holiness of many of them is confirmed by heavenly signs, and their virtues by miracles; and having no doubt that they are Saints, I shall never cease to emulate their lives, customs, and discipline."

"It is well established that Anatolius was a most holy, learned, and worthy man," answered Wilfrid; "but how can you claim his authority when you do not follow his directions? For he followed the correct rule about Easter, and observed a cycle of nineteen years; but either you do not know of this general custom of the Christian Church, or else you ignore it. He calculated the fourteenth day of the moon at Easter according to the Egyptian method, making it the evening of the fifteenth day; similarly, he assigned the twentieth to Easter Sunday, regarding it after sunset as the twenty-first day. But it appears that you do not realize this distinction, since you sometimes keep Easter before full moon, that is, on the thirteenth day. And with regard to your Father Columba and his followers, whose holiness you imitate and whose rules and customs you claim to have been supported by heavenly signs, I can only say that when many shall say to our Lord at the day of judgment: 'Have we not prophesied in Thy name, and cast out devils, and done many wonderful works?' the Lord will reply, 'I never knew you.' Far be it from me to apply these words to your fathers, for it is more just to believe good rather than evil of those whom one does not know. So I do not deny that they were true servants of God and dear to Him, and that they loved Him in primitive simplicity. Nor do I think that their ways of keeping Easter were in any way harmful, so long as no one came to show them a more perfect way. Nevertheless, I feel certain that if any Catholic adviser had come to them, they would readily have

[11] St. Anatolius (d. c. 282) was Bishop of Laodicea and compiled an influential treatise on the dating of Easter.
[12] St. Columba (c. 521-597) founded the famous monastery of Iona around 563 and began the work of converting the Scots.

accepted his guidance, since we know that they readily observed such of God's ordinances as they already knew. But you and your colleagues are most certainly guilty of sin if you reject the decrees of the Apostolic See and the universal Church which are confirmed by these Letters. For although your Fathers were holy men, do you imagine that they, a few men in a corner of a remote island, are to be preferred before the universal Church of Christ throughout the world? And even if your Columba—or, may I say, ours also if he was the servant of Christ—was a Saint of potent virtues, can he take precedence before the most blessed Prince of the Apostles, to whom our Lord said: "Thou are Peter, and upon this rock I will build my Church, and the gates of hell shall not prevail against it, and to thee I will give the keys of the kingdom of heaven'?"

When Wilfrid had ended, the king asked: "Is it true, Colman, that these words were spoken to Peter by our Lord?" He answered: "It is true, Your Majesty." Then the king said: "Can you show that a similar authority was given to your Columba?" "No," replied Colman. "Do you both agree," the king continued, "that these words were indisputably addressed to Peter in the first place, and that our Lord gave him the keys of the kingdom of heaven?" Both answered: "We do." At this, the king concluded: "Then, I tell you, Peter is guardian of the gates of heaven, and I shall not contradict him. I shall obey his commands in everything to the best of my knowledge and ability; otherwise, when I come to the gates of heaven, he who holds the keys may not be willing to open them."

All present, both high and low, signified their agreement with what the king had said, and abandoning their imperfect customs, readily accepted those which they had learned to be better.

7. ST. BONIFACE (WYNFRITH) AND HIS MISSION[1]

St. Wynfrith, renamed Boniface (680-754), was perhaps the greatest of all English missionaries. Born in Wessex, he did most of his work on the European continent, reforming and establishing numerous churches and monasteries in France and Germany. Not more ardent or fearless than Columban, and certainly not more learned, he far surpassed the Irishman in organizing ability. Boniface was, moreover, the product of a monasticism which had always remained in close touch

[1] Reprinted by permission of the publishers from Willibald, *Life of St. Boniface,* trans. by G. W. Robinson (Cambridge, Mass., Harvard University Press, 1916), pp. 57-64, and *The Letters of St. Boniface,* trans. by E. Emerton, *Records of Civilization,* No. XXXI (New York, Columbia University Press, 1940), pp. 78-83.

with Rome. It was natural for him to seek papal authorization for his German missions and bishoprics and for his remarkably successful attempt to impose a stricter Roman discipline on the Frankish church. Columban, on the other hand, had tried to maintain and extend the divergent usages of the Celts. The difference between them was dramatized by the results of their activities in Gaul: Columban was driven into exile, but Boniface served as the instrument which forged the momentous alliance between the Carolingian house and the Papacy, sealed by the anointing of Pepin the Short as king in 754 at the hands of Pope Stephen II (reigned 752-757). Yet both Columban and Boniface left behind them great and enduring monasteries that became centers of religious and cultural life: Columban, Luxeuil and Bobbio; Boniface, Fulda.

Willibald wrote his life of Boniface only a few years after the saint's death, and it is therefore strange that he does not seem to know much about Boniface's later career. For example, he tells of Boniface's close cooperation with Popes Gregory II (reigned 715-731) and Gregory III (reigned 731-741), but fails to mention his similar letters to Pope Zacharias (reigned 741-752), one of which is given below.

WILLIBALD: FROM *LIFE OF ST. BONIFACE* (c. 760)

When he had brought unto the Lord a vast people among the Frisians, and many, educated by him in spiritual learning, had come to knowledge of the truth in the beaming rays of the true light; then indeed, protected by the Lord, he went to other parts of Germany for the sake of preaching, and, with the Lord's help, came to Amanaburch. There twin brothers ruled, Dettic namely and Deorulf. The saint summoned them from the sacrilegious worship of idols, which they wrongfully practised under a kind of name of Christianity; and withdrew a very great multitude of people from the malevolent superstition of heathenism, having disclosed to them the way of right understanding, and caused them to put aside their horrible errors; and, having gathered a congregation of God's servants, built a cell for a monastery. And in like wise, near to the borders of the Saxons, by preaching the gospel injunctions he set free from the captivity of devils the people of the Hessians, who yet wandered in pagan rites.

When he had cleansed many thousand people from their inveterate paganism and given them baptism, he directed to Rome a fit messenger, a faithful bearer of his letter, Bynna by name; and by the service of the voiceless word disclosed in order to the venerable father, the bishop of the apostolic see, all the things which by God's gift had been brought to pass in him; and showed how a great multitude of people, illuminated by the divine spirit, had received the sacrament of regeneration. But also, writing further, he asked concerning things which pertained to the daily need of the church of God and the progress of the people: that he might obtain the counsel of the apostolic see. When Bynna the messenger had remained at Rome for some days, and the time of his return was already at hand, he received in exchange from the bishop of the apostolic see an answer to his embassy. And immediately returning, he now brought to his master, after the passage of no long time, a letter written by the apostolic see.

When the saint had read the letter that was brought, he gathered that he was invited to Rome, and sought in haste to fulfil the highest degree of obedience. Without delay, attended by a throng of clients and surrounded by a train of the brethren, he traversed the lands of the Franks and the Burgundians, and, having surmounted the ridges of the Alps, the territories of the marches of Italy[2] and the boundaries of the soldiers.[3] And when he beheld the walls of the Roman city, quickly he returned deserved praise and thanks to God on high; and presently, reaching the church of Saint Peter, he fortified himself by diligent prayer. But when he had rested his wearied limbs for a little time, it was announced to the blessed Gregory, bishop of the apostolic see, that our servant of God had arrived. And he was received kindly and conducted to the pilgrims' lodge.

When a suitable day for their conference arrived, and the glorious bishop of the apostolic see came to the church of Saint Peter the apostle, immediately our servant of God was summoned. After they had exchanged a few peaceful words of salutation, the apostolic bishop questioned him concerning the creed and the tradition of the faith of the church. Anon our man of God answered him humbly, saying: "Apostolic lord! I, stranger as I am, know that I have no skill in your familiar language; but I beg that thou grant me leisure and time to write down my confession of faith, and that only the voiceless word may make a reasonable presentation of my faith." The bishop at once consented, and commanded him to bring this writing speedily. And after some space of time had glided away, the saint brought his confession of faith in the Holy Trinity, written down in polished, eloquent, and learned language, and rendered it to the aforesaid bishop. Nevertheless he waited yet some days.

At last he was summoned again. Having been conducted within the Lateran, immediately he cast himself humbly prostrate on his face at the feet of the apostolic bishop, beseeching his benediction: who quickly raised him from the ground, and returned to our servant of God the writing in which the sound and incorrupt truth of faith was manifest, and made him sit by his side. And he instructed him, with wholesome teaching and admonition, to preserve ceaselessly inviolate this bulwark of faith, and to preach it earnestly unto others to the limit of his strength. And he brought forward many other matters relating to the holy religion and the true faith and questioned the saint concerning them, so that they spent almost the whole day in mutual conversation. And at last the pope inquired how the peoples who before had wandered in error and crime received the lessons of the faith through his teaching. And when he had learned for a certainty that the saint had admitted an exceeding great multitude of the commonalty from the sacrilegious worship

---

[2] Lombardy.
[3] The Byzantine Exarchate of Ravenna.

of devils to the fellowship of the holy church, he intimated to him that he had purposed to impose upon him the office of bishop, and to set him over the peoples that before had lacked a shepherd's care, and in the words of the Lord our God, fainted, as sheep having no shepherd. But the saint, because he dared not contradict this great bishop set over the apostolic see, consented and obeyed. And so the most high bishop of holy authority appointed a day of ordination, namely the thirtieth of November.[4]

After the sacred day of the holy solemnity had dawned, being the natal day of Saint Andrew and the day set for the ordination, the holy bishop of the apostolic see imposed upon the saint the dignity of the episcopacy and of the name Boniface; and brought him the book in which the most sacred laws of the constitution of the church have been compiled at the assemblies of the bishops; commanding, that thenceforth this order of episcopal discipline and customs should remain unshaken in his hands, and that the subject peoples should be instructed by these examples. But also he gave to him and to all subject to him the friendship of the holy apostolic see thenceforth forever. And by his most sacred letter he placed our saint, now a bishop, under the protection and pious care of the sovereignty of glorious Duke Charles.[5]

After Boniface by long and devious ways had visited the territories of great peoples, he came to the aforesaid prince of the Franks, and was received by him with veneration. He delivered to Duke Charles the letters of the abovementioned Roman bishop and of the apostolic see, and, subject to his lordship and patronage, returned, with the consent of Duke Charles, to the land of the Hessians where before he had tarried.

Now at that time many of the Hessians, brought under the Catholic faith and confirmed by the grace of the sevenfold spirit, received the laying on of hands; . . . others indeed, not yet strengthened in soul, refused to accept in their entirety the lessons of the inviolate faith. Moreover some were wont secretly, some openly to sacrifice to trees and springs; some in secret, others openly practised inspections of victims and divinations, legerdemain and incantations; some turned their attention to auguries and auspices and various sacrificial rites; while others, with sounder minds, abandoned all the profanations of heathenism, and committed none of these things. With the advice and counsel of these last, the saint attempted, in the place called Gaesmere, while the servants of God stood by his side, to fell a certain oak of extraordinary size, which is called, by an old name of the pagans, the Oak of Jupiter.[6] And when in the strength of his steadfast heart he had cut the lower notch, there was present a great multitude of pagans, who in their souls were most earnestly cursing the enemy of their gods. But when the fore side of the tree was notched only a little, suddenly the oak's vast bulk, driven by a divine blast from above, crashed to the ground, shivering its crown of branches as it fell; and, as if by

---

[4] Boniface was ordained November 30, 722.
[5] Charles Martel.
[6] Thor.

the gracious dispensation of the Most High, it was also burst into four parts, and four trunks of huge size, equal in length, were seen, unwrought by the brethren who stood by. At this sight the pagans who before had cursed now, on the contrary, believed, and blessed the Lord, and put away their former reviling. Then moreover the most holy bishop, after taking counsel with the brethren, built from the timber of the tree a wooden oratory, and dedicated it in honor of Saint Peter the apostle.

ST. BONIFACE: *LETTER* 50: TO POPE ZACHARIAS (742)

TO OUR BEST BELOVED LORD ZACHARIAS, THE APOSTOLIC MAN WEARING THE INSIGNIA OF THE SUPREME PONTIFICATE, BONIFACE, A SERVANT OF THE SERVANTS OF GOD.

We must confess, our father and lord, that after we learned from messengers that your predecessor in the apostolate, Gregory of reverend memory, pontiff of the Apostolic See, had been set free from the prison of the body and had passed on to God, nothing gave us greater joy or happiness than the knowledge that the Supreme Arbiter had appointed your fatherly clemency to administer the canon law and to govern the Apostolic See. We gave thanks to God with uplifted hands. And so, just as if we were kneeling at your feet, we most earnestly pray that, as we have been devoted servants and willing disciples of your predecessors under the authority of St. Peter, so also we may be worthy to be the obedient servants of Your Holiness under the canon law. It is our earnest desire to maintain the catholic faith and the unity of the Roman Church. As many hearers or learners as God shall grant me in my missionary work, I will not cease to summon and urge them to render obedience to the Apostolic See.

We have also to inform Your Paternity that by the grace of God we have appointed three bishops over those peoples in Germany who have been to a certain extent won over and converted and we have divided the province into three dioceses. The bishoprics of these three towns or cities where they were ordained we beg you to confirm and establish by your authority in writing. We have appointed one episcopal see in the fortress called Würzburg, another in the town of Buraburg, and a third in a place called Erfurt, which was formerly a city of heathen rustics. The choice of these three places we earnestly pray you to strengthen and confirm by your own charter and by authority of your apostolic office, so that, God willing, there may be in Germany three episcopal sees founded and established by apostolic order and under the authority and direction of St. Peter. And may neither the present nor any future generation presume to break up these dioceses or to defy the orders of the Apostolic See.

Be it known also to Your Paternity that Karlmann, duke of the Franks, summoned me to him and requested me to bring together a council in the part of the Frankish kingdom which is under his rule. He promised that he would do something toward reforming and reëstablishing the ecclesiastical discipline, which for a long time, not less than sixty or seventy years, has been despoiled and trampled upon. If, therefore, he is really willing, under divine inspiration, to carry out this purpose, I should have the advice and direction of your authority—that is, the authority of the Apostolic See. The Franks, according to their elders, have not held a council for more than eighty years, nor have they had an archbishop or established or restored anywhere the canon law of the Church. For the most part the episcopal sees in cities are in the hands of greedy laymen or are exploited by adulterous and vicious clergymen and publicans for secular uses. If, then, I am to undertake this business by your orders and at the instance of the aforesaid duke, I desire to have at once the command and the suggestions of the Apostolic See, together with the Church canons.

If I find among these men certain so-called deacons who have spent their lives since boyhood in debauchery, adultery, and every kind of filthiness, who entered the diaconate with this reputation, and who now, while they have four or five concubines in their beds, still read the Gospel and are not ashamed or afraid to call themselves deacons—nay rather, entering upon the priesthood, they continue in the same vices, add sin to sin, declare that they have a right to make intercession for the people in the priestly office and to celebrate Mass, and, still worse, with such reputations advancing from step to step to nomination and appointment as bishops—may I have the formal prescription of your authority as to your procedure in such cases so that they may be convicted by an apostolic judgment and dealt with as sinners? And certain bishops are to be found among them who, although they deny that they are fornicators or adulterers, are drunkards and shiftless men, given to hunting and to fighting in the army like soldiers and by their own hands shedding blood, whether of heathens or Christians. Since I am the recognized servant and legate of the Apostolic See, my word here and your word there ought to agree, in case I should send messengers, as I have done in the past, to learn the decision of your authority.

In another matter, also, I have to ask your advice and permission. Your predecessor of reverend memory directed me in your presence, to name, God willing, a [certain] priest as my heir and successor in the service of the Church in case of my death. If this be the will of God, it is agreeable to me. But now I am in doubt and do not know whether it can be done, because since then a brother of that priest has killed an uncle of the duke of the Franks and up to the present time we do not know how and when that quarrel will be settled. I pray you, therefore, to give me your authority to act in this choice, with the approval of the servants of God, as may seem best to us all for God and for the advantage and spiritual profit of the Church and the protection of religion. May I have your consent to act in this matter as God shall deign to inspire me, since it does not seem possible to accomplish it against the wishes of the prince?

I have further to seek the advice of Your Paternity in regard to a certain perplexing and scandalous report which has come to us recently and has greatly disturbed us, filling with confusion the priests of our churches. A certain layman of high station came to us and said that Gregory of sainted memory, pontiff of the Apostolic See, had granted him permission to marry the widow of his uncle. She had formerly been the wife of her own cousin but had left him during his lifetime. She is known to be related in the third degree to the man who now desires her and who declares that permission was granted him. She formerly made a vow of chastity before God and took the veil but laid it aside and was married.

The aforesaid man declares that he has a license from the Apostolic See for such a marriage as this! But we do not believe this to be true; for a synod of the church of the Saxons beyond the sea, in which I was born and reared, namely the synod of London [605], convoked and directed by disciples of St. Gregory, the archbishops—Augustine, Laurentius, Justus, and Miletus— declared such a marriage union, on the authority of Holy Scripture, to be a heinous crime, an incestuous and horrible offense, and a damnable sin. Wherefore, I beg Your Paternity to deign to enlighten us as to the true doctrine in this case, that scandals and schisms or new errors may not arise and increase therefrom among the clergy and the Christian people.

Some of the ignorant common people, Alemanians, Bavarians, and Franks, hearing that many of the offenses prohibited by us are practiced in the city of Rome, imagine that they are allowed by the priests there and reproach us for causing them to incur blame in their own lives. They say that on the first day of January year after year, in the city of Rome and in the neighborhood of St. Peter's church by day or night, they have seen bands of singers parading the streets in pagan fashion, shouting and chanting sacrilegious songs and loading tables with food day and night, while no one in his own house is willing to lend his neighbor fire or tools or any other convenience. They say also that they have seen there women with amulets and bracelets of heathen fashion on their arms and legs, offering them for sale to willing buyers. All these things, seen by evil-minded and ignorant people, are a cause of reproach to us and a hindrance to our preaching and teaching. It is of such things that the Apostle says reprovingly: "Ye observe days and times; I fear I have labored with you in vain." And St. Augustine said:

He who believes in such evil things, as incantations or diviners or soothsayers, or amulets, or any kind of prophesies, even though he fast, or pray, or run to church continually, and though he give alms generously, or torment his body with all kinds of tortures, it shall profit him nothing so long as he does not abandon these sacrilegious rites.

If Your Paternity would prohibit these heathen practices at Rome, it would bring rewards to you and the greatest advantage to us in our teaching.

Some bishops and priests of the Frankish nation who were adulterers and fornicators of the worst kind, whose children born during their episcopate or priesthood bear witness against them, now declare, on returning from the Apostolic See, that the Roman Pontiff has given them permission to carry on their episcopal service in the Church. Against this we maintain that we have never heard that the Apostolic See had ever given a decision contrary to canonical decrees.

All these things, beloved master, we make known to you that we may give an answer to these people upon your authority and that under guidance of your instruction the sheep of the Church may not be led astray and that the ravening wolves may be overcome and destroyed.

We are sending you some trifling gifts, not as being worthy of Your Paternity, but as a token of our affection and our devoted obedience, a warm rug and a little silver and gold.

May God's hand protect your Holiness and may you have health and length of days in Christ.

> May God enthroned on High for long preserve
> In His holy Temple the ruler of the Apostolic See,
>   May the honey-sweet doctrine visit the grateful earth
> And make it worthy of God for Christ's blessed sake,
>   May the blooming Mother rejoice,
> And may the House of the Lord be joyful with abundant offering!

III

BYZANTIUM AND RUSSIA

In spite of surface instability, tenacity and endurance are the keynotes of Byzantine history. Except for fifty-seven years of Latin rule after the Crusader sack of 1204, the imperial capital of Constantinople beat off all attacks between its founding in 330 and its final capitulation to the Turks in 1453. Its success was due to its strategic position as fortress and seaport and also to the fact that it was the heart of a highly organized state, governed by an emperor who was at the same time supreme judge and sole legislator, commander of the armed forces, absolute master of the bureaucracy, and protector and overseer of the Church. Individual emperors might come and go, sometimes with bewildering rapidity. They might even die violent and unseemly deaths. But the imperial authority remained. Since considerations of space exclude an adequate treatment of the various aspects of Byzantine life, it is perhaps best to concentrate on this crucial center of East Roman existence.

The last two selections in this section deal with the emergence of Kievan Russia, whose Scandinavian overlords received their religion and their culture from the city on the Bosporus, which both here and in the Balkans played a primary role in the making of Eastern Europe.

1. PROCOPIUS: JUSTINIAN AS RULER AND BUILDER[1]

The Emperor Justinian I (reigned 527-565) is an ambiguous figure to modern historians. His accomplishments included the codifying of Roman law and the building of the great church Hagia Sophia. Together with his formidable wife, Theodora, he gave the Empire a long period of vigorous and assiduous rule. Yet his expensive attempt to reconquer Italy and the western Mediterranean weakened the defense of the eastern frontier against the Persians, and his persecution of heretics alienated large groups of his subjects. The writings of the contemporary historian Procopius, who served as secretary to Belisarius, one of the best of Justinian's generals, contain contrasting judgments. In his *Histories* of the Persian, Vandal, and Italian wars Procopius eulogizes Belisarius, in his *Buildings* he eulogizes Justinian, in his *Secret History* he defames them both. Perhaps he wrote the latter in revenge for personal disappointments. But the reasons he gives for his praise and condemnation must be considered in any attempt to form a just estimate of this most famous of Byzantine Emperors.

FROM *BUILDINGS* (c. 558)

In our own age there has been born the Emperor Justinian, who, taking over the State when it was harrassed by disorder, has not only made it greater in extent, but also much more illustrious, by expelling from it those barbarians who had from of old pressed hard upon it, as I have made clear in detail in the Books on the Wars. Indeed they say that Themistocles, the son of Neocles, once boastfully said that he did not lack the ability to make a small state large. But this Sovereign does not lack the skill to produce completely transformed states—witness the way he has already added to the Roman domain many states which in his own times had belonged to others, and has created countless cities which did not exist before. And finding that the belief in God was, before his time, straying into errors and being forced to go in many directions, he completely destroyed all the paths leading to such errors, and brought it about that it stood on the firm foundation of a single faith. Moreover, finding the laws obscure because they had become far more numerous than they

¹ Reprinted by permission of the publishers from Procopius, *Buildings*, I, 1-2, trans. by H. B. Dewing, LOEB CLASSICAL LIBRARY edition, Vol. 7 (Cambridge, Mass., Harvard University Press, 1940, pp. 5-13, 17-23, 25-27, 33-37. Reprinted from *Secret History* by Procopius, trans. by Richard Atwater (Ann Arbor, 1961) by permission of The University of Michigan Press. Pp. 42-44.

should be, and in obvious confusion because they disagreed with each other, he preserved them by cleansing them of the mass of their verbal trickery, and by controlling their discrepancies with the greatest firmness; as for those who plotted against him, he of his own volition dismissed the charges against them, and causing those who were in want to have a surfeit of wealth, and crushing the spiteful fortune that oppressed them, he wedded the whole State to a life of prosperity. Furthermore, he strengthened the Roman domain, which everywhere lay exposed to the barbarians, by a multitude of soldiers, and by constructing strongholds he built a wall along all its remote frontiers.

However, most of the Emperor's other achievements have been described by me in my other writings, so that the subject of the present work will be the benefits which he wrought as a builder. They do indeed say that the best king of whom we know by tradition was the Persian Cyrus, and that he was chiefly responsible for the founding of the kingdom of Persia for the people of his race. But whether that Cyrus was in fact such a man as he whose education from childhood up is described by Xenophon the Athenian, I have no means of knowing. For it may well be that the skill of the writer of that description was quite capable, such was his exquisite eloquence, of coming to be a mere embellishment of the facts. But in the case of the king of our times, Justinian (whom one would rightly, I think, call a king by nature as well as by inheritance, since he is, as Homer says, "as gentle as a father"), if one should examine his reign with care, he will regard the rule of Cyrus as a sort of child's play. The proof of this will be that the Roman Empire, as I have just said, has become more than doubled both in area and in power generally, while, on the other hand, those who treacherously formed the plot against him, going so far even as to plan his assassination, are not only living up to the present moment, and in possession of their own property, even though their guilt was proved with absolute certainty, but are actually still serving as generals of the Romans, and are holding the consular rank to which they had been appointed.

But now we must proceed, as I have said, to the subject of the buildings of this Emperor, so that it may not come to pass in the future that those who see them refuse, by reason of their great number and magnitude, to believe that they are in truth the works of one man. For already many works of men of former times which are not vouched for by a written record have aroused incredulity because of their surpassing merit. And with good reason the buildings in Byzantium, beyond all the rest, will serve as a foundation for my narrative. For "o'er a work's beginnings," as the old saying has it, "we needs must set a front that shines afar."

Some men of the common herd, all the rubbish of the city, once rose up against the Emperor Justinian in Byzantium, when they brought about the rising called the Nika Insurrection, which has been described by me in detail and without any concealment in the Book on the Wars.[2] And by way of

[2] *Wars*, I, 24.

shewing that it was not against the Emperor alone that they had taken up
arms, but no less against God himself, unholy wretches that they were, they
had the hardihood to fire the Church of the Christians, which the people of
Byzantium call "Sophia,"[3] an epithet which they have most appropriately invented for God, by which they call His temple; and God permitted them to
accomplish this impiety, foreseeing into what an object of beauty this shrine
was destined to be transformed. So the whole church at that time lay a
charred mass of ruins. But the Emperor Justinian built not long afterwards a
church so finely shaped, that if anyone had enquired of the Christians before
the burning if it would be their wish that the church should be destroyed and
one like this should take its place, shewing them some sort of model of the
building we now see, it seems to me that they would have prayed that they
might see their church destroyed forthwith, in order that the building might
be converted into its present form. At any rate the Emperor, disregarding all
questions of expense, eagerly pressed on to begin the work of construction, and
began to gather all the artisans from the whole world. And Anthemius of
Tralles, the most learned man in the skilled craft which is known as the art
of building, not only of all his contemporaries, but also when compared with
those who had lived long before him, ministered to the Emperor's enthusiasm,
duly regulating the tasks of the various artisans, and preparing in advance
designs of the future construction; and associated with him was another mas-
ter-builder, Isidorus by name, a Milesian by birth, a man who was intelligent
and worthy to assist the Emperor Justinian. Indeed this also was an indication
of the honour in which God held the Emperor, that He had already provided
the men who would be most serviceable to him in the tasks which were waiting to be carried out. And one might with good reason marvel at the discernment of the Emperor himself, in that out of the whole world he was able to
select the men who were most suitable for the most important of his enter-
prises.

So the church has become a spectacle of marvellous beauty, overwhelm-
ing to those who see it, but to those who know it by hearsay altogether incredible. For it soars to a height to match the sky, and as if surging up from
amongst the other buildings it stands on high and looks down upon the remainder of the city, adoring it, because it is a part of it, but glorying in its own
beauty, because, though a part of the city and dominating it, it at the same
time towers above it to such a height that the whole city is viewed from there
as from a watch-tower. Both its breadth and its length have been so carefully
proportioned, that it may not improperly be said to be exceedingly long and
at the same time unusually broad. And it exults in an indescribable beauty.

.   .   .   .   .

For it proudly reveals its mass and the harmony of its proportions, having
neither any excess nor deficiency, since it is both more pretentious than the

3 "Wisdom."

buildings to which we are accustomed, and considerably more noble than those which are merely huge, and it abounds exceedingly in sunlight and in the reflection of the sun's rays from the marble. Indeed one might say that its interior is not illuminated from without by the sun, but that the radiance comes into being within it, such an abundance of light bathes this shrine. And the face itself of the church, which would be the part which faces the rising sun, that portion of the building in which they perform the mysteries in worship of God, was constructed in the following manner. A structure of masonry is built up from the ground, not made in a straight line, but gradually curving inward on its flanks and receding at the middle, so that it forms the shape of half a circle, which those who are skilled in such matters call a half-cylinder, and so it rises precipitously to a height. The upper part of this structure ends in the fourth part of a sphere, and above it another crescent-shaped structure rises, fitted to the adjoining parts of the building, marvellous in its grace, but by reason of the seeming insecurity of its composition altogether terrifying. For it seems somehow to float in the air on no firm basis, but to be poised aloft to the peril of those inside it. Yet actually it is braced with exceptional firmness and security. On either side of this are columns arranged on the pavement; these likewise do not stand in a straight line, but they retreat inward in the pattern of the semicircle as if they were yielding to one another in a choral dance, and above them hangs a structure of crescent shape. And on the side opposite the east is reared a wall containing the entrances, and on either side of this there stand in a semicircle not only the columns themselves but also the structure above them, all this being very similar to the columns and structure I have just described. And in the centre of the church stand four man-made eminences, which they call piers, two on the north side and two on the south, opposite and equal to each other, each pair having between them just four columns. The piers are composed of huge stones joined together, carefully selected and skilfully fitted to one another by the masons, and rising to a great height. One might suppose that they were sheer mountain-peaks. From these spring four arches, which rise over the four sides of a square, and their ends come together in pairs and are made fast to each other on top of these piers, while the other portions rise and soar to an infinite height. And while two of the arches rise over empty air, those namely on the east and the west sides, the other two have under them certain structural elements, including a number of rather small columns. Upon the crowns of the arches rests a circular structure, cylindrical in shape; it is through this that the light of day always first smiles. For it towers above the whole earth, as I believe, and the structure is interrupted at short intervals, openings having been left intentionally, in the spaces where the perforation of the stone-work takes place, to be channels for the admission of light in sufficient measure. And since the arches where they are joined together are so constructed as to form a four-cornered plan, the stonework between the arches produces four triangles. And while each supporting end of a triangle, having been contracted to a point by the coming together of each pair of arches, makes the lower point an acute angle, yet as the triangle rises and its width is extended by the intermediate surface, it ends in the segment of a circle which it supports, and forms the remaining angles at that level. And upon this circle rests the huge spherical dome which makes the structure exceptionally beautiful. Yet it seems not to rest upon solid masonry, but to cover the space with its golden dome suspended from Heaven. All these details, fitted together with incredible skill in mid-air and floating off from each other and resting only on the parts next to them, produce a single and most extraordinary harmony in the work, and yet do not permit the spectator to linger much over the study of any one of them, but each detail attracts the eye and draws it on irresistibly to itself. So the vision constantly shifts suddenly, for the beholder is utterly unable to select which particular detail he should admire more than all the others. But even so, though they turn their attention to every side and look with contracted brows upon every detail, observers are still unable to understand the skilful craftsmanship, but they always depart from there overwhelmed by the bewildering sight.

.   .   .   .   .

The whole ceiling is overlaid with pure gold, which adds glory to the beauty, yet the light reflected from the stones prevails, shining out in rivalry with the gold. And there are two stoa-like colonnades, one on each side, not separated in any way from the structure of the church itself, but actually making the effect of its width greater, and reaching along its whole length, to the very end, while in height they are less than the interior of the building. And they too have vaulted ceilings and decorations of gold. One of these two colonnaded stoas has been assigned to men worshippers, while the other is reserved for women engaged in the same exercise. But they have nothing to distinguish them, nor do they differ from one another in any way, but their very equality serves to beautify the church, and their similarity to adorn it. But who could fittingly describe the galleries of the women's side, or enumerate the many colonnades and the colonnaded aisles by means of which the church is surrounded? Or who could recount the beauty of the columns and the stones with which the church is adorned? One might imagine that he had come upon a meadow with its flowers in full bloom. For he would surely marvel at the purple of some, the green tint of others, and at those on which the crimson glows and those from which the white flashes, and again at those which Nature, like some painter, varies with the most contrasting colours. And whenever anyone enters this church to pray, he understands at once that it is not by any human power or skill, but by the influence of God, that this work has been so finely turned. And so his mind is lifted up toward God and exalted, feeling that He cannot be far away, but must especially love to dwell in this place which He has chosen.

.   .   .   .   .

Before the Senate House there happened to be a sort of market-place, which the people of Byzantium call the Augustaeum. In that place there is a structure of stones, which is made up of not less than seven courses, laid in a rectangle, all fitted to each other at their ends, but each course being narrower than that beneath, and set back, with the result that each of the stones becomes, from the way it is set, a projecting step, so that people assembled there sit upon them as upon seats. And at the top of the stones there rises a column of extraordinary size, not a monolith, however, but composed of large stones in circular courses, cut so as to form angles on their inner faces, and fitted to one another by the skill of the masons. And finest brass, cast in panels and garlands, covers the stones on every side, both serving to bind them securely, and covering them with adornment, and giving the shaft throughout, but particularly at the base and the capital, the appearance of a column. This brass, in its colour, is softer than pure gold, and its value is not much less than that of an equal weight of silver. And on the summit of the column stands a gigantic bronze horse, facing toward the east, a very noteworthy sight. He seems about to advance, and to be splendidly pressing forward. Indeed he holds his left fore foot in the air, as though it were about to take a forward step on the ground before him, while the other is pressed down upon the stone on which he stands, as if ready to take the next step; his hind feet he holds close together, so that they may be ready whenever he decides to move. Upon this horse is mounted a colossal bronze figure of the Emperor. And the figure is habited like Achilles, that is, the costume he wears is known by that name. He wears half-boots and his legs are not covered by greaves. Also he wears a breastplate in the heroic fashion, and a helmet covers his head and gives the impression that it moves up and down, and a dazzling light flashes forth from it. One might say, in poetic speech, that here is that star of Autumn. And he looks toward the rising sun, directing his course, I suppose, against the Persians. And in his left hand he holds a globe, by which the sculptor signifies that the whole earth and sea are subject to him, yet he has neither sword nor spear nor any other weapon, but a cross stands upon the globe which he carries, the emblem by which alone he has obtained both his Empire and his victory in war. And stretching forth his right hand toward the rising sun and spreading out his fingers, he commands the barbarians in that quarter to remain at home and to advance no further.

FROM *SECRET HISTORY* (c. 558)

Now such was Justinian in appearance; but his character was something I could not fully describe. For he was at once villainous and amenable; as people say colloquially, a moron. He was never truthful with anyone, but always guileful in what he said and did, yet easily hoodwinked by any who wanted to deceive him. His nature was an unnatural mixture of folly and wickedness. What in olden times a peripatetic philosopher said was also true of him, that opposite qualities combine in a man as in the mixing of colors. I will try to portray him, however, insofar as I can fathom his complexity.

This Emperor, then, was deceitful, devious, false, hypocritical, two-faced, cruel, skilled in dissembling his thought, never moved to tears by either joy or pain, though he could summon them artfully at will when the occasion demanded, a liar always, not only offhand, but in writing, and when he swore sacred oaths to his subjects in their very hearing. Then he would immediately break his agreements and pledges, like the vilest of slaves, whom indeed only the fear of torture drives to confess their perjury. A faithless friend, he was a treacherous enemy, insane for murder and plunder, quarrelsome and revolutionary, easily led to anything evil, but never willing to listen to good counsel, quick to plan mischief and carry it out, but finding even the hearing of anything good distasteful to his ears.

How could anyone put Justinian's ways into words? These and many even worse vices were disclosed in him as in no other mortal: nature seemed to have taken the wickedness of all other men combined and planted it in this man's soul. And besides this, he was too prone to listen to accusations; and too quick to punish. For he decided such cases without full examination, naming the punishment when he had heard only the accuser's side of the matter. Without hesitation he wrote decrees for the plundering of countries, sacking of cities, and slavery of whole nations, for no cause whatever. So that if one wished to take all the calamities which had befallen the Romans before this time and weigh them against his crimes, I think it would be found that more men had been murdered by this single man than in all previous history.

He had no scruples about appropriating other people's property, and did not even think any excuse necessary, legal or illegal, for confiscating what did not belong to him. And when it was his, he was more than ready to squander it in insane display, or give it as an unnecessary bribe to the barbarians. In short, he neither held on to any money himself nor let anyone else keep any: as if his reason were not avarice, but jealousy of those who had riches. Driving all wealth from the country of the Romans in this manner, he became the cause of universal poverty.

Now this was the character of Justinian, so far as I can portray it.

2. JUSTINIAN: THE CIVIL LAW[1]

The *Corpus Iuris Civilis*, or Body of Civil Law, is the supreme expression of the Emperor's function as judge and legislator. It consists of four parts: 1. the *Codex*, containing all valid imperial edicts since Hadrian (drawn up 529, revised

---

[1] *The Civil Law*, trans. by S. P. Scott (Cincinnati, The Central Trust Company, 1932), II, 179-182; 3-7, reprinted with permission of the Trustee of the Trust under the Will of Elizabeth W. Scott, Deceased, and of The Jefferson Medical College of Philadelphia.

534); 2. the *Digest*, a great anthology of the opinions of classical jurists (completed 533); 3. the *Institutes*, a textbook for students (533); 4. the *Novellae*, new laws enacted by Justinian after the promulgation of the *Codex*. Most of the *Novellae* were written in Greek, the rest of the *Corpus* in Latin. This was the fundamental law by which the Empire lived, though it was supplemented by various later codes and thoroughly revised by the *Basilica*, promulgated under Leo VI (reigned 886-912). From the eleventh century the whole *Corpus* was eagerly studied in the West, and it still forms the basis of the law of much of continental Europe. Many would call it the highest achievement of the Byzantine genius for order.

THE PLAN OF *THE DIGEST* (530)

The Emperor Caesar, Flavius, Justinianus, Pious, Fortunate, Renowned, Conquerer and Triumpher, Ever Augustus, to Tribonianus His Quaestor: Greeting.

With the aid of God governing Our Empire which was delivered to Us by His Celestial Majesty, We carry on war successfully, We adorn peace and maintain the Constitution of the State, and have such confidence in the protection of Almighty God that We do not depend upon Our arms, or upon Our soldiers, or upon those who conduct Our Wars, or upon Our own genius, but We solely place Our reliance upon the providence of the Holy Trinity, from which are derived the elements of the entire world and their disposition throughout the globe.

Therefore, since there is nothing to be found in all things so worthy of attention as the authority of the law, which properly regulates all affairs both divine and human, and expels all injustice; We have found the entire arrangement of the law which has come down to us from the foundation of the City of Rome and the times of Romulus, to be so confused that it is extended to an infinite length and is not within the grasp of human capacity; and hence We were first induced to begin by examining what had been enacted by former most venerated princes, to correct their constitutions, and make them more easily understood; to the end that being included in a single Code, and having had removed all that is superfluous in resemblance and all iniquitous discord, they may afford to all men the ready assistance of their true meaning.

After having concluded this work and collected it all in a single volume under Our illustrious name, raising Ourself above small and comparatively insignificant matters, We have hastened to attempt the most complete and thorough amendment of the entire law, to collect and revise the whole body of Roman jurisprudence, and to assemble in one book the scattered treatises of so many authors; which no one else has heretofore ventured to hope for or to expect, and it has indeed been considered by Ourselves a most difficult undertaking, nay, one that was almost impossible; but with Our hands raised to heaven, and having invoked the Divine aid, We have kept this object in

Our mind, confiding in God who can grant the accomplishment of things which are almost desperate, and can Himself carry them into effect by virtue of the greatness of His power.

We have also taken into consideration your marked integrity as disclosed by your labors, and have committed this work to you, after having already received the evidence of your talents in the preparation of Our Code; and We have ordered you in the prosecution of your task, to select as your assistants whomever you might approve of from among the most eloquent professors of law, as well as from the most learned men belonging to the bar of this great city. These, therefore, having been collected and introduced into Our palace, and accepted by Us upon your statements, We have permitted the entire work to be accomplished; it being provided, however, that it should be conducted under the supervision of your most vigilant mind.

Therefore We order you to read and revise the books relating to the Roman law drawn up by the jurists of antiquity, upon whom the most venerated princes conferred authority to write and interpret the same; so that from these all the substance may be collected, and, as far as may be possible, there shall remain no laws either similar to or inconsistent with one another, but that there may be compiled from them a summary which will take the place of all. And while others have written books relating to the law, for the reason that their writings have not been adopted by any authorities, or made use of in practice, We do not deem their treatises worthy of Our consideration.

Since this compilation is to be ascribed to the extraordinary liberality of Our Imperial will, it ought to constitute a most excellent work and, as it were, be revered as a peculiar and most holy temple of justice. You shall divide the entire law into fifty books, and into a certain number of titles following, as far as may be convenient for you, the arrangement of Our Code, as well as that of the Perpetual Edict, so that nothing may be omitted from the above mentioned collection; and that all the ancient law which has been in a confused condition for almost fourteen hundred years shall be embraced in the said fifty books, and this ancient law, purified by Us, shall be, so to speak, surrounded by a wall, and shall have nothing beyond it. All legal authors shall possess equal authority, and no preference shall be given to any, because all of them are neither superior nor inferior to one another in every respect, but some are of greater or less weight as far as certain subjects are concerned.

But you must neither base your judgment as to what is best and most equitable upon the number of authors, as perhaps on some points the opinion of one who is inferior may be preferable to that of many and greater ones; and therefore you must not entirely reject what was formerly included in the notes to Aemilius Papinianus,[2] taken from Ulpianus,[3] Paulus, and Marcianus,[4] al-

---

[2] A very influential Roman jurist during the reigns of the Emperors Marcus Aurelius and Septimius Severus (late second century A.D.). The *Digest* contains many excerpts from his writings.

[3] Papinian's most famous student.

[4] Other jurists.

though the said notes have hitherto had but little force, on account of the distinction of the most renowned Papinianus; but if you perceive that anything from them is required to supplement the labors of Papinianus, that man of eminent genius, or necessary for their interpretation, you must not hesitate, after having selected it, to give it the force of law; so that all those most learned men whose opinions are included in this book may have the same authority as if their studies had been based upon the Imperial Constitutions promulgated by Our own Divine power; for We very properly consider all those things to be Ours which have obtained their sanction from Us; for he who corrects what has not been skilfully done is more praiseworthy than he who is the original author of the same.

We desire you to be careful with regard to the following: if you find in the old books anything that is not suitably arranged, superfluous, or incomplete, you must remove all superfluities, supply what is lacking, and present the entire work in regular form, and with as excellent an appearance as possible. You must also observe the following, namely: if you find anything which the ancients have inserted in their old laws or constitutions that is incorrectly worded, you must correct this, and place it in its proper order, so that it may appear to be true, expressed in the best language, and written in this way in the first place; so that by comparing it with the original text, no one can venture to call in question as defective what you have selected and arranged. Since by an ancient law, which is styled the *Lex Regia,* all the rights and power of the Roman people were transferred to the Emperor, We do not derive Our authority from that of other different compilations, but wish that it shall all be entirely Ours, for how can antiquity abrogate our laws?

We wish that all these matters after they have been arranged in place shall be observed to such an extent that, although they may have been written by the ancients in a different way than appears in Our collection, no blame shall be imputed to the text, but it shall be ascribed to our selection.

Therefore, in no part of the aforesaid treatise, shall there be any place for *antinomia,* . . . but there must be such conformity and consistency therein that there will be no opportunity for contradiction.

We desire, as has already been stated, that all repetition shall also be banished from this compilation, and whatever has been provided by the most Sacred Constitutions which We have included in our Code We do not permit again to be considered as a part of the ancient law, since the sanction of the Imperial Constitutions is sufficient to confer authority upon them; unless perhaps this should take place either for the purpose of division, or supplement, or in order to secure greater exactness; and even this must be done very rarely, lest where this repetition occurs, something thorny may grow up in this meadow.

However, by no means do We allow you to insert into your treatise laws that appearing in ancient works have now fallen into desuetude; since We only desire that legal procedure to prevail which has been most frequently employed, or which long custom has established in this benign City; in accordance with the work of Salvius Julianus which declares that all states should follow the custom of Rome, which is the head of the world, and not that Rome should follow the example of other states; and by Rome is to be understood not only the ancient city, but Our own royal metropolis also, which by the grace of God was founded under the best auguries.

Therefore We order that everything shall be governed by these two works, one that of the Imperial Constitutions, the other, that of the law to be interpreted and compiled in a future Code; so that if anything else should be promulgated by Us in the form of an elementary treatise, the uninstructed mind of the student, being nourished by simple matters, may the more readily be conducted to a knowledge of the higher principles of jurisprudence.

We desire Our compilation which, God willing, is to be drawn up by you, to bear the name of the Digest or Pandects, and no person learned in the law shall dare hereafter to add any commentaries thereto, and to confuse by his own prolixity the abridgement of the aforesaid work, as was done in former times, for almost all law was thrown into confusion by the opposite opinions of those interpreting it; but it is sufficient merely by indexes, and a skilful use of titles which are called παράτιτλα, to give such warning that no change may take place in the interpretation of the same.

And in order that no doubt may arise hereafter on account of the writing, We order that the text of the said work shall not be written with abbreviated words, and that obscure and compendious expressions shall not be employed, which by themselves and through the defects which they have occasioned have brought about many contradictions, even where the number of the book or something else is meant; for We do not permit such things to be indicated by special abbreviations of numbers but they must be designated by regular letters.

Let it be your earnest desire, therefore, to do all these things, God willing, by the aid of your own wisdom and that of those other most eloquent men, and bring the work to as excellent and rapid a conclusion as possible; so that it having been completed and digested into fifty books may remain a monument to the great and eternal memory of the undertaking, a proof of the wisdom of Almighty God, to the glory of Our Empire and of your service. Given on the eighteenth day of the Kalends of January,[5] during the Consulship of those most illustrious men Lampadius and Orestes, 530.

[5] December 15.

FROM *THE INSTITUTES* (533)

Preamble

Of the Institutes or Elements of Our Lord the
Most Holy Emperor Justinian.

In the Name of Our Lord Jesus Christ.

THE EMPEROR CAESAR, FLAVIUS, JUSTINIANUS, ALEMANNICUS, GOTHICUS,
FRANCICUS, GERMANICUS, ANTICUS, ALANICUS, VANDALICUS, AFRICANUS,
PIOUS, HAPPY, RENOWNED, VICTOR AND TRIUMPHER, EVER AUGUSTUS,
TO THE YOUTH DESIROUS OF LEARNING THE LAWS.

It is expedient that the Imperial Majesty not only be distinguished by
arms, but also be protected by laws, so that government may be justly administered in time of both war and peace, and the Roman Sovereign not only
may emerge victorious from battle with the enemy, but also by legitimate
measures may defeat the evil designs of wicked men and appear as strict in
the administration of justice as triumphant over conquered foes.

This twofold task We have now accomplished, by means of the greatest
attention and care, and with the assistance of God. For barbarous nations,
subjected to Our authority, acknowledge Our warlike exploits, and Africa, as
well as other numerous provinces after so long a period of time have submitted
to the Roman domination, and have again become a portion of Our Empire by
means of Our conquests through the aid of Celestial Power, and all peoples
in fact, are now governed by laws either promulgated or compiled by Us.

After having brought into perfect harmony the Imperial Constitutions
hitherto involved in confusion, We have directed Our attention to the immense volumes of ancient jurisprudence, and have finally accomplished this
most difficult task, proceeding, as it were, through the depths of the ocean, and
aided by the favor of heaven.

This having been concluded through the Grace of God, We summoned
the illustrious Tribonian, Master and former Quaestor of Our Sacred Palace,
along with Theophilus and Dorotheus, eminent men and professors, whose
skill, familiarity with the laws, and fidelity in obeying Our orders We have
proved on many occasions, and especially directed them to draw up Institutes
by Our authority, and with Our advice, that you may be able to learn the
first principles of the law, not from ancient fables, but acquire them from the
Imperial Splendor; so that your ears as well as your minds may absorb nothing that is useless or incorrect, but whatever is in accordance with reason in
all things. And while, in former times, it was scarcely possible for those who
preceded you to read the Imperial Constitutions in the course of four years,

you may, now, from the very beginning, proceed to do so; being found worthy of such honor and happiness that both the beginning and the end of your instruction in the laws issue from the mouth of your Sovereign.

Therefore, after the completion of the fifty books of the Digest or Pandects, in which all the ancient law has been collected, and which We have caused to be compiled by the said distinguished personage Tribonian and other eminent and most illustrious men, We have ordered these Institutes to be divided into the following four books, that they may constitute the first elements of the entire science of jurisprudence.

In them a brief explanation has been made both of the principles which formerly obtained, as well as of those which, after having been obscured by disuse, have been illuminated once more by Imperial restoration.

These Institutes collected from all those of the ancients and especially from the Commentaries of Our Gaius,[6] embracing not only what is contained in his Institutes but also those of his work relating to daily transactions and compiled from those of many others, the three learned men aforesaid submitted to Us, and, after having read and examined them, We have accorded to them the full authority of Our Constitutions.

Accept, therefore, with the greatest ardor and alacrity, these Our laws, and prove yourselves so well informed in them that, when your course of law has been completed, the fairest hope may inspire you of being competent to govern Our dominions in whatever parts of the same the administration may be entrusted to you.

Given at Constantinople, on the eleventh day of the Kalends of December, during the third Consulship of Our Lord Justinian, ever Augustus.[7]

The Institutes of Our Lord Justinian.
BOOK I.

TITLE I.

Concerning Justice and Law.

Justice is the constant and perpetual desire to give to each one that to which he is entitled.

Jurisprudence is the knowledge of matters divine and human, and the comprehension of what is just and what is unjust.

These divisions being generally understood, and We being about to explain the laws of the Roman people, it appears that this may be most conveniently done if separate subjects are at first treated in a clear and simple

---

[6] Roman jurist who lived c. A.D. 110-c. 180, author of a famous textbook also called *Institutiones.*

[7] November 21, 533.

manner, and afterwards with greater care and exactness; for if We, at once, in the beginning, load the still uncultivated and inexperienced mind of the student with a multitude and variety of details, We shall bring about one of two things; that is, We shall either cause him to abandon his studies, or, by means of excessive labor—and also with that distrust which very frequently discourages young men—conduct him to that point to which, if led by an easier route, he might have been brought more speedily without much exertion and without misgiving.

The following are the precepts of the Law: to live honestly, not to injure another, and to give to each one that which belongs to him.

There are two branches of this study, namely: public and private. Public Law is that which concerns the administration of the Roman government; Private Law relates to the interests of individuals. Thus Private Law is said to be threefold in its nature, for it is composed of precepts of Natural Law, of those of the Law of Nations, and of those of the Civil Law.

Title II.

Concerning Natural Law, the Law of Nations, and the Civil Law.

Natural Law is that which nature has taught to all animals, for this law is not peculiar to the human race, but applies to all creatures which originate in the air, or the earth, and in the sea. Hence arises the union of the male and the female which we designate marriage; and hence are derived the procreation and the education of children; for we see that other animals also act as though endowed with knowledge of this law.

The Civil Law and the Law of Nations are divided as follows. All peoples that are governed by laws and customs make use of the law which is partly peculiar to themselves and partly pertaining to all men; for what each people has established for itself is peculiar to that State, and is styled the Civil Law; being, as it were, the especial law of that individual commonwealth. But the law which natural reason has established among all mankind and which is equally observed among all peoples, is called the Law of Nations, as being that which all nations make use of. The Roman people also employ a law which is in part peculiar to them, and in part common to all men. We propose to set forth their distinctions in their proper places.

The Civil Law derives its name from each state, as, for example, that of the Athenians; for if anyone wishes to designate the laws of Solon[8] or of Draco[9] as the Civil Law of Athens, he will not commit an error; for in this manner We call the law which the Roman people use the Civil Law of the

---

[8] Famous Athenian statesman and poet (*c.* 640 - *c.* 558 B.C.).

[9] Athenian legislator who drew up a code of laws (621 B.C.) proverbial for its severity.

Romans, or the *Jus Quiritium* employed by Roman citizens, as the Romans are styled *Quirites* from Quirinus.[10] When, however, We do not add the name of the state, We mean Our own law; just as when We mention *the poet* but do not give his name, the illustrious Homer is understood among the Greeks, and Virgil among us.

The Law of Nations, however, is common to the entire human race, for all nations have established for themselves certain regulations exacted by custom and human necessity. For wars have arisen, and captivity and slavery, which are contrary to natural law, have followed as a result, as, according to Natural Law, all men were originally born free; and from this law nearly all contracts, such as purchase, sale, hire, partnership, deposit, loan, and innumerable others have been derived.

Our Law, which We make use of, is either written or unwritten, just as among the Greeks written and unwritten laws exist. The written law consists of the Statutes, the *Plebiscita,* the Decrees of the Senate, the Decisions of the Emperors, the Orders of the Magistrates and the Answers of Jurisconsults.

A Statute is what the Roman people have established as the result of an interrogatory of a senatorial magistrate, for example, a consul. The *Plebiscitum* is what the plebeians have established upon the interrogatory of a plebeian magistrate, for instance, a tribune. Plebeians differ from the people as a species does from a genus; for all citizens, including even patricians, and senators, are understood by the word people, and by the term plebeians all other citizens, exclusive of patricians and senators, are designated. *Plebiscita* have had the same force as statutes since the passage of the *Lex Hortensia.*[11]

A Decree of the Senate is what the Senate orders and establishes, for since the Roman people have increased in numbers to such an extent that it is difficult for them to be convoked in an assembly for the purpose of adopting a law, it has seemed advisable for the Senate to be consulted instead of the people.

Whatever is approved by the sovereign has also the force of law, because by the *Lex Regia,* from when his power is derived, the people have delegated to him all their jurisdiction and authority. Therefore, whatever the Emperor establishes by means of a Rescript or decrees as a magistrate, or commands by an Edict, stands as law, and these are called Constitutions. Some of these are personal and are not considered as precedents, because the sovereign does not wish them to be such; for any favor he grants on account of merit, or where he inflicts punishment upon anyone or affords him unusual assistance, this affects only the individual concerned; the others, however, as they are of general application unquestionably are binding upon all.

The Edicts of the Praetors[12] also possess more than ordinary authority, and

---

[10] Quirinus was the god of the Sabines, who lived on the Quirinal hill and who were later made part of Rome. *Quirites* therefore denotes the old inhabitants of Rome.

[11] In 287 B.C.

[12] Roman magistrates elected annually by the citizens.

we are accustomed to designate them "honorary" laws, because they derive their force from those who are invested with honors, that is to say magistrates. The Curule Aediles,[13] likewise, formerly published edicts relative to certain matters which also constitute part of the honorary law.

The Answers of Jurisconsults are the decisions and opinions of persons upon whom has been conferred authority to establish laws; for it was decided in ancient times that the laws should be publicly interpreted by those to whom the right to answer had been granted by the Emperor, and who were called jurisconsults, and the unanimous decisions and opinions of the latter had such force that, according to the Constitutions, a judge was not permitted to deviate from what they had determined.

The unwritten law is that which usage has confirmed, for customs long observed and sanctioned by the consent of those who employ them, resemble law.

Not improperly does the Civil Law appear to have been divided into two branches; since in its origin it seems to have been derived from the institutions of two states, namely, Athens, and Lacedaemon; for in these states it was the practice for the Lacedaemonians to commit to memory the rules which served them as laws, and the Athenians, on the other hand, observed whatever legal regulations which they had reduced to writing.

Natural Laws that are observed without distinction by all nations and have been established by Divine Providence remain always fixed and unchangeable; but those which every State establishes for itself are often changed either by the tacit consent of the people, or by some other law subsequently enacted.

3. THE FIRST ICONOCLASTIC CONTROVERSY

Jewish opposition to the use of images in worship was inherited by the Christian Church. Christians first limited themselves to veneration of the cross and of relics, but in the years after the conversion of Constantine the pagan cult of the ruler's portrait was adapted to portrayals of Christ, Mary, and the saints. Despite opposition, there was a great intensification of the use and veneration of Christian images after Justinian's reign. Attitudes of those later called by their enemies iconodules, or image-worshippers, ranged from the merely didactic and emotional to the belief that icons were mediators between the prototype and the observer, and to the superstition that they possessed magical powers. Reaction against such veneration, particularly on the part of Monophysites[1] and other oriental inhabitants of

[13] Plebeian magistrates representing the whole populace.
[1] Heretics who thought Christ's human nature was swallowed up in his divinity.

border regions of the Empire, was correspondingly violent. It reached a climax in the Iconoclastic, or Image-breaking, Controversy, in which a series of emperors attempted to put an end to practices they regarded as idolatrous and also as harmful to the loyalty of important border areas. This controversy revealed both the extent and the limits of imperial power.

The struggle was begun in 726 by the great soldier-emperor Leo III (reigned 717-741) with sermons against the iconodules, and with the removal of a famous icon of Christ which stood in Constantinople. The riot this action provoked was the beginning of a long period of disorder, repression, and bloodshed. It reached its height under Leo's son, Constantine V (reigned 741-775), and finally ended in the victory of the iconodules at the Seventh Ecumenical Council at Nicaea in 787. The conflict broke out again early in the ninth century and lasted until the final defeat of iconoclasm in 843. Its outcome showed that while the Emperor could interfere with impunity in ecclesiastical administration, he would be wise not to meddle with theological doctrine.

One of the most formidable opponents of the iconoclasts was John of Damascus (c. 675 - c. 749), who served as a high official of the Moslem caliph in Damascus and later entered the monastery of St. Sabas near Jerusalem. He is most famous for his great *summa*, the *Fount of Wisdom*, divided into three main sections, which discuss philosophy, heresy, and the orthodox faith. It holds much the same position in the thought of the Eastern Church as the writings of Aquinas in the West. A chapter from it, setting forth John's view of images, is reprinted below, as is a longer discussion of this question from a treatise dealing specifically with the subject. Extracts from the decrees of the Iconoclastic Synod of Constantinople in 754 and the orthodox Second Council of Nicaea in 787 are also included in order to give a summary view of the arguments on both sides.

ST. JOHN OF DAMASCUS: FROM
ON HOLY IMAGES (c. 730)[2]

Now, as we are talking of images and worship, let us analyse the exact meaning of each. An image is a likeness of the original with a certain difference, for it is not an exact reproduction of the original. Thus, the Son is the living, substantial, unchangeable Image of the invisible God, bearing in Himself the whole Father, being in all things equal to Him, differing only in being begotten by the Father, who is the Begetter; the Son is begotten. The Father does not proceed from the Son, but the Son from the Father. It is through the Son, though not after Him, that He is what He is, the Father who generates. In God, too, there are representations and images of His future acts,—that is to say, His counsel from all eternity, which is ever unchangeable. That which is divine is immutable; there is no change in Him,

[2] *St. John Damascene on Holy Images*, trans. by Mary H. Allies (London, Thomas Baker, 1898), pp. 10-17. Reprinted by kind permission of the publishers, Burns & Oates Ltd., London.

nor shadow of change. Blessed Denis,[3] who has made divine things in God's presence his study, says that these representations and images are marked out beforehand. In His counsels, God has noted and settled all that He would do, the unchanging future events before they came to pass. In the same way, a man who wished to build a house would first make and think out a plan. Again, visible things are images of invisible and intangible things, on which they throw a faint light. Holy Scripture clothes in figure God and the angels, and the same holy man (Blessed Denis) explains why. When sensible things sufficiently render what is beyond sense, and give a form to what is intangible, a medium would be reckoned imperfect according to our standard, if it did not fully represent material vision, or if it required effort of mind. If, therefore, Holy Scripture, providing for our need, ever putting before us what is intangible, clothes it in flesh, does it not make an image of what is thus invested with our nature, and brought to the level of our desires, yet invisible? A certain conception through the senses thus takes place in the brain, which was not there before, and is transmitted to the judicial faculty, and added to the mental store. Gregory, who is so eloquent about God, says that the mind, which is set upon getting beyond corporeal things, is incapable of doing it. For the invisible things of God since the creation of the world are made visible through images. We see images in creation which remind us faintly of God, as when, for instance, we speak of the holy and adorable Trinity, imaged by the sun, or light, or burning rays, or by a running fountain, or a full river, or by the mind, speech, or the spirit within us, or by a rose tree, or a sprouting flower, or a sweet fragrance.

Again, an image is expressive of something in the future, mystically shadowing forth what is to happen. For instance, the ark represents the image of Our Lady, Mother of God, so does the staff and the earthen jar. The serpent brings before us Him who vanquished on the Cross the bite of the original serpent; the sea, water, and the cloud the grace of baptism.

Again, things which have taken place are expressed by images for the remembrance either of a wonder, or an honour, or dishonour, or good or evil, to help those who look upon it in after times that we may avoid evils and imitate goodness. It is of two kinds, the written image in books, as when God had the law inscribed on tablets, and when He enjoined that the lives of holy men should be recorded and sensible memorials be preserved in remembrance; as, for instance, the earthen jar and the staff in the ark. So now we preserve in writing the images and the good deeds of the past. Either, therefore, take away images altogether and be out of harmony with God who made these regulations, or receive them with the language and in the manner which befits them. In speaking of the manner let us go into the question of worship.

Worship is the symbol of veneration and of honour. Let us understand that there are different degrees of worship. First of all the worship of latreia,

---

[3] Dionysius the pseudo-Areopagite, author of works of mystical theology composed c. 500, attributed to that Dionysius the Areopagite mentioned by St. Paul in Acts 17:34.

which we show to God, who alone by nature is worthy of worship. Then, for the sake of God who is worshipful by nature, we honour His saints and servants, as Josue and Daniel worshipped an angel, and David His holy places, when he says, "Let us go to the place where His feet have stood." Again, in His tabernacles, as when all the people of Israel adored in the tent, and standing round the temple in Jerusalem, fixing their gaze upon it from all sides, and worshipping from that day to this, or in the rulers established by Him, as Jacob rendered homage to Esau, his elder brother, and to Pharaoh, the divinely established ruler. Joseph was worshipped by his brothers. I am aware that worship was based on honour, as in the case of Abraham and the sons of Emmor. Either, then, do away with worship, or receive it altogether according to its proper measure.

Answer me this question. Is there only one God? You answer, "Yes, there is only one Law-giver." Why, then, does He command contrary things? The cherubim are not outside of creation; why, then, does He allow cherubim carved by the hand of man to overshadow the mercy-seat? Is it not evident that as it is impossible to make an image of God, who is uncircumscribed and impassible, or of one like to God, creation should not be worshipped as God. He allows the image of the cherubim who are circumscribed, and prostrate in adoration before the divine throne, to be made, and thus prostrate to overshadow the mercy-seat. It was fitting that the image of the heavenly choirs should overshadow the divine mysteries. Would you say that the ark and staff and mercy-seat were not made? Are they not produced by the hand of man? Are they not due to what you call contemptible matter? What was the tabernacle itself? Was it not an image? Was it not a type and a figure? Hence the holy Apostle's words concerning the observances of the law, "Who serve unto the example and shadow of heavenly things." As it was answered to Moses, when he was to finish the tabernacle: "See" (He says), "that thou make all things according to the pattern which was shown thee on the Mount." But the law was not an image. It shrouded the image. In the words of the same Apostle, the law contains the shadow of the goods to come, not the image of those things. For if the law should forbid images, and yet be itself a forerunner of images, what should we say? If the tabernacle was a figure, and the type of a type, why does the law not prohibit image-making? But this is not in the least the case. There is a time for everything.

Of old, God the incorporeal and uncircumscribed was never depicted. Now, however, when God is seen clothed in flesh, and conversing with men, I make an image of the God whom I see. I do not worship matter, I worship the God of matter, who became matter for my sake, and deigned to inhabit matter, who worked out my salvation through matter. I will not cease from honouring that matter which works my salvation. I venerate it, though not as God. How could God be born out of lifeless things? And if God's body is God by union, it is immutable. The nature of God remains the same as before, the flesh created in time is quickened by a logical and reasoning soul.

I honour all matter besides, and venerate it. Through it, filled, as it were, with a divine power and grace, my salvation has come to me. Was not the thrice happy and thrice blessed wood of the Cross matter? Was not the sacred and holy mountain of Calvary matter? What of the life-giving rock, the Holy Sepulchre, the source of our resurrection: was it not matter? Is not the most holy book of the Gospels matter? Is not the blessed table matter which gives us the Bread of Life? Are not the gold and silver matter, out of which crosses and altar-plate and chalices are made? And before all these things, is not the body and blood of our Lord matter? Either do away with the veneration and worship due to all these things, or submit to the tradition of the Church in the worship of images, honouring God and His friends, and following in this the grace of the Holy Spirit.

ST. JOHN OF DAMASCUS: FROM *THE FOUNT OF WISDOM* (AFTER 742)[4]

But since some find fault with us for worshipping and honouring the image of our Saviour and that of our Lady, and those, too, of the rest of the saints and servants of Christ, let them remember that in the beginning God created man after His own image. On what grounds, then, do we shew reverence to each other unless because we are made after God's image? For as Basil,[5] that much-versed expounder of divine things, says, the honour given to the image passes over to the prototype. Now a prototype is that which is imaged, from which the derivative is obtained. Why was it that the Mosaic people honoured on all hands the tabernacle which bore an image and type of heavenly things, or rather of the whole creation? God indeed said to Moses, "Look that thou make them after their pattern which was shewed thee in the mount." The Cherubim, too, which o'ershadow the mercy seat, are they not the work of men's hands? What, further, is the celebrated temple at Jerusalem? Is it not hand-made and fashioned by the skill of men?

Moreover the divine Scripture blames those who worship graven images, but also those who sacrifice to demons. The Greeks sacrificed and the Jews also sacrificed: but the Greeks to demons and the Jews to God. And the sacrifice of the Greeks was rejected and condemned, but the sacrifice of the just was very acceptable to God. For Noah sacrificed, and "God smelled a sweet savour," receiving the fragrance of the right choice and good-will towards Him. And so the graven images of the Greeks, since they were images of deities, were rejected and forbidden.

---

[4] John of Damascus, *Exposition of the Orthodox Faith,* trans. by S. D. F. Salmon, *A Select Library of Nicene and Post-Nicene Fathers of the Christian Church,* Series II, ed. by P. Schaff and H. Wace (reprinted Grand Rapids, Mich., Wm. B. Eerdmans Publishing Company, 1955), IX, p. 88.

[5] St. Basil (c. 330 - 379), successor of Eusebius as Bishop of Caesarea and one of the greatest of the early Church fathers.

But besides this who can make an imitation of the invisible, incorporeal, uncircumscribed, formless God? Therefore to give form to the Deity is the height of folly and impiety. And hence it is that in the Old Testament the use of images was not uncommon. But after God in His bowels of pity became in truth man for our salvation, not as He was seen by Abraham in the semblance of a man, nor as He was seen by the prophets, but in being truly man, and after He lived upon the earth and dwelt among men, worked miracles, suffered, was crucified, rose again and was taken back to Heaven, since all these things actually took place and were seen by men, they were written for the remembrance and instruction of us who were not alive at that time in order that though we saw not, we may still, hearing and believing, obtain the blessing of the Lord. But seeing that not every one has a knowledge of letters nor time for reading, the Fathers gave their sanction to depicting these events on images as being acts of great heroism, in order that they should form a concise memorial of them. Often, doubtless, when we have not the Lord's passion in mind and see the image of Christ's crucifixion, His saving passion is brought back to remembrance, and we fall down and worship not the material but that which is imaged: just as we do not worship the material of which the Gospels are made, nor the material of the Cross, but that which these typify. For wherein does the cross, that typifies the Lord, differ from a cross that does not do so? It is just the same also in the case of the Mother of the Lord. For the honour which we give to her is referred to Him Who was made of her incarnate. And similarly also the brave acts of holy men stir us up to be brave and to emulate and imitate their valour and to glorify God. For as we said, the honour that is given to the best of fellow-servants is a proof of good-will towards our common Lady, and the honour rendered to the image passes over to the prototype. But this is an unwritten tradition, just as is also the worshipping towards the East and the worship of the Cross, and very many other similar things.

A certain tale, too, is told, how that when Augarus[6] was king over the city of the Edessenes, he sent a portrait painter to paint a likeness of the Lord, and when the painter could not paint because of the brightness that shone from His countenance, the Lord Himself put a garment over His own divine and life-giving face and impressed on it an image of Himself and sent this to Augarus, to satisfy thus his desire.

Moreover that the Apostles handed down much that was unwritten, Paul, the Apostle of the Gentiles, tells us in these words: "Therefore, brethren, stand fast and hold the traditions which ye have been taught of us, whether by word or by epistle." And to the Corinthians he writes, "Now I praise you, brethren, that ye remember me in all things, and keep the traditions as I have delivered them to you."

[6] Abgar V (4 B.C. to A.D. 50), King of Edessa, supposed, according to legend, to have exchanged letters with Christ.

THE ICONOCLASTIC CONCILIABULUM (754)[7]

The Definition of the Holy, Great, and Ecumenical Seventh Synod.

The holy and Ecumenical synod, which by the grace of God and most pious command of the God-beloved and orthodox Emperors, Constantine and Leo, now assembled in the imperial residence city, in the temple of the holy and inviolate Mother of God and Virgin Mary, surnamed in Blachernae, have decreed as follows.

Satan misguided men, so that they worshipped the creature instead of the Creator. The Mosaic law and the prophets cooperated to undo this ruin; but in order to save mankind thoroughly, God sent his own Son, who turned us away from error and the worshipping of idols, and taught us the worshipping of God in spirit and in truth. As messengers of his saving doctrine, he left us his Apostles and disciples, and these adorned the Church, his Bride, with his glorious doctrines. This ornament of the Church the holy Fathers and the six Ecumenical Councils have preserved inviolate. But the before-mentioned demiurgos of wickedness could not endure the sight of this adornment, and gradually brought back idolatry under the appearance of Christianity. As then Christ armed his Apostles against the ancient idolatry with the power of the Holy Spirit, and sent them out into all the world, so has he awakened against the new idolatry his servants our faithful Emperors, and endowed them with the same wisdom of the Holy Spirit. Impelled by the Holy Spirit they could no longer be witnesses of the Church being laid waste by the deception of demons, and summoned the sanctified assembly of the God-beloved bishops, that they might institute at a synod a scriptural examination into the deceitful colouring of the pictures ($\delta\mu\omega\mu\acute{\alpha}\tau\omega\nu$) which draws down the spirit of man from the lofty adoration ($\lambda\alpha\tau\rho\epsilon\acute{\iota}\alpha\varsigma$) of God to the low and material adoration ($\lambda\alpha\tau\rho\epsilon\acute{\iota}\alpha\nu$) of the creature, and that they, under divine guidance, might express their view of the subject.

Our holy synod therefore assembled, and we, its 338 members, follow the older synodal decrees, and accept and proclaim joyfully the dogmas handed down, principally those of the six holy Ecumenical Synods. In the first place the holy and ecumenical great synod assembled at Nice, etc.

After we had carefully examined their decrees under the guidance of the Holy Spirit, we found that the unlawful art of painting living creatures blasphemed the fundamental doctrine of our salvation—namely, the Incarnation of Christ, and contradicted the six holy synods. These condemned Nestorius

---

[7] *The Seven Ecumenical Councils of the Undivided Church*, trans. by H. R. Percival, *A Select Library of Nicene and Post-Nicene Fathers of the Christian Church*, Series II, ed. by P. Schaff and H. Wace (reprinted Grand Rapids, Mich., Wm. B. Eerdmans Publishing Company, 1955), XIV, pp. 543-544.

because he divided the one Son and Word of God into two sons, and on the other side, Arius, Dioscorus, Eutyches, and Severus, because they maintained a mingling of the two natures of the one Christ.

Wherefore we thought it right, to shew forth with all accuracy in our present definition the error of such as make and venerate these, for it is the unanimous doctrine of all the holy Fathers and of the six Ecumenical Synods, that no one may imagine any kind of separation or mingling in opposition to the unsearchable, unspeakable, and incomprehensible union of the two natures in the one hypostasis or person. What avails, then, the folly of the painter, who from sinful love of gain depicts that which should not be depicted—that is, with his polluted hands he tries to fashion that which should only be believed in the heart and confessed with the mouth? He makes an image and calls it Christ. The name *Christ* signifies *God and man*. Consequently it is an image of God and man, and consequently he has in his foolish mind, in his representation of the created flesh, depicted the Godhead which cannot be represented, and thus mingled what should not be mingled. Thus he is guilty of a double blasphemy—the one in making an image of the Godhead, and the other by mingling the Godhead and manhood. Those fall into the same blasphemy who venerate the image, and the same woe rests upon both, because they err with Arius, Dioscorus, and Eutyches, and with the heresy of the Acephali. When, however, they are blamed for undertaking to depict the divine nature of Christ, which should not be depicted, they take refuge in the excuse: We represent only the flesh of Christ which we have seen and handled. But that is a Nestorian error. For it should be considered that that flesh was also the flesh of God the Word, without any separation, perfectly assumed by the divine nature and made wholly divine. How could it now be separated and represented apart? So is it with the human soul of Christ which mediates between the Godhead of the Son and the dullness of the flesh. As the human flesh is at the same time flesh of God the Word, so is the human soul also soul of God the Word, and both at the same time, the soul being deified as well as the body, and the Godhead remained undivided even in the separation of the soul from the body in his voluntary passion. For where the soul of Christ is, there is also his Godhead; and where the body of Christ is, there too is his Godhead. If then in his passion the divinity remained inseparable from these, how do the fools venture to separate the flesh from the Godhead, and represent it by itself as the image of a mere man? They fall into the abyss of impiety, since they separate the flesh from the Godhead, ascribe to it a subsistence of its own, a personality of its own, which they depict, and thus introduce a fourth person into the Trinity. Moreover, they represent as not being made divine, that which has been made divine by being assumed by the Godhead. Whoever, then, makes an image of Christ, either depicts the Godhead which cannot be depicted, and mingles it with the manhood (like the Monophysites), or he represents the body of Christ as not made divine and separate and as a person apart, like the Nestorians.

The only admissible figure of the humanity of Christ, however, is bread and wine in the holy Supper. This and no other form, this and no other type, has he chosen to represent his incarnation. Bread he ordered to be brought, but not a representation of the human form, so that idolatry might not arise. And as the body of Christ is made divine, so also this figure of the body of Christ, the bread, is made divine by the descent of the Holy Spirit; it becomes the divine body of Christ by the mediation of the priest who, separating the oblation from that which is common, sanctifies it.

The evil custom of assigning names to the images does not come down from Christ and the Apostles and the holy Fathers; nor have these left behind them any prayer by which an image should be hallowed or made anything else than ordinary matter.

If, however, some say, we might be right in regard to the images of Christ, on account of the mysterious union of the two natures, but it is not right for us to forbid also the images of the altogether spotless and ever-glorious Mother of God, of the prophets, apostles, and martyrs, who were mere men and did not consist of two natures; we may reply, first of all: If those fall away, there is no longer need of these. But we will also consider what may be said against these in particular. Christianity has rejected the *whole* of heathenism, and so not merely heathen sacrifices, but also the heathen worship of images. The Saints live on eternally with God, although they have died. If anyone thinks to call them back again to life by a dead art, discovered by the heathen, he makes himself guilty of blasphemy. Who dares attempt with heathenish art to paint the Mother of God, who is exalted above all heavens and the Saints? It is not permitted to Christians, who have the hope of the resurrection, to imitate the customs of demon-worshippers, and to insult the Saints, who shine in so great glory, by common dead matter. . . .

DECREE OF THE SECOND COUNCIL OF NICAEA (787)[8]

. . . . .

We, therefore, following the royal pathway and the divinely inspired authority of our Holy Fathers and the traditions of the Catholic Church (for, as we all know, the Holy Spirit indwells her), define with all certitude and accuracy that just as the figure of the precious and life-giving Cross, so also the venerable and holy images, as well in painting and mosaic as of other fit materials, should be set forth in the holy churches of God, and on the sacred vessels and on the vestments and on hangings and in pictures both in houses and by the wayside, to wit, the figure of our Lord God and Saviour Jesus Christ, of our spotless Lady, the Mother of God, of the honourable Angels, of all Saints and of all pious people: For by so much more frequently as they

[8] *The Seven Ecumenical Councils of the Undivided Church,* trans. by H. R. Percival, *A Select Library of Nicene and Post-Nicene Fathers of the Christian Church,* Series II, ed. by P. Schaff and H. Wace (reprinted Grand Rapids, Mich., Wm. B. Eerdmans Publishing Company, 1955), XIV, p. 550.

are seen in artistic representation, by so much more readily are men lifted up
to the memory of their prototypes, and to a longing after them; and to these
should be given due salutation and honourable reverence (ἀσπασμὸν καὶ
τιμητικὴν προσκίνησιν), not indeed that true worship of faith (λατρείαν) which
pertains alone to the divine nature; but to these, as to the figure of the
precious and life-giving Cross and to the Book of the Gospels and to the
other holy objects, incense and lights may be offered according to ancient
pious custom. For the honour which is paid to the image passes on to that
which the image represents, and he who reveres the image reveres in it the
subject represented. For thus the teaching of our holy Fathers, that is the
tradition of the Catholic Church, which from one end of the earth to the
other hath received the Gospel, is strengthened. Thus we follow Paul, who
spake in Christ, and the whole divine Apostolic company and the holy Fathers, holding fast the traditions which we have received. So we sing prophetically the triumphal hymns of the Church, "Rejoice greatly, O daughter
of Sion; Shout, O daughter of Jerusalem. Rejoice and be glad with all thy
heart. The Lord hath taken away from thee the oppression of thy adversaries; thou art redeemed from the hand of thine enemies. The Lord is a
King in the midst of thee; thou shalt not see evil any more, and peace be
unto thee forever."

Those, therefore, who dare to think or teach otherwise, or as wicked
heretics to spurn the traditions of the Church and to invent some novelty, or
else to reject some of those things which the Church hath received (*e.g.*, the
Book of the Gospels, or the image of the cross, or the pictorial icons, or the
holy reliques of a martyr), or evilly and sharply to devise anything subversive
of the lawful traditions of the Catholic Church or to turn to common uses
the sacred vessels or the venerable monasteries, if they be Bishops or Clerics,
we command that they be deposed; if religious or laics, that they be cut off
from communion.

4. CONSTANTINE VII: ADVICE ON GOVERNING THE EMPIRE (*c.* 950)[1]

Constantine VII (reigned 905-959) was one of the most learned of Byzantine emperors and a great patron of education. Shy and studious, he exercised
little power during the reign of his co-emperor and father-in-law, Romanus I

[1] Constantine Porphyrogenitus, *De Administrando Imperio*, ed. by G. Moravcsik,
with Eng. trans. and commentary by R. J. H. Jenkins (Budapest, Tudományegyetemi
Görög Filológiai Intézet, 1949-1962), I, pp. 45-57, 65-77.

Lecapenus (920-944). Even after Romanus' exile in 944, Constantine did not distinguish himself as a strong ruler and is chiefly remembered today as a scholar and author. Among his writings the most important are a life of his grandfather Basil I (reigned 867-886), the *Book of Ceremonies,* containing much information about the finery and protocol of the Byzantine court, and a treatise of advice to his son Romanus. Untitled but usually called *De Administrando Imperio* or *On Administering the Empire,* the latter attempts to acquaint Romanus with the knowledge necessary for his future task: recent history, the geography and inhabitants of neighboring lands, the principles of Byzantine foreign policy and diplomacy. Because of his frankness, we may assume that the Emperor was writing confidentially. Not many documents allow one to penetrate so deeply into the purposes and methods of a government.

CONSTANTINE IN CHRIST THE ETERNAL EMPEROR EMPEROR OF THE ROMANS TO HIS SON ROMANUS[2] THE EMPEROR CROWNED OF GOD AND BORN IN THE PURPLE

Proem

A wise son maketh glad a father, and an affectionate father taketh delight in a prudent son. For the Lord giveth wit to speak in season, and addeth thereto an ear to hear; with Him is the treasure of wisdom, and from him cometh every perfect gift; He setteth kings upon the throne and giveth unto them the lordship over all. Now therefore hearken unto me, my son, and being adept in this my teaching thou shalt be wise among the prudent, and be accounted prudent among the wise; the peoples shall bless thee, and the multitudes of the nations shall call thee blessed. Be instructed in what it behoves thee before all else to know, and lay hold skilfully upon the helm of the rule. Study the things that are now, and be instructed concerning the things that are to be, so that thou mayst amass experience with sound judgment, and thou shalt be most competent in thine affairs. Lo, I set a doctrine before thee, so that being sharpened thereby in experience and knowledge, thou shalt not stumble concerning the best counsels and the common good: first, in what each nation has power to advantage the Romans, and in what to hurt, and how and by what other nation each severally may be encountered in arms and subdued; then, concerning their ravenous and insatiate temper and the gifts they demand inordinately; next, concerning also the difference between other nations, their origins and customs and manner of life, and the position and climate of the land they dwell in, its geographical description and measurement, and moreover concerning events which have occurred at various times between the Romans and different nations; and thereafter, what reforms have been introduced from time to time in our state, and also through-

[2] Later Romanus II (reigned 959-963).

out the Roman empire. These things have I discovered of my own wisdom, and have decreed that they shall be made known unto thee, my beloved son, in order that thou mayst know the difference between each of these nations, and how either to treat with and conciliate them, or to make war upon and oppose. For so shall they quake before thee as one mighty in wisdom, and as from fire shall they flee from thee; their lips shall be bridled, and as darts shall thy words wound them unto death. Thou shalt appear terrible unto them, and at thy face shall trembling take hold upon them. And the Almighty shall cover thee with his shield, and thy Creator shall endue thee with understanding; He shall direct thy steps, and shall establish thee upon a sure foundation. Thy throne shall be as the sun before Him, and His eyes shall be looking towards thee, and naught of harm shall touch thee, for He hath chosen thee and set thee apart from thy mother's womb, and hath given unto thee His rule as unto one excellent above all men, and hath set thee as a refuge upon a hill and as a statue of gold upon an high place, and as a city upon a mountain hath He raised thee up, that the nations may bring to thee their gifts and thou mayst be adored of them that dwell upon the earth. But Thou, O Lord my God, whose rule abideth unharmed for ever, prosper him in his ways who through Thee was begotten of me, and may the visitation of Thy face be toward him, and Thine ear be inclined to his supplications. May Thy hand cover him, and may he rule because of truth, and may Thy right hand guide him; may his ways be directed before Thee to keep thy statutes. May foes fall before his face, and his enemies lick the dust. May the stem of his race be shady with leaves of many offspring, and the shadow of his fruit cover the kingly mountains; for by Thee do kings rule, glorifying Thee for ever and ever.

Hear now, my son, those things of which I think you should not be ignorant, and be wise that you may attain to government. For I maintain that while learning is a good thing for all the rest as well, who are subjects, yet it is especially so for you, who are bound to take thought for the safety of all, and to steer and guide the laden ship of the world. And if in setting out my subject I have followed the plain and beaten track of speech and, so to say, idly running and simple prose, do not wonder at that, my son. For I have not been studious to make a display of fine writing or of an Atticizing style, swollen with the sublime and lofty, but rather have been eager by means of every-day and conversational narrative to teach you those things of which I think you should not be ignorant, and which may without difficulty provide that intelligence and prudence which are the fruit of long experience.

I conceive, then, that it is always greatly to the advantage of the emperor of the Romans to be minded to keep the peace with the nation of the Pechenegs and to conclude conventions and treaties of friendship with them and to send every year to them from our side a diplomatic agent with presents befitting and suitable to that nation, and to take from their side sureties, that is, hostages and a diplomatic agent, who shall come, together with the competent minister, to this city protected of God, and shall enjoy all imperial benefits and gifts suitable for the emperor to bestow.

This nation of the Pechenegs is neighbour to the district of Cherson,[3] and if they are not friendly disposed towards us, they may make excursions and plundering raids against Cherson, and may ravage Cherson itself and the so-called Regions.

The Pechenegs are neighbours to and march with the Russians also, and often, when the two are not at peace with one another, raid Russia, and do her considerable harm and outrage.

The Russians also are much concerned to keep the peace with the Pechenegs. For they buy of them horned cattle and horses and sheep, whereby they live more easily and comfortably, since none of the aforesaid animals is found in Russia. Moreover, the Russians are quite unable to set out for wars beyond their borders unless they are at peace with the Pechenegs, because while they are away from their homes, these may come upon them and destroy and outrage their property. And so the Russians, both to avoid being harmed by them and because of the strength of that nation, are the more concerned always to be in alliance with them and to have them for support, so as both to be rid of their enmity and to enjoy the advantage of their assistance.

Nor can the Russians come at this imperial city of the Romans, either for war or for trade, unless they are at peace with the Pechenegs, because when the Russians come with their ships to the barrages of the river and cannot pass through unless they lift their ships off the river and carry them past by porting them on their shoulders, then the men of this nation of the Pechenegs set upon them, and, as they cannot do two things at once, they are easily routed and cut to pieces.

The tribe of the Turks, too, trembles greatly at and fears the said Pechenegs, because they have often been defeated by them and brought to the verge of complete annihilation. Therefore the Turks always look on the Pechenegs with dread, and are held in check by them.

So long as the emperor of the Romans is at peace with the Pechenegs, neither Russians nor Turks can come upon the Roman dominions by force of arms, nor can they exact from the Romans large and inflated sums in money and goods as the price of peace, for they fear the strength of this nation which the emperor can turn against them while they are campaigning against the Romans. For the Pechenegs, if they are leagued in friendship with the emperor and won over by him through letters and gifts, can easily come upon the country both of the Russians and of the Turks, and enslave their women and children and ravage their country.

To the Bulgarians also the emperor of the Romans will appear more formidable, and can impose on them the need for tranquillity, if he is at peace with the Pechenegs, because the said Pechenegs are neighbours to these Bulgarians also, and when they wish, either for private gain or to do a favour

[3] A Byzantine city in the Crimea.

to the emperor of the Romans, they can easily march against Bulgaria, and with their preponderating multitude and their strength overwhelm and defeat them. And so the Bulgarians also continually struggle and strive to maintain peace and harmony with the Pechenegs. For from having frequently been crushingly defeated and plundered by them, they have learned by experience the value and advantage of being always at peace with them.

Yet another folk of these Pechenegs lies over against the district of Cherson; they trade with the Chersonites, and perform services for them and for the emperor in Russia and Chazaria and Zichia and all the parts beyond: that is to say, they receive from the Chersonites a prearranged remuneration in respect of this service proportionate to their labour and trouble, in the form of pieces of purple cloth, ribbons, silks, gold brocade, pepper, scarlet or "Parthian" leather, and other commodities which they require, according to a contract which each Chersonite may make or agree to with an individual Pecheneg. For these Pechenegs are free men and, so to say, independent, and never perform any service without remuneration.

When an imperial agent goes over to Cherson on this service, he must at once send to Patzinacia and demand hostages and an escort, and on their arrival he must leave the hostages under guard in the city of Cherson, and himself go off with the escort to Patzinacia and carry out his instructions. Now these Pechenegs, who are ravenous and keenly covetous of articles rare among them, are shameless in their demands for generous gifts, the hostages demanding this for themselves and that for their wives, and the escort something for their own trouble and some more for the wear and tear of their cattle. Then, when the imperial agent enters their country, they first ask for the emperor's gifts, and then again, when these have glutted the menfolk, they ask for the presents for their wives and parents. Also, all who come with him to escort him on his way back to Cherson demand payment from him for their trouble and the wear and tear of their cattle.

In the region of Bulgaria also is settled a folk of the Pechenegs, toward the region of the Dnieper and the Dniester and the other rivers of those parts. And when an imperial agent is dispatched from here with ships of war, he may, without going to Cherson, shortly and swiftly find these same Pechenegs here; and when he has found them, the imperial agent sends a message to them by his man, himself remaining on board the ships of war, carrying along with him and guarding in the ships of war the imperial goods. And they come down to him, and when they come down, the imperial agent gives them hostages of his men, and himself takes other hostages of these Pechenegs, and holds them in the ships of war, and then he makes agreement with them; and when the Pechenegs have taken their oaths to the imperial agent according to their "zakana," he presents them with the imperial gifts, and takes from among them as many "friends" as he sees fit, and returns. Agreement must be made with them on this condition, that wherever the emperor calls upon them, they are to serve him, whether among the Russians, or among the Bulgarians, or again among the Turks. For they are able to make war upon all these, and as they have often come against them, are now regarded by them with dread. And this is clear from what follows. For once when the cleric Gabriel was dispatched by imperial mandate to the Turks and said to them, "The emperor declares that you are to go and expel the Pechenegs from their place and settle yourselves there (for in former days you used to be settled there yourselves) so that you may be near to my imperial majesty, and when I wish, I may send and find you speedily," then all the chief men of the Turks cried aloud with one voice, "We are not putting ourselves on the track of the Pechenegs; for we cannot fight them, because their country is great and their people numerous and they are the devil's brats; and do not say this to us again; for we do not like it!"

When spring is over, the Pechenegs cross to the far side of the Dnieper river, and always pass the summer there. . . .

These nations are adjacent to the Turks: on their western side Francia; on their northern the Pechenegs; and on the south side great Moravia, the country of Sphendoplokos, which has now been totally devastated by these Turks, and occupied by them. On the side of the mountains the Croats are adjacent to the Turks.

The Pechenegs too can attack the Turks, and plunder and harm them greatly, as has been said above in the chapter on the Pechenegs.

Fix, my son, your mind's eye upon my words, and learn those things which I command you, and you will be able in due season as from ancestral treasures to bring forth the wealth of wisdom, and to display the sap of a sharp wit. Know therefore that all the tribes of the north have, as it were implanted in them by nature, a ravening greed of money, never satiated, and so they demand everything and hanker after everything and have desires that know no limit or circumscription, but are always eager for more, and desirous to acquire great profits in exchange for a small service. And so these importunate demands and brazenly submitted claims must be turned back and rebutted by plausible speeches and prudent and clever excuses which, in so far as our experience has enabled us to arrive at them, will, to speak summarily, run more or less as follows:

Should they ever require and demand, whether they be Chazars, or Turks, or again Russians, or any other nation of the northerners and Scythians, as frequently happens, that some of the imperial vesture or diadems or state robes should be sent to them in return for some service or office performed by them, then thus you shall excuse yourself:

These robes of state and the diadems, which you call "kamelaukia," were not fashioned by men, nor by human arts devised or elaborated, but, as we find it written in secret stories of old history, when God made emperor that famous Constantine the great, who was the first Christian emperor, He sent him these robes of state by the hand of His angel, and the diadems which you call "kamelaukia," and charged him to lay them in the great and holy church of

God, which, after the name of that very wisdom which is the property of God, is called St. Sophia; and not to clothe himself in them every day, but only when it is a great public festival of the Lord. And so by God's command he laid them up, and they hang above the holy table in the sanctuary of this same church, and are for the ornament of the church. And the rest of the imperial vestments and cloaks lie spread out upon this holy table. And when a festival of our Lord and God Jesus Christ comes round, the patriarch takes up such of these robes of state and diadems as are suitable and appropriate to that occasion, and sends them to the emperor, and he wears them in the procession, and only in it, as the servant and minister of God, and after use returns them again to the church, and they are laid up in it. Moreover, there is a curse of the holy and great emperor Constantine engraved upon this holy table of the church of God, according as he was charged by God through the angel, that if an emperor for any use or occasion or unseasonable desire be minded to take of them and either himself misuse them or give them to others, he shall be anathematized as the foe and enemy of the commands of God, and shall be excommunicated from the church; moreover, if he himself be minded to make others like them, these too the church of God must take, with the freely expressed approval of all the archbishops and of the senate; and it shall not be in the authority either of the emperor, or of the patriarch, or of any other, to take these robes of state or the diadems from the holy church of God. And mighty dread hangs over them who are minded to transgress any of these divine ordinances. For one of the emperors, Leo by name, who also married a wife from Chazaria,[4] out of his folly and rashness took up one of these diadems when no festival of the Lord was toward, and without the approval of the patriarch put it about his head. And straightway a carbuncle came forth upon his forehead so that in torment at the pains of it he evilly departed his evil life, and ran upon death untimely. And, this rash act being summarily avenged, thereafter a rule was made, that when he is about to be crowned the emperor must first swear and give surety that he will neither do nor conceive anything against what has been ordained and kept from ancient times, and then may he be crowned by the patriarch and perform and execute the rites appropriate to the established festival.

Similar care and thought you shall take in the matter of the liquid fire which is discharged through tubes,[5] so that if any shall ever venture to demand this too, as they have often made demands of us also, you may rebut and dismiss them in words like these:

This too was revealed and taught by God through an angel to the great and holy Constantine, the first Christian emperor, and concerning this too he received great charges from the same angel, as we are assured by the faithful witness of our fathers and grandfathers, that it should be manufactured among the Christians only and in the city ruled by them, and nowhere else at all, nor should it be sent nor taught to any other nation whatsoever. And so, for the confirmation of this among those who should come after him, this great em-

---

[4] Not Leo III, but his son Constantine V married a Khazar princess.
[5] The famous Greek fire.

peror caused curses to be inscribed on the holy table of the church of God, that he who should dare to give of this fire to another nation should neither be called a Christian, nor be held worthy of any rank or office; and if he should be the holder of any such, he should be expelled therefrom and be anathematized and made an example for ever and ever, whether he were emperor, or patriarch, or any other man whatever, either ruler or subject, who should seek to transgress this commandment. And he adjured all who had the zeal and fear of God to be prompt to make away with him who attempted to do this, as a common enemy and a transgressor of this great commandment, and to dismiss him to a death most hateful and cruel. And it happened once, as wickedness will still find room, that one of our military governors, who had been most heavily bribed by certain infidels, handed over some of this fire to them; and, since God could not endure to leave unavenged this transgression, as he was about to enter the holy church of God, fire came down out of heaven and devoured and consumed him utterly. And thereafter mighty dread and terror were implanted in the hearts of all men, and never since then has anyone, whether emperor, or noble, or private citizen, or military governor, or any man of any sort whatever, ventured to think of such a thing, far less to attempt to do it or bring it to pass.

"But come, now, turn," and to meet another sort of demand, monstrous and unseemly, seemly and appropriate words discover and seek out. For if any of these shifty and dishonourable tribes of the north shall ever demand a marriage alliance with the emperor of the Romans, and either to take his daughter to wife, or to give a daughter of their own to be wife to the emperor or to the emperor's son, this monstrous demand of theirs also you shall rebut with these words, saying:

Concerning this matter also a dread and authentic charge and ordinance of the great and holy Constantine is engraved upon the sacred table of the catholic church of the Christians, St. Sophia, that never shall an emperor of the Romans ally himself in marriage with a nation of customs differing from and alien to those of the Roman order, especially with one that is infidel and unbaptized, unless it be with the Franks alone; for they alone were excepted by that great man, the holy Constantine, because he himself drew his origin from those parts; for there is much relationship and converse between Franks and Romans. And why did he order that with them alone the emperors of the Romans should intermarry? Because of the traditional fame of those lands and the nobility of those tribes. But with any other nation whatsoever it was not to be in their power to do this, and he who dared to do it was to be condemned as an alien from the ranks of the Christians and subject to the anathema, as a transgressor of ancestral laws and imperial ordinances. And that emperor Leo aforesaid, who also, as has been described above, unlawfully and rashly, without the consent of him who was then patriarch, took from the church the diadem and put it about his head and was summarily punished in full for his wicked attempt, dared to make light of and to disregard this commandment also of that holy emperor, which, as has already been made clear, is engraved on the holy table; and as he had once put himself outside the fear of God and His commandments, so also he contracted an alliance in marriage with the chagan of Chazaria, and received his daughter to be his wife, and thereby attached great shame to the empire of the Romans and to himself, because he annulled and disregarded the ancestral injunctions; yet he, however, was not even an orthodox Christian, but an heretic and a destroyer of images. And so for these his unlawful impieties he is continually excommunicated and anathematized in the church of God, as a transgressor and perverter of the ordinance of God and of the holy and great emperor Constantine. For how can it be admissible that Christians should form marriage associations and ally themselves by marriage with infidels, when the canon forbids it and the whole church regards it as alien to and outside the Christian order? Or which of the illustrious or noble or wise emperors of the Romans has admitted it?

But if they reply: "How then did the lord Romanus[6] the emperor, ally himself in marriage with the Bulgarians, and give his grand-daughter to the lord Peter the Bulgarian?", this must be the defence:

The lord Romanus, the emperor, was a common, illiterate fellow, and not from among those who have been bred up in the palace, and have followed the Roman national customs from the beginning; nor was he of imperial and noble stock, and for this reason in most of his actions he was too arrogant and despotic, and in this instance he neither heeded the prohibition of the church, nor followed the commandment and ordinance of the great Constantine, but out of a temper arrogant and self-willed and untaught in virtue and refusing to follow what was right and good, or to submit to the ordinances handed down by our forefathers, he dared to do this thing; offering, that is, this alone by way of specious excuse, that by this action so many Christian prisoners were ransomed, and that the Bulgarians too are Christians and of like faith with us, and that in any case she who was given in marriage was not daughter of the monarch and lawful emperor, but of the third and most junior, who was still subordinate and had no share of authority in matters of government; but this was no different from giving any other of the ladies of the imperial family, whether more distantly or closely related to the imperial nobility, nor did it make any difference that she was given for some service to the commonweal, or was daughter of the most junior, who had no authority to speak of. And because he did this thing contrary to the canon and to ecclesiastical tradition and the ordinance and commandment of the great and holy emperor Constantine, the aforesaid lord Romanus was in his lifetime much abused, and was slandered and hated by the senatorial council and all the commons and the church herself, so that their hatred became abundantly clear in the end to which he came; and after his death he is in the same way vilified and slandered and condemned inasmuch as he too introduced an unworthy and unseemly innovation into the noble polity of the Romans.

For each nation has different customs and divergent laws and institutions, and should consolidate those things that are proper to it, and should

---

[6] Romanus I Lecapenus (reigned 920-944), Constantine VII's father-in-law.

form and develop out of the same nation the associations for the fusion of its life. For just as each animal mates with its own tribe, so it is right that each nation also should marry and cohabit not with those of other race and tongue but of the same tribe and speech. For hence arise naturally harmony of thought and intercourse among one another and friendly converse and living together; but alien customs and divergent laws are likely on the contrary to engender enmities and quarrels and hatreds and broils, which tend to beget not friendship and association but spite and division. Mark, too, that it is not for those who wish to govern lawfully to copy and emulate what has been ill done by some out of ignorance or arrogance, but rather to have the glorious deeds of those who have ruled lawfully and righteously as noble pictures set up for an example to be copied, and after their pattern to strive himself also to direct all that he does; since the end which came upon him, I mean, the lord Romanus, through these his headstrong acts is a sufficient warning to restrain anyone who is minded to emulate his evil deeds.

But now, with the rest, you must know also what follows, my well-loved son, since knowledge of it may greatly advantage you and render you the object of greater admiration. That is, once again, knowledge "of the difference between other nations, their origins and customs and manner of life, and the position and climate of the land they dwell in, and its geographical description and measurement," as they are more widely expounded hereafter.

5. LIUDPRAND OF CREMONA: A WESTERN VIEW OF BYZANTIUM[1]

A vivid picture of the Byzantine court, betraying a mixture of admiration, envy, and hostility characteristic of the rawer and poorer West, is given by Bishop Liudprand of Cremona (c. 922 - c. 972). Born of a wealthy Lombard family, he undertook embassies to Constantinople as the servant of two kings, Berengar of Italy and Otto I of Germany. A passage from the *Antapodosis*, or *Tit-for-Tat*, tells of his first mission, in 949, to Constantine VII. The *Legatio* or *Embassy* is a report to Otto on the failure of his last journey (968) to the Emperor Nicephorus Phocas (reigned 963-969) to try to secure an imperial princess for Otto's son. From reading Liudprand no one would guess that Nicephorus was a vigorous ruler and one of the great generals of his age.

[1] Liudprand of Cremona, *Antapodosis*, VI, 2-10; *Legatio*, 2-12, reprinted by permission of Routledge and Kegan Paul Ltd. from *The Works of Liudprand of Cremona*, trans. by F. A. Wright (London, Routledge and Sons Ltd., 1930), pp. 206-212, 236-243.

FROM *ANTAPODOSIS* (c. 950)

After the death of King Hugh in Provence[2] the fame of Berengar[3] spread abroad in many lands, and especially among the Greek peoples. By virtue of his abilities he was the chief man in Italy, while Lothair[4] was king only in name. So Constantine,[5] who after the downfall of Romanos[6] and his sons had become emperor at Constantinople, hearing that in actual power Berengar was superior to Lothair, sent him a letter by the hand of a certain Andreas, who from his functions had the title of "prefect of the guard." In this letter he said that he was very desirous of a visit from an envoy of Berengar's, that the latter on his messenger's return might know with what affection he was regarded. He also wrote him another letter on Lothair's behalf, commending him to his care and begging him to be faithful in administering the realm, to whose governance by God's favour he had been appointed. Constantine indeed had no small regard for Lothair's welfare and made it a subject of scrupulous thought, owing to the affection he felt for his son's wife who was Lothair's sister.

Accordingly Berengar, who was a man stuffed full of cunning, began to consider whom he could best send without contributing anything himself to the expense of the long journey. He therefore sent for my stepfather, under whose care I was then living, and addressed him thus:—"What a boon it would be to me if your stepson knew Greek!" My stepfather replied: "I would spend half my estate to give him that knowledge." "Nay," said Berengar, "you need not spend one hundredth part of it. The emperor of Constantinople begs me in this letter to send an envoy to his court. As far as courage goes, no one could be better than your stepson, and on the score of eloquence no one could be more satisfactory than he will be. And I need not tell you how easily there he will imbibe the learning of Greece, he who in his youth has drunk so deep of Latin knowledge." At this my stepfather was fired by hope, contributed all the expenses of the journey, and sent me off, the bearer of handsome gifts, to Constantinople.

On the first of August[7] I left Pavia and sailing down the Po arrived in three days at Venice. There I met a Greek envoy, the eunuch Salemo, chamberlain of the palace, who had just returned from Spain and Saxony. He was anxious to sail for Constantinople and was taking there with him an envoy from my present master, who was then king and is now emperor. This man, who was the bearer of costly presents, was a rich merchant of Mainz, called

---

[2] King Hugh of Arles died in 948.

[3] Berengar, marquess of Ivrea, seized power in Italy in 945, was elected king in 950, and was overthrown and imprisoned by Otto I of Germany in 964.

[4] Son of Hugh of Arles.

[5] Constantine VII.

[6] Romanus I Lecapenus.

[7] A.D. 949.

Liutefred. Finally we left Venice on the twenty-fifth of August and reached Constantinople on the seventeenth of September. It will be a pleasant task to describe the marvellous and unheard of manner of our reception.

Next to the imperial residence at Constantinople there is a palace of remarkable size and beauty which the Greeks call Magnavra, the letter v taking the place of the digamma, and the name being equivalent to "Fresh breeze." In order to receive some Spanish envoys, who had recently arrived, as well as myself and Liutefred, Constantine gave orders that this palace should be got ready and the following preparations made.

Before the emperor's seat stood a tree, made of bronze gilded over, whose branches were filled with birds, also made of gilded bronze, which uttered different cries, each according to its varying species. The throne itself was so marvellously fashioned that at one moment it seemed a low structure, and at another it rose high into the air. It was of immense size and was guarded by lions, made either of bronze or of wood covered over with gold, who beat the ground with their tails and gave a dreadful roar with open mouth and quivering tongue. Leaning upon the shoulders of two eunuchs I was brought into the emperor's presence. At my approach the lions began to roar and the birds to cry out, each according to its kind; but I was neither terrified nor surprised, for I had previously made enquiry about all these things from people who were well acquainted with them. So after I had three times made obeisance to the emperor with my face upon the ground, I lifted my head, and behold! the man whom just before I had seen sitting on a moderately elevated seat had now changed his raiment and was sitting on the level of the ceiling. How it was done I could not imagine, unless perhaps he was lifted up by some such sort of device as we use for raising the timbers of a wine press. On that occasion he did not address me personally, since even if he had wished to do so the wide distance between us would have rendered conversation unseemly, but by the intermediary of a secretary he enquired about Berengar's doings and asked after his health. I made a fitting reply and then, at a nod from the interpreter, left his presence and retired to my lodging.

It would give me some pleasure also to record here what I did then for Berengar, so that all may recognize what affection I showed to him and what recompense I have received from him for my services. The Spanish envoys and the aforesaid Liutefred, who represented my present master who was then King Otto,[8] had brought handsome gifts from their masters to the emperor Constantine. I for my part had brought nothing from Berengar except a letter and that was full of lies. I was very greatly disturbed and shamed at this and began to consider anxiously what I had better do. In my doubt and perplexity it finally occurred to me that I might offer the gifts, which on my own account I had brought for the emperor, as coming from Berengar, and trick out my humble present with fine words. I therefore presented him with nine excellent cuirasses, seven excellent shields with gilded bosses, two silver gilt cauldrons,

[8] Otto I of Germany.

some swords, spears and spits, and what was more precious to the emperor than anything, four carzimasia; that being the Greek name for young eunuchs who have had both their testicles and their penis removed. This operation is performed by traders at Verdun, who take the boys into Spain and make a huge profit.

Three days after I had presented my gifts the emperor summoned me to the palace and personally invited me to dinner with him, after the banquet bestowing a handsome present on myself and my attendants. As the opportunity has occurred to describe the appearance of the emperor's table, particularly on a feast day, and also the entertainments that are given there, I think it best not to pass the matter over in silence but to give an account.

There is a palace near the Hippodrome looking northwards, wonderfully lofty and beautiful, which is called "Decanneacubita," "The house of the nineteen couches." The reason of its name is obvious: "deca" is Greek for ten, "ennea" for nine, and "cubita" are couches with curved ends; and on the day when Our Lord Jesus Christ was born according to the flesh nineteen covers are always laid here at the table. The emperor and his guests on this occasion do not sit at dinner, as they usually do, but recline on couches: and everything is served in vessels, not of silver, but of gold. After the solid food fruit is brought on in three golden bowls, which are too heavy for men to lift and come in on carriers covered over with purple cloth. Two of them are put on the table in the following way. Through openings in the ceiling hang three ropes covered with gilded leather and furnished with golden rings. These rings are attached to the handles projecting from the bowls, and with four or five men helping from below, they are swung on to the table by means of a moveable device in the ceiling and removed again in the same fashion. As for the various entertainments I saw there, it would be too long a task to describe them all, and so for the moment I pass them by. One, however, was so remarkable that it will not be out of place to insert an account of it here.

A man came in carrying on his head, without using his hands, a wooden pole twenty-four feet or more long, which a foot and a half from the top had a cross piece three feet wide. Then two boys appeared, naked except for loin cloths round their middle, who went up the pole, did various tricks on it, and then came down head first, keeping the pole all the time as steady as though it were rooted in the earth. When one had come down, the other remained on the pole and performed by himself, which filled me with even greater astonishment and admiration. While they were both performing their feat seemed barely possible; for, wonderful as it was, the evenness of their weights kept the pole up which they climbed balanced. But when one remained at the top and kept his balance so accurately that he could both do his tricks and come down again without mishap, I was so bewildered that the emperor himself noticed my astonishment. He therefore called an interpreter, and asked me which seemed the more wonderful, the boy who had moved so carefully that the pole remained firm, or the man who had so deftly balanced it on his head that neither the boys' weight nor their performance had disturbed it in the least. I said that I did not know which I thought *plus merveilleux*[9] that is, more wonderful; and he burst into a loud laugh and said he was in the same case, he did not know either.

I do not think that I ought to pass over in silence another strange and wonderful sight that I saw there. In the week before the feast Vaiophoron, which we call the Feast of Palms, the emperor makes a payment in gold coins to his vassals and to the different officers of his court, each one receiving a sum proportionate to his office. As I wished to be present at the ceremony, the emperor bade me attend it. The procedure was as follows. A table was brought in, fifteen feet long and six feet broad, which had upon it parcels of money tied up in bags, according to each man's due, the amount being written on the outside of the bag. The recipients then came in and stood before the king, advancing in order as they were called up by a herald. The first to be summoned was the marshal of the palace, who carried off his money, not in his hands but on his shoulders, together with four cloaks of honour. After him came the commander in chief of the army and the lord high admiral of the fleet. These being of equal rank received an equal number of money bags and cloaks, which they did not carry off on their shoulders but with some assistance dragged laboriously away. After them came twenty-four controllers, who each received twenty-four pounds of gold coins together with two cloaks. Then followed the order of patricians, of whom every one in turn was given twelve pounds of gold and one cloak. As I do not know how many patricians there are, I do not know the total amount that was paid; but every one received an equal share. After them came a huge crowd of minor dignitaries; knights of the sword of the first, second and third class, chamberlains, treasury and admiralty officials. Some of these received seven pounds of gold, others six, five, four, three, two and one, according to their rank. I would not have you think that this was all done in one day. It began on the fifth day of the week at six o'clock in the morning and went on till ten, and the emperor finished his part in the proceedings on the sixth and seventh day. Those who take less than a pound receive their share, not from the emperor, but from the chief chamberlain during the week before Easter. While I was standing and marvelling at the proceedings the emperor sent his chancellor to me and asked me how the ceremony pleased me. "It would please me," I replied, "if it did me any good. When Dives was in torment the rest that he saw Lazarus enjoying would have pleased him, if it had come his way. As it did not, how, pray, could it have pleased him?" The emperor smiled in some confusion, and motioned me to come to him. He then presented me with a large cloak and a pound of gold coins; a gift which he willingly made and I even more willingly accepted. . . .

[9] The translator uses French phrases as a rough equivalent for the Greek expressions with which Liudprand sprinkles his work.

FROM *EMBASSY TO CONSTANTINOPLE* (c. 969)

. . . On the fourth of June, as I said above, we arrived at Constantinople and waited with our horses in heavy rain outside the Carian gate until five o'clock in the afternoon. At five o'clock Nicephorus ordered us to be admitted on foot, for he did not think us worthy to use the horses with which your clemency had provided us, and we were escorted to the aforesaid hateful, waterless, draughty stone house. On the sixth of June, which was the Saturday before Pentecost, I was brought before the emperor's brother Leo, marshal of the court and chancellor; and there we tired ourselves with a fierce argument over your imperial title. He called you not emperor, which is Basileus in his tongue, but insultingly Rex, which is king in ours. I told him that the thing meant was the same though the word was different, and he then said that I had come not to make peace but to stir up strife. Finally he got up in a rage, and really wishing to insult us received your letter not in his own hand but through an interpreter. He is a man commanding enough in person but feigning humility: whereon if a man lean it will pierce his hand.

On the seventh of June, the sacred day of Pentecost, I was brought before Nicephorus himself in the palace called Stephana, that is, the Crown Palace. He is a monstrosity of a man, a dwarf, fat-headed and with tiny mole's eyes; disfigured by a short, broad, thick beard half going gray; disgraced by a neck scarcely an inch long; piglike by reason of the big close bristles on his head; in colour an Ethiopian and, as the poet says, "you would not like to meet him in the dark"; a big belly, a lean posterior, very long in the hip considering his short stature, small legs, fair sized heels and feet; dressed in a robe made of fine linen, but old, foul smelling, and discoloured by age; shod with Sicyonian slippers; bold of tongue, a fox by nature, in perjury and falsehood a Ulysses. My lords and august emperors, you always seemed comely to me; but how much more comely now! Always magnificent; how much more magnificent now! Always mighty; how much more mighty now! Always clement; how much more clement now! Always full of virtues; how much fuller now! At his left, not on a line with him, but much lower down, sat the two child emperors, once his masters, now his subjects. He began his speech as follows:—

"It was our duty and our desire to give you a courteous and magnificent reception. That, however, has been rendered impossible by the impiety of your master, who in the guise of an hostile invader has laid claim to Rome; has robbed Berengar and Adalbert[10] of their kingdom contrary to law and right; has slain some of the Romans by the sword, some by hanging, while others he has either blinded or sent into exile; and furthermore has tried to subdue to himself by massacre and conflagration cities belonging to our empire. His wicked attempts have proved unsuccessful, and so he has sent you, the insti-

[10] The son of Berengar of Ivrea.

gator and furtherer of this villainy, under pretence of peace to act *comme un espion,* that is, as a spy upon us."

To him I made this reply: "My master did not invade the city of Rome by force nor as a tyrant; he freed her from a tyrant's yoke, or rather from the yoke of many tyrants. Was she not ruled by effeminate debauchers, and what is even worse and more shameful, by harlots? Your power, methinks, was fast asleep then; and the power of your predecessors, who in name alone are called emperors of the Romans, while the reality is far different. If they were powerful, if they were emperors of the Romans, why did they allow Rome to be in the hands of harlots? Were not some of the holy popes banished, others so distressed that they could not procure their daily supplies nor money wherewith to give alms? Did not Adalbert send insulting letters to your predecessors, the emperors Romanos and Constantine? Did he not rob and plunder the churches of the holy apostles? Who of you emperors, led by zeal for God, troubled to punish so heinous a crime and bring back the holy church to its proper state? You neglected it, my master did not. From the ends of the world he rose, and came to Rome, and drove out the ungodly, and gave back to the vicars of the holy apostles all their power and honour. Those who afterwards rose against him and the lord pope, as being violators of their oath, sacrilegious robbers and torturers of their lords the popes, in accordance with the decrees of such Roman emperors as Justinian, Valentinian, Theodosius etc., he slew, beheaded, hanged, or exiled. If he had not done so, he himself would be an impious, unjust, cruel tyrant. It is a known fact that Berengar and Adalbert became his vassals and received the kingdom of Italy with a golden sceptre from his hand and that they promised fealty under oath in the presence of your servants, men still alive and now dwelling in this city. At the devil's prompting they perfidiously broke their word, and therefore he justly took their kingdom from them, as being deserters and rebels. You yourself would have done the same to men who had sworn fealty and then revolted against you."

"But," said he, "there is one of Adalbert's vassals here, and he does not acknowledge the truth of this." "If he denies it," I replied, "one of my men, at your command, will prove to him to-morrow in single combat that it is so." "Well," said he, "he may, as you declare, have acted justly in this. Explain now why he attacked the borders of our empire with war and conflagration. We were friends and were thinking by marriage to enter into a partnership that would never be broken."

"The land," I answered, "which you say belongs to your empire, is proved by race and language to be part of the kingdom of Italy. The Lombards held it in their power, and Louis, emperor of the Lombards or Franks, freed it from the grip of the Saracens with great slaughter. For seven years also Landulf, prince of Benevento and Capua, held it under his control. Nor would it even now have passed from the yoke of slavery to him and his descendants, had not your emperor Romanos bought at a great price the friendship of our King

Hugh. It was for this reason also that he made a match between King Hugh's bastard daughter and his own nephew and namesake. I see now that you think it shows weakness in my master, not generosity, when after winning Italy and Rome he for so many years left them to you. The friendly partnership, which you say you wished to form by a marriage, we hold to be a fraud and a snare: you ask for a truce, but you have no real reason to want it nor we to grant it. Come, let us clear away all trickeries and speak the plain truth. My master has sent me to you to see if you will give the daughter of the emperor Romanos and the empress Theophano to his son, my master the august emperor Otto. If you give me your oath that the marriage shall take place, I am to affirm to you under oath that my master in grateful return will observe to do this and this for you. Moreover he has already given you, his brother ruler, the best pledge of friendship by handing over Apulia, which was subject to his rule. I, to whose suggestion you declare this mischief was due, intervened in this matter, and there are as many witnesses to this as there are people in Apulia."

"It is past seven o'clock," said Nicephorus "and there is a church procession which I must attend. Let us keep to the business before us. We will give you a reply at some convenient season."

I think that I shall have as much pleasure in describing this procession as my masters will have in reading of it. A numerous company of tradesmen and low-born persons, collected on this solemn occasion to welcome and honour Nicephorus, lined the sides of the road, like walls, from the palace to Saint Sophia, tricked out with thin little shields and cheap spears. As an additional scandal, most of the mob assembled in his honour had marched there with bare feet, thinking, I suppose, that thus they would better adorn the sacred procession. His nobles for their part, who with their master passed through the plebeian and barefoot multitude, were dressed in tunics that were too large for them and were also because of their extreme age full of holes. They would have looked better if they had worn their ordinary clothes. There was not a man among them whose grandfather had owned his tunic when it was new. No one except Nicephorus wore any jewels or golden ornaments, and the emperor looked more disgusting than ever in the regalia that had been designed to suit the persons of his ancestors. By your life, sires, dearer to me than my own, one of your nobles' costly robes is worth a hundred or more of these. I was taken to the procession and given a place on a platform near the singers.

As Nicephorus, like some crawling monster, walked along, the singers began to cry out in adulation: "Behold the morning star approaches: the day star rises: in his eyes the sun's rays are reflected: Nicephorus our prince, the pale death of the Saracens." And then they cried again: "Long life, long life to our prince Nicephorus. Adore him, ye nations, worship him, bow the neck to his greatness." How much more truly might they have sung:—"Come, you miserable burnt-out coal; old woman in your walk, wood-devil in your look; clodhopper, haunter of byres, goat-footed, horned, double-limbed; bristly, wild, rough, barbarian, harsh, hairy, a rebel, a Cappadocian!" So, puffed up by these lying ditties, he entered St. Sophia, his masters the emperors following at a distance and doing him homage on the ground with the kiss of peace. His armour bearer, with an arrow for pen, recorded in the church the era in progress since the beginning of his reign. So those who did not see the ceremony know what era it is.

On this same day he ordered me to be his guest. But as he did not think me worthy to be placed above any of his nobles, I sat fifteenth from him and without a table cloth. Not only did no one of my suite sit at table with me; they did not even set eyes upon the house where I was entertained. At the dinner, which was fairly foul and disgusting, washed down with oil after the fashion of drunkards and moistened also with an exceedingly bad fish liquor, the emperor asked me many questions concerning your power, your dominions and your army. My answers were sober and truthful; but he shouted out:— "You lie. Your master's soldiers cannot ride and they do not know how to fight on foot. The size of their shields, the weight of their cuirasses, the length of their swords, and the heaviness of their helmets, does not allow them to fight either way." Then with a smile he added: "Their gluttony also prevents them. Their God is their belly, their courage but wind, their bravery drunkenness. Fasting for them means dissolution, sobriety, panic. Nor has your master any force of ships on the sea. I alone have really stout sailors, and I will attack him with my fleets, destroy his maritime cities and reduce to ashes those which have a river near them. Tell me, how with his small forces will he be able to resist me even on land? His son was there: his wife was there: his Saxons, Swabians, Bavarians and Italians were all there with him: and yet they had not the skill nor the strength to take one little city[11] that resisted them. How then will they resist me when I come followed by as many forces as there are

> Corn fields on Gargarus, grapes on Lesbian vine,
> Waves in the ocean, stars in heaven that shine?"

I wanted to answer and make such a speech in our defence as his boasting deserved; but he would not let me and added this final insult: "You are not Romans but Lombards." He even then was anxious to say more and waved his hand to secure my silence, but I was worked up and cried: "History tells us that Romulus, from whom the Romans get their name, was a fratricide born in adultery. He made a place of refuge for himself and received into it insolvent debtors, runaway slaves, murderers and men who deserved death for their crimes. This was the sort of crowd whom he enrolled as citizens and gave them the name of Romans. From this nobility are descended those men whom you style 'rulers of the world.' But we Lombards, Saxons, Franks, Lotharingians, Bavarians, Swabians and Burgundians, so despise these fellows that when we are angry with an enemy we can find nothing more insulting to say than

[11] The Byzantine city of Bari.

—'You Roman!' For us in the word Roman is comprehended every form of lowness, timidity, avarice, luxury, falsehood and vice. You say that we are unwarlike and know nothing of horsemanship. Well, if the sins of the Christians merit that you keep this stiff neck, the next war will prove what manner of men you are, and how warlike we."

6. MICHAEL PSELLUS: PORTRAIT OF BASIL II (*c. 1060*)[1]

The *Chronographia* of the great Byzantine scholar and subtle historian Michael Psellus (1018 - *c.* 1078) covers the period 976-1077. Although it deals mainly with the decadence and decline of the Macedonian imperial house during the eleventh century, it begins with an account of the reign which was the apogee of Byzantine power, that of Basil II (reigned 976-1025), the conqueror of the Bulgars, the most dangerous rivals of Constantinople to the North. One would search in vain the historical literature of contemporary western Europe to find a match for the delicate shadings of Psellus' portrait.

. . . In his dealings with his subjects, Basil behaved with extraordinary circumspection. It is perfectly true that the great reputation he built up as a ruler was founded rather on terror than on loyalty. As he grew older and became more experienced he relied less on the judgment of men wiser than himself. He alone introduced new measures, he alone disposed his military forces. As for the civil administration, he governed, not in accordance with the written laws, but following the unwritten dictates of his own intuition, which was most excellently equipped by nature for the purpose. Consequently he paid no attention to men of learning: on the contrary, he affected utter scorn—towards the learned folk, I mean. It seems to me a wonderful thing, therefore, that while the emperor so despised literary culture, no small crop of philosophers and orators sprang up in those times. One solution of the paradox, I fancy, is that the men of those days did not devote themselves to the study of letters for any ulterior purpose: they cultivated literature for its own sake and as an end in itself, whereas the majority nowadays do not approach the subject of education in this spirit, but consider personal profit to be the first reason for study.

[1] Reprinted by permission of Routledge and Kegan Paul Ltd. from *The Chronographia of Michael Psellus*, trans. by E. R. A. Sewter (London, Routledge and Kegan Paul Ltd., 1953), pp. 23-28.

Perhaps I should add, that though gain is the object of their zeal for literature, if they do not immediately achieve this goal, then they desist from their studies at once. Shame on them!

However, we must return to the emperor. Having purged the Empire of the barbarians, he dealt with his own subjects and completely subjugated them too—I think *subjugate* is the right word to describe it. He decided to abandon his former policy, and after the great families had been humiliated and put on an equal footing with the rest, Basil found himself playing the game of power-politics with considerable success. He surrounded himself with favourites who were neither remarkable for brilliance of intellect, nor of noble lineage, nor too learned. To them were entrusted the imperial rescripts, and with them he was accustomed to share the secrets of state. However, since at that time the emperor's comments on memoranda or requests for favour were never varied, but only plain, straightforward statements, for Basil, whether writing or speaking, eschewed all elegance of composition, he used to dictate to his secretaries just as the words came to his tongue, stringing them all together, one after the other. There was no sublety, nothing superfluous, in his speech.

By humbling the pride or jealousy of his people, Basil made his own road to power an easy one. He was careful, moreover, to close the exit-doors on the monies contributed to the treasury. So a huge sum of money was built up, partly by the exercise of strict economy, partly by fresh additions from abroad. Actually, the sum accumulated in the imperial treasury reached the grand total of 200,000 talents. As for the rest of his gains, it would indeed be hard to find words adequately to describe them. All the treasures amassed in Iberia and Arabia, all the riches found among the Celts or contained in the land of the Scyths—in brief, all the wealth of the barbarians who surround our borders—all were gathered together in one place and deposited in the emperor's coffers. In addition to this, he carried off to his treasure-chambers and sequestrated there all the money of those who rebelled against him and were afterwards subdued. And since the vaults of the buildings made for this purpose were not big enough, he had spiral galleries dug underground, after the Egyptian style, and there he kept safe a considerable proportion of his treasures. He himself took no pleasure in any of it: quite the reverse indeed, for the majority of the precious stones, both the white ones which we call pearls and the coloured brilliants, far from being inlaid in diadems or collars, were hidden away in his underground vaults. Meanwhile Basil took part in his processions and gave audience to his governors clothed merely in a robe of purple, not the very bright purple, but simply purple of a dark hue, with a handful of gems as a mark of distinction. As he spent the greater part of his reign serving as a soldier on guard at our frontiers and keeping the barbarians from raiding our territories, not only did he draw nothing from his reserves of wealth, but even multiplied his riches many times over.

On his expedition against the barbarians, Basil did not follow the customary procedure of other emperors, setting out at the middle of spring and returning home at the end of summer. For him the time to return was when the task in hand was accomplished. He endured the rigours of winter and the heat of summer with equal indifference. He disciplined himself against thirst. In fact, all his natural desires were kept under stern control, and the man was as hard as steel. He had an accurate knowledge of the details of army life, and by that I do not mean the general acquaintance with the composition of his army, the relative functions of individual units in the whole body, or the various groupings and deployments suited to the different formations. His experience of army matters went further than that: the duties of the *protostate,* the duties of the *hemilochites,*[2] the tasks proper to the rank immediately junior to them—all these were no mysteries to Basil, and the knowledge stood him in good stead in his wars. Accordingly, jobs appropriate to these ranks were not devolved on others, and the emperor, being personally conversant with the character and combat duties of each individual, knowing to what each man was fitted either by temperament or by training, used him in this capacity and made him serve there.

Moreover, he knew the various formations suited to his men. Some he had read of in books, others he devised himself during the operations of war, the result of his own intuition. He professed to conduct his wars and draw up the troops in line of battle, himself planning each campaign, but he preferred not to engage in combat personally. A sudden retreat might otherwise prove embarrassing. Consequently, for the most part he kept his troops immobile. He would construct machines of war and skirmish at a distance, while the manoeuvring was left to his light-armed soldiers. Once he had made contact with the enemy, a regular military liaison was established between the different formations of the Roman army. The whole force was formed up like a solid tower, headquarters being in touch with the cavalry squadrons, who were themselves kept in communication with the light infantry, and these again with the various units of heavy-armed foot. When all was ready, strict orders were given that no soldier should advance in front of the line or break rank under any circumstance. If these orders were disobeyed, and if some of the most valiant or daring soldiers did ride out well in front of the rest, even in cases where they engaged the enemy successfully, they could expect no medals or rewards for valour when they returned. On the contrary, Basil promptly discharged them from the army, and they were punished on the same level as common criminals. The decisive factors in the achievement of victory was, in his opinion, the massing of troops in one coherent body, and for this reason alone he believed the Roman armies to be invincible. The careful inspections he made before battle used to aggravate the soldiers and they abused him openly, but the emperor met their scorn with common sense. He would listen quietly, and then, with a gay smile, point out that if he neglected these precautions, their battles would go on for ever.

Basil's character was two-fold, for he readily adapted himself no less to

2 Junior officers.

the crises of war than to the calm of peace. Really, if the truth be told, he was more of a villain in wartime, more of an emperor in time of peace. Outbursts of wrath he controlled, and like the proverbial "fire under the ashes," kept anger hid in his heart, but if his orders were disobeyed in war, on his return to the palace he would kindle his wrath and reveal it. Terrible then was the vengeance he took on the miscreant. Generally, he persisted in his opinions, but there were occasions when he did change his mind. In many cases, too, he traced crimes back to their original causes, and the final links in the chain were exonerated. So most defaulters obtained forgiveness, either through his sympathetic understanding, or because he showed some other interest in their affairs. He was slow to adopt any course of action, but never would he willingly alter the decision, once it was taken. Consequently, his attitude to friends was unvaried, unless perchance he was compelled by necessity to revise his opinion of them. Similarly, where he had burst out in anger against someone, he did not quickly moderate his wrath. Whatever estimate he formed, indeed, was to him an irrevocable and divinely-inspired judgment.

So much for his character. As for his personal appearance, it betrayed the natural nobility of the man, for his eyes were light-blue and fiery, the eyebrows not overhanging nor sullen, nor yet extended in one straight line, like a woman's, but well-arched and indicative of his pride. The eyes were neither deep-set, a sign of knavishness and cunning, nor yet too prominent, a sign of frivolity, but they shone with a brilliance that was manly. His whole face was rounded off, as if from the centre into a perfect circle, and joined to the shoulders by a neck that was firm and not too long. His chest was neither thrust out in front of him, nor hanging on him, so to speak, nor again was it concave and, as it were, cramped: rather was it the mean between the two extremes, and the rest of his body was in harmony with it.

As for height, he was of less than normal stature, but it was proportionate to the separate parts of his body, and he held himself upright. If you met him on foot, you would find him much like some other men, but on horseback he afforded a sight that was altogether incomparable, for in the saddle he reminded one of the statues which the great sculptors carved, with their riders adopting a similar pose. When he gave rein to his horse and rode in the assault, he was erect and firm in his saddle, riding uphill and downhill alike, and when he checked his steed, reining it in, he would leap on high as though he had wings, and he mounted or dismounted alike with equal grace. In his old age the beard under his chin went bald, but the hair from his cheeks poured down, the growth on either side being thick and very profuse, so that wound round on both sides it was made into a perfect circle and he appeared to possess a full beard. It was a habit of his to roll it between his fingers, a gesture to which he was particularly prone when roused to anger or giving audience, or when he was engaged in deep thought. That was a frequent habit; another was to put his fingers on his hips, arms akimbo. He was not a fluent speaker. The phrases were not rounded off, nor were they lengthened out into periods. In fact, he clipped his words, with little pauses between them, more like a peasant than a man of good education. He had a loud laugh, which convulsed the whole of his body.

The emperor seems to have lived a very long time, more than all the other sovereigns, for from birth up to his twentieth year he shared imperial power with his father[3] and Phocas Nicephorus, and later with John Tzimisces, the latter's successor. During this period he occupied a subordinate position, but for the next fifty-two years he ruled supreme. He was therefore in his seventy-second year when he died.

7. IBN FADLAN: DESCRIPTION OF THE RUSSIAN VIKINGS (921-922)[1]

Ibn Fadlan was a Moslem sent on a diplomatic mission from Baghdad to the Volga region in 921-922. The "Rus folk" who aroused his interest were of Swedish origin and in many parts of Russia formed a military ruling class. His is a remarkable eye-witness account of a rough, savage, pagan folk, but one already interested in trade.

I saw the Rus folk when they arrived on their trading-mission and settled at the river Atul (Volga). Never had I seen people of more perfect physique. They are tall as date-palms, and reddish in colour. They wear neither coat nor *kaftan,* but each man carried a cape which covers one half of his body, leaving one hand free. No one is ever parted from his axe, sword, and knife. Their swords are Frankish in design, broad, flat, and fluted. Each man has a number of trees, figures, and the like from the finger-nails to the neck. Each woman carries on her bosom a container made of iron, silver, copper, or gold—its size and substance depending on her man's wealth. Attached to the container is a ring carrying her knife which is also tied to her bosom. Round her neck she wears gold or silver rings: when a man collects 10,000 dirhams he gives his wife a neck-ring, when he has 20,000 he gives two rings, and so the wife gets a new ring for each 10,000 dirhams added to the husband's wealth. One woman often has many neck-rings. Their finest ornament is the green clay-

---

[3] Romanus II.

[1] J. Brøndsted, *The Vikings,* trans. by E. Bannister-Good (Harmondsworth, Middlesex, Penguin Books Ltd., 1960), pp. 247-248, 280-284.

pearl on the ships. To provide this they go to great trouble; they buy one pearl for a dirham and combine the pearls into necklaces for their women.

They are the filthiest of God's creatures. They do not wash after discharging their natural functions, neither do they wash their hands after meals. They are as lousy as donkeys. They arrive from their distant lands and lay their ships alongside the banks of the Atul, which is a great river, and there they build big houses on its shores. Ten or twenty of them may live together in one house, and each of them has a couch of his own where he sits and diverts himself with the pretty slave girls whom he has brought along for sale. He will make love with one of them while a comrade looks on; sometimes they indulge in a communal orgy, and, if a customer should turn up to buy a girl, the Rus man will not let her go till he has finished with her.

They wash their hands and faces every day in incredibly filthy water. Every morning the girl brings her master a large bowl of water in which he washes his hands and face and hair, then blows his nose into it and spits into it. When he has finished the girl takes the bowl to his neighbour—who repeats the performance. Thus the bowl goes the rounds of the entire household.

On beaching their vessels, each man goes ashore carrying bread, meat, onions, milk, and *nabid* (beer?) and these he takes to a large wooden post with a face like that of a human being, surrounded by smaller figures, and behind them there are high poles in the ground. Each man prostrates himself before the large post and recites: "O Lord, I have come from distant parts with so many girls, so many sable furs (and whatever other commodities are in his catalogue). I now bring you this offering." He then presents his gift, and continues. "Please send me a merchant who has many dinars and dirhams and who will trade favourably with me without contradicting me." If after this his business does not proceed quickly and well, he returns to the statue and presents further gifts. If results continue slow, he then presents gifts to the minor figures and begs their intercession. . . . If his pleas prevail, and trade picks up, he says, "My Lord has requited my needs, and now it is my duty to repay him"; and, on this, he sacrifices goats or cattle, some of which he distributes as alms. The rest he lays before the statues, large and small, and the heads of the beasts he plants upon the pole. After dark, of course, the dogs come and devour the lot—and the successful trader says, "My Lord is pleased with me, and has eaten my offerings."

If one of the Rus folk falls sick they put him in a tent by himself and leave bread and water for him. They do not visit him, however, or speak to him, especially if he is a serf. Should he recover he rejoins the others; if he dies they burn him. But if he happens to be a serf they leave him for the dogs and vultures to devour. If they catch a robber they hang him to a tree until he is torn to shreds by wind and weather. . . .

I was always told that when their chiefs died cremation was the least part of what they undertook and I was, therefore, very much interested to find out more about this. One day I heard that one of their great men had died. They laid him forthwith in a grave which they covered up for ten days till they had finished cutting out and sewing his costume. If the dead man is poor they make a little ship, put him in it, and conduct a cremation. But if he is wealthy they split his property and goods into three parts: one for his family, one to pay for his costume, and one to make *nabid* (probably a Nordic beer) which they drink on the day when the slave woman of the dead man kills herself and is burned together with her lord. They are deeply addicted to *nabid*, drinking it night and day. Often one of them has died with a beaker in his hand. When a chief among them had died his family demands of his slave women and servants: "Which of you wishes to die with him?" Then one of them says: "I do" and having said that the person concerned is forced to do so and no drawing back is possible. Even if he wished to he would not be allowed to. Those who are willing are mostly the slave women.

So when this man died they said to his slave women "Which of you wants to die with him?" One of them answered, "I do." From that moment she was put in the constant care of two other women servants who took care of her even to the extent of washing her feet with their own hands. Then they began to get things ready for the dead man, to cut his costume and so on, while every day the doomed woman drank and sang as though in anticipation of a joyous event.

When the day arrived on which he and his slave woman were going to be burnt, I went to the river where his ship lay. It had been dragged ashore and four posts were made for it of birch and other wood. Furthermore there was arranged around it what resembled a big store of wood. Then the ship was dragged near and laid on the wood. And people began to walk about talking in a language I could not understand, and the corpse still lay in the grave, they had not taken it away. They then produced a wooden bench, placed it on the ship, and covered it with carpets of Byzantine dibag (painted silk) and with cushions of Byzantine dibag. Then came an old woman whom they call "the Angel of Death," and spread the said cushions out over the bench. She was in charge of the whole business of dressing the corpse, and her function included that of killing the slave woman. I saw that she was an old giant-woman, a massive and grim figure. When they came to his grave they removed the earth from the wooden frame and they also took the frame away. Then they divested the corpse of the clothes in which he had died. The body, I noticed, had turned black because of the intense frost. When they had first put him in the grave, they had furnished him with beer, fruit, and a lute, all of which they now removed. Strangely enough the corpse did not smell, nor had anything about him changed save the colour of his flesh. They now dressed him in hose, and trousers, boots, coat, and mantle of dibag adorned with gold buttons, put on his head a hood of dibag and sable fur, and carried him to the tent on to the ship where they put him on the carpet and supported him with the cushions. Then they produced *nabid,* fruit, and aromatic plants and put these around the body; and they also brought bread, meat, and onions which they flung before him. Next they took a dog, cut it in half, and flung the pieces into the ship, and after this they took all his weapons and placed them beside him. Next they brought two horses and ran them about until they were in a sweat, after which they cut them to pieces with swords and flung their meat into the ship. They took two cows as well. These also they cut into pieces and threw them into the ship. Then they produced a cock and a hen, killed them, and threw them in. Meanwhile the slave woman who wished to be killed walked up and down, going into one tent after the other, and the owner of each tent had sexual intercourse with her, saying: "Tell your master: I did this out of love for him."

On the Friday afternoon they took the slave woman away to something which they had made resembling a door-frame. Then she placed her legs on the palms of the men and reached high enough to overlook the frame, and she said something in some language. Then they took her down. And they lifted her again and she did the same as the first time. Then they took her down and lifted her a third time and she did the same as the first and second times. Then they gave her a chicken and she cut its head off and threw it away; they took the hen and threw it into the ship. Then I asked the interpreter what she had done. He answered: "The first time they lifted her she said: 'look! I see my father and mother.' The second time she said: 'look! I see all my dead relatives sitting around.' The third time she said: 'look! I see my master sitting in Paradise, and Paradise is beautiful and green and together with him are men and young boys. He calls on me. Let me join him then!' "

They now led her towards the ship. Then she took off two bracelets she was wearing and gave them to the old woman, "the Angel of Death," the one who was going to kill her. She next took off two anklets she was wearing and gave them to daughters of that woman known by the name "the Angel of Death." They then led her to the ship but did not allow her inside the tent. Then a number of men carrying wooden shields and wooden sticks arrived, and gave her a beaker with a *nabid*. She sang over it and emptied it. The interpreter then said to me: "Now with that she is bidding farewell to all her women friends." Then she was given another beaker. She took it and sang a lengthy song; but the old woman told her to hurry, to drink up and enter the tent where her master was. Then I regarded her and she looked completely bewildered. She wanted to enter the tent and she put her head between it and the ship. There the woman took her head and managed to get it inside the tent, and the woman herself followed. Then the men began to beat the shields with the wooden sticks, to deaden her shrieks, so that the other girls would not become afraid and shrink from dying with their masters. Six men now entered the tent and all of them had intercourse with the girl. Thereafter they laid her by the side of her dead master. Two held her hands and two her feet. And the woman called the Angel of Death put a cord round the girl's neck, the ends twisted to both sides, and gave it to two men to pull. Then she advanced holding a small dagger with a broad blade and began to plunge it between the girl's ribs to and fro while the two men choked her with the cord till she died.

The dead man's nearest kinsman now appeared. He took a piece of wood and ignited it. Then he walked backwards, his back towards the ship, his face towards the crowd, holding in one hand the wooden piece while the other lay on his behind; and he was naked. In this way the wood was ignited which they had placed under the ship after they had laid the slave woman, whom they had killed, beside her master. Then people came with branches and wood; each brought a burning brand and threw it on the pyre, so that the fire took hold of the wood, then the ship, then the tent and the man and the slave woman and all. Thereafter a strong and terrible wind rose so that the flame stirred and the fire blazed still more.

I heard one of the Rus folk, standing by, say something to my interpreter, and on inquiring what he had said my interpreter answered: "He said: 'You Arabs are foolish.' 'Why?' I asked.— 'Well, because you throw those you love and honour into the ground where the earth and the beasts and the fields devour them, whereas we on the other hand burn them up quickly and they go to Paradise that very moment.' The man burst out laughing, and on being asked why, he said: 'His Lord, out of love for him, has sent this wind to take him away within the hour!'" And so it proved, for within that time the ship and the pyre, the girl and the corpse had all become ashes and then dust. On the spot where the ship stood after having been dragged ashore they built something like a round mound. In the middle of that they raised a large post of birch-wood. Thereon they wrote the names of the dead man and of the king of the Rus folk. On this they broke up.

8. *THE RUSSIAN PRIMARY CHRONICLE:* THE CONVERSION OF VLADIMIR (*c.* 987)[1]

The Russian Primary Chronicle, sometimes called *The Chronicle of Nestor* or *The Tale of Bygone Years,* is of uncertain authorship, though it was certainly completed in the early twelfth century. It covers the period 852-1110. The account of Vladimir's conversion perhaps represents the fusion of two traditions, one that he was converted by a Byzantine missionary and by the report of his own envoys

[1] *The Russian Primary Chronicle,* trans. and ed. by S. H. Cross and O. P. Sherbowitz-Wetzor (Cambridge, Mass., The Mediaeval Academy of America, Publication No. 60, 1953), pp. 96-97, 109-117. Vladimir was Great Prince of Kiev from 978 to 1015.

describing the glories of Constantinople, the other that his baptism was a political act and was linked to his marriage with the Princess Anna. It is likely that the latter tradition is closer to the truth. The sequence of events was probably as follows: Vladimir agreed to become a Christian and to help Basil II put down a rebellion in exchange for the almost unprecedented favor of a royal Byzantine bride. Having fulfilled (early in 988) his part of the bargain, he found Basil unwilling to do likewise. He then attacked Cherson to force Basil to send him the Princess Anna, as had been agreed. But even if this is not an entirely accurate reconstruction, the fact that the ruler of Kiev was baptized according to the Greek rite and the momentousness of that event for the future of Russia are indisputable.

. . . Vladimir was visited by Bulgars of Mohammedan faith,[2] who said, "Though you are a wise and prudent prince, you have no religion. Adopt our faith, and revere Mahomet." Vladimir inquired what was the nature of their religion. They replied that they believed in God, and that Mahomet instructed them to practice circumcision, to eat no pork, to drink no wine, and, after death, promised them complete fulfillment of their carnal desires. "Mahomet," they asserted, "will give each man seventy fair women. He may choose one fair one, and upon that woman will Mahomet confer the charms of them all, and she shall be his wife. Mahomet promises that one may then satisfy every desire, but whoever is poor in this world will be no different in the next." They also spoke other false things which out of modesty may not be written down. Vladimir listened to them, for he was fond of women and indulgence, regarding which he heard with pleasure. But circumcision and abstinence from pork and wine were disagreeable to him. "Drinking," said he, "is the joy of the Russes. We cannot exist without that pleasure."

Then came the Germans, asserting that they were come as emissaries of the Pope. They added, "Thus says the Pope: 'Your country is like our country, but your faith is not as ours. For our faith is the light. We worship God, who has made heaven and earth, the stars, the moon, and every creature, while your gods are only wood.'" Vladimir inquired what their teaching was. They replied, "Fasting according to one's strength. But whatever one eats or drinks is all to the glory of God, as our teacher Paul has said." Then Vladimir answered, "Depart hence; our fathers accepted no such principle."

The Jewish Khazars heard of these missions, and came themselves saying, "We have learned that Bulgars and Christians came hither to instruct you in their faiths. The Christians believe in him whom we crucified, but we believe in the one God of Abraham, Isaac, and Jacob." Then Vladimir inquired what their religion was. They replied that its tenet included circumcision, not eating pork or hare, and observing the Sabbath. The Prince then asked where their native land was, and they replied that it was in Jerusalem.

[2] The account of these successive embassies is probably apocryphal.

When Vladimir inquired where that was, they made answer, "God was angry at our forefathers, and scattered us among the gentiles on account of our sins. Our land was then given to the Christians." The Prince then demanded, "How can you hope to teach others while you yourselves are cast out and scattered abroad by the hand of God? If God loved you and your faith, you would not be thus dispersed in foreign lands. Do you expect us to accept that fate also?"

Then the Greeks sent to Vladimir a scholar, who spoke thus:[3]

. . . . .

Now that the Apostles have taught men throughout the world to believe in God, we Greeks have inherited their teaching, and the world believes therein. God hath appointed a day, in which he shall come from heaven to judge both the quick and the dead, and to render to each according to his deeds; to the righteous, the kingdom of heaven and ineffable beauty, bliss without end, and eternal life; but to sinners, the torments of hell and a worm that sleeps not, and of their torments there shall be no end. Such shall be the penalties for those who do not believe in our Lord Jesus Christ. The unbaptized shall be tormented with fire.

As he spoke thus, he exhibited to Vladimir a canvas on which was depicted the Judgment Day of the Lord, and showed him, on the right, the righteous going to their bliss in Paradise, and on the left, the sinners on their way to torment. Then Vladimir sighed and said, "Happy are they upon the right, but woe to those upon the left!" The scholar replied, "If you desire to take your place upon the right with the just, then accept baptism!" Vladimir took this counsel to heart, saying, "I shall wait yet a little longer," for he wished to inquire about all the faiths. Vladimir then gave the scholar many gifts, and dismissed him with great honor.

Vladimir summoned together his boyars and the city-elders, and said to them, "Behold, the Bulgars came before me urging me to accept their religion. Then came the Germans and praised their own faith; and after them came the Jews. Finally the Greeks appeared, criticizing all other faiths but commending their own, and they spoke at length, telling the history of the whole world from its beginning. Their words were artful, and it was wondrous to listen and pleasant to hear them. They preach the existence of another world. 'Whoever adopts our religion and then dies shall arise and live forever. But whosoever embraces another faith, shall be consumed with fire in the next world.' What is your opinion on this subject, and what do you answer?" The boyars and the elders replied, "You know, oh Prince, that no man condemns his own possessions, but praises them instead. If you desire to make certain, you have servants at your disposal. Send them to inquire about the ritual of each and how he worships God."

Their counsel pleased the prince and all the people, so that they chose

[3] [There follows a précis of the Bible.]

good and wise men to the number of ten, and directed them to go first among the Bulgars and inspect their faith. The emissaries went their way, and when they arrived at their destination they beheld the disgraceful actions of the Bulgars and their worship in the mosque; then they returned to their country. Vladimir then instructed them to go likewise among the Germans, and examine their faith, and finally to visit the Greeks. They thus went into Germany, and after viewing the German ceremonial, they proceeded to Tsar'grad, where they appeared before the Emperor. He inquired on what mission they had come, and they reported to him all that had occurred. When the Emperor heard their words, he rejoiced, and did them great honor on that very day.

On the morrow, the Emperor sent a message to the Patriarch to inform him that a Russian delegation had arrived to examine the Greek faith, and directed him to prepare the church and the clergy, and to array himself in his sacerdotal robes, so that the Russes might behold the glory of the God of the Greeks. When the Patriarch received these commands, he bade the clergy assemble, and they performed the customary rites. They burned incense, and the choirs sang hymns. The Emperor accompanied the Russes to the church, and placed them in a wide space, calling their attention to the beauty of the edifice, the chanting, and the pontifical services and the ministry of the deacons, while he explained to them the worship of his God. The Russes were astonished, and in their wonder praised the Greek ceremonial. Then the Emperors Basil and Constantine invited the envoys to their presence, and said, "Go hence to your native country," and dismissed them with valuable presents and great honor.

Thus they returned to their own country, and the Prince called together his boyars and the elders. Vladimir then announced the return of the envoys who had been sent out, and suggested that their report be heard. He thus commanded them to speak out before his retinue. The envoys reported, "When we journeyed among the Bulgars, we beheld how they worship in their temple, called a mosque, while they stand ungirt. The Bulgar bows, sits down, looks hither and thither like one possessed, and there is no happiness among them, but instead only sorrow and a dreadful stench. Their religion is not good. Then we went among the Germans, and saw them performing many ceremonies in their temples; but we beheld no glory there. Then we went to Greece, and the Greeks led us to the edifices where they worship their God, and we knew not whether we were in heaven or on earth. For on earth there is no such splendor or such beauty, and we are at a loss how to describe it. We only know that God dwells there among men, and their service is fairer than the ceremonies of other nations. For we cannot forget that beauty. Every man, after tasting something sweet, is afterward unwilling to accept that which is bitter, and therefore we cannot dwell longer here." Then the boyars spoke and said, "If the Greek faith were evil, it would not have been adopted by your grandmother Olga who was wiser than all other men."[4] Vladimir then in-

---

[4] Olga was baptized in Constantinople in 957.

quired where they should all accept baptism, and they replied that the decision rested with him.

After a year had passed, in 6496 (988), Vladimir proceeded with an armed force against Kherson, a Greek city, and the people of Kherson barricaded themselves therein. Vladimir halted at the farther side of the city beside the harbor, a bowshot from the town, and the inhabitants resisted energetically while Vladimir besieged the town. Eventually, however, they became exhausted, and Vladimir warned them that if they did not surrender, he would remain on the spot for three years. When they failed to heed this threat, Vladimir marshalled his troops and ordered the construction of an earthwork in the direction of the city. While this work was under construction, the inhabitants dug a tunnel under the city-wall, stole the heaped-up earth, and carried it into the city, where they piled it up in the center of the town. But the soldiers kept on building, and Vladimir persisted. Then a man of Kherson, Anastasius by name, shot into the Russ camp an arrow on which he had written, "There are springs behind you to the east, from which water flows in pipes. Dig down and cut them off." When Vladimir received this information, he raised his eyes to heaven and vowed that if this hope was realized, he would be baptized. He gave orders straightway to dig down above the pipes, and the water-supply was thus cut off. The inhabitants were accordingly overcome by thirst, and surrendered.

Vladimir and his retinue entered the city, and he sent messages to the Emperors Basil and Constantine,[5] saying, "Behold, I have captured your glorious city. I have also heard that you have an unwedded sister. Unless you give her to me to wife, I shall deal with your own city as I have with Kherson." When the Emperors heard this message they were troubled, and replied, "It is not meet for Christians to give in marriage to pagans. If you are baptized, you shall have her to wife, inherit the kingdom of God, and be our companion in the faith. Unless you do so, however, we cannot give you our sister in marriage." When Vladimir learned their response, he directed the envoys of the Emperors to report to the latter that he was willing to accept baptism, having already given some study to their religion, and that the Greek faith and ritual, as described by the emissaries sent to examine it, had pleased him well. When the Emperors heard this report, they rejoiced, and persuaded their sister Anna to consent to the match. They then requested Vladimir to submit to baptism before they should send their sister to him, but Vladimir desired that the Princess should herself bring priests to baptize him. The Emperors complied with his request, and sent forth their sister, accompanied by some dignitaries and priests. Anna, however, departed with reluctance. "It is as if I were setting out into captivity," she lamented; "better were it for me to die at home." But her brothers protested, "Through your agency God turns the land of Rus' to repentance, and you will relieve Greece from the danger of grievous

[5] Constantine VIII, co-emperor with Basil II from 963 to 1025, sole ruler from 1025 to 1028.

war. Do you not see how much harm the Russes have already brought upon the Greeks? If you do not set out, they may bring on us the same misfortunes." It was thus that they overcame her hesitation only with great difficulty. The Princess embarked upon a ship, and after tearfully embracing her kinfolk, she set forth across the sea and arrived at Kherson. The natives came forth to greet her, and conducted her into the city, where they settled her in the palace.

By divine agency, Vladimir was suffering at that moment from a disease of the eyes, and could see nothing, being in great distress. The Princess declared to him that if he desired to be relieved of this disease, he should be baptized with all speed, otherwise it could not be cured. When Vladimir heard her message, he said, "If this proves true, then of a surety is the God of the Christians great," and gave order that he should be baptized. The Bishop of Kherson, together with the Princess's priests, after announcing the tidings, baptized Vladimir, and as the Bishop laid his hand upon him, he straightway received his sight. Upon experiencing this miraculous cure, Vladimir glorified God, saying, "I have now perceived the one true God." When his followers beheld this miracle, many of them were also baptized.

Vladimir was baptized in the Church of St. Basil, which stands at Kherson upon a square in the center of the city, where the Khersonians trade. The palace of Vladimir stands beside this church to this day, and the palace of the Princess is behind the altar. After his baptism, Vladimir took the Princess in marriage. Those who do not know the truth say he was baptized in Kiev, while others assert this event took place in Vasil'ev, while still others mention other places.

Hereupon Vladimir took the Princess and Anastasius and the priests of Kherson, together with the relics of St. Clement and of Phoebus his disciple, and selected also sacred vessels and images for the service. In Kherson he thus founded a church on the mound which had been heaped up in the midst of the city with the earth removed from his embankment; this church is standing at the present day. Vladimir also found and appropriated two bronze statues and four bronze horses, which now stand behind the Church of the Holy Virgin, and which the ignorant think are made of marble. As a wedding present for the Princess, he gave Kherson over to the Greeks again, and then departed for Kiev.

When the Prince arrived at his capital, he directed that the idols should be overthrown, and that some should be cut to pieces and others burned with fire. He thus ordered that Perun[6] should be bound to a horse's tail and dragged down Borichev to the stream. He appointed twelve men to beat the idol with sticks, not because he thought the wood was sensitive, but to affront the demon who had deceived man in this guise, that he might receive chastisement at the hands of men. Great art thou, oh Lord, and marvelous are thy works! Yesterday he was honored of men, but today held in derision. While the idol was being dragged along the stream to the Dnieper, the unbelievers wept over it,

[6] An old Slavic god.

for they had not yet received holy baptism. After they had thus dragged the idol along, they cast it into the Dnieper. But Vladimir had given this injunction "If it halts anywhere, then push it out from the bank, until it goes over the falls. Then let it loose." His command was duly obeyed. When the men let the idol go, and it passed through the rapids, the wind cast it out on the bank, which since that time has been called Perun's sandbank, a name that it bears to this very day.

Thereafter Vladimir sent heralds throughout the whole city to proclaim that if any inhabitants, rich or poor, did not betake himself to the river, he would risk the Prince's displeasure. When the people heard these words, they wept for joy, and exclaimed in their enthusiasm, "If this were not good, the Prince and his boyars would not have accepted it." On the morrow, the Prince went forth to the Dnieper with the priests of the Princess and those from Kherson, and a countless multitude assembled. They all went into the water: some stood up to their necks, others to their breasts, and the younger near the bank, some of them holding children in their arms, while the adults waded farther out. The priests stood by and offered prayers. There was joy in heaven and upon earth to behold so many souls saved. But the devil groaned, lamenting, "Woe is me! how am I driven out hence! For I thought to have my dwelling-place here, since the apostolic teachings do not abide in this land. Nor did this people know God, but I rejoiced in the service they rendered unto me. But now I am vanquished by the ignorant, not by apostles and martyrs, and my reign in these regions is at an end."

IV

ISLAM

Mohammed created a great religion. His followers founded upon it a great culture, but not a great state. The Caliphates of Damascus and of Baghdad, despite their wealth and glitter and military success, lacked the political permanence and cohesion of Byzantium. The Moslems glossed the Koran and developed an imposing body of religious law; they produced no *Corpus Iuris Civilis*. Their rivalries soon split Islam into a number of irreconcilable units, though the bonds of religion and language still made all Moslems in a sense the members of one society.

Their impact on Christendom was not confined to one sphere. Militarily they dealt Byzantium a crippling blow and swarmed along the southern coast the Mediterranean to engulf even faraway Spain. Checked by Charles Martel at the Battle of Poitiers in 733, they still managed in subsequent years to conquer most of the Mediterranean islands, to establish a base at Fraxinet in southern France, and to raid deep into the mainland with monotonous and ferocious regularity. Yet warfare did not preclude trade, even trade with enemies; the example of Venetian relations with Egypt is no isolated case. Moreover, they proved themselves to be indefatigable middlemen in the commerce of ideas. They absorbed the philosophy and science of the Greeks and Hindus and played a leading role in introducing Aristotle to the West. They were eager borrowers and fertile innovators in such fields as business, agriculture, optics, medicine, architecture, and literature. They developed a civilization more adventurous than that of Byzantium and more sophisticated than that of the contemporary West.

The following selections have been chosen to represent various facets of that civilization—religion (the Koran), war, political theory and political reality, and the conflict between philosophy and mysticism. The resulting picture is of necessity partial and fragmentary, but it affords a glimpse of the richness and variety of the Moslem world.

1. MOHAMMED: FROM THE *KORAN* (*EARLY SEVENTH CENTURY*)[1]

Moslems believe that the real author of the *Koran*, which means the *Recitation*, was not Mohammed but Allah and that Mohammed was God's prophet in the most literal sense, receiving revelations during periods of religious trance and then communicating them to others. These revelations came to Mohammed over a period of years, down to his death in 632. The dates of many are obscure, for the *sûrahs,* or chapters, of the *Koran* are arranged not according to time but according to length, from the longest (with the exception of the initial brief prayer to Allah) to the shortest. The four *sûrahs* chosen here indicate that Mohammed was strongly influenced by Jewish and Christian traditions and by the Christian concept of a Last Judgment.

Mary

Revealed at Mecca

IN THE NAME OF ALLAH, THE BENEFICENT, THE MERCIFUL.

1. Kâf. Hâ. Yâ. A'în. Sad.[2]
2. A mention of the mercy of thy Lord unto His servant Zachariah.
3. When he cried unto his Lord a cry in secret,
4. Saying: My Lord! Lo! the bones of me wax feeble and my head is shining with grey hair, and I have never been unblest in prayer to Thee, my Lord.
5. Lo! I fear my kinsfolk after me, since my wife is barren. Oh, give me from Thy presence a successor
6. Who shall inherit of me and inherit (also) of the house of Jacob. And make him, my Lord, acceptable (unto Thee).

[1] *The Meaning of the Glorious Koran,* trans. by M. M. Pickthall (London, George Allen & Unwin Ltd., 1930), pp. 221-226, 384-386, 387-389, 439-440.
[2] Many sûrahs of the Koran began with letters of the Arabic alphabet. Their significance is uncertain.

7. (It was said unto him): O Zachariah! Lo! We bring thee tidings of a son whose name is John;[3] We have given the same name to none before (him).

8. He said: My Lord! How can I have a son when my wife is barren and I have reached infirm old age?

9. HE said: So (it will be). Thy Lord saith: It is easy for Me, even as I created thee before, when thou wast naught.

10. He said: My Lord! Appoint for me some token. HE said: Thy token is that thou, with no bodily defect, shalt not speak unto mankind three nights.

11. Then he came forth unto his people from the sanctuary, and signified to them: Glorify your Lord at break of day and fall of night.

12. (And it was said unto his son): O John! Hold fast the Scripture. And We gave him wisdom when a child,

13. And compassion from Our presence, and purity; and he was devout,

14. And dutiful toward his parents. And he was not arrogant, rebellious.

15. Peace on him the day he was born, and the day he dieth and the day he shall be raised alive!

16. And make mention of Mary in the Scripture, when she had withdrawn from her people to a chamber looking East,

17. And had chosen seclusion from them. Then We sent unto her Our spirit and it assumed for her the likeness of a perfect man.

18. She said: Lo! I seek refuge in the Beneficent One from thee, if thou art God-fearing.

19. He said: I am only a messenger of thy Lord, that I may bestow on thee a faultless son.

20. She said: How can I have a son when no mortal hath touched me, neither have I been unchaste?

21. He said: So (it will be). Thy Lord saith: It is easy for Me. And (it will be) that We may make of him a revelation for mankind and a mercy from Us, and it is a thing ordained.

22. And she conceived him, and she withdrew with him to a far place.

23. And the pangs of childbirth drove her unto the trunk of the palm-tree. She said: Oh, would that I had died ere this and had become a thing of naught, forgotten!

24. Then (one) cried unto her from below her, saying: Grieve not! Thy Lord hath placed a rivulet beneath thee,

25. And shake the trunk of the palm-tree toward thee, thou wilt cause ripe dates to fall upon thee.

26. So eat and drink and be consoled. And if thou meetest any mortal, say: Lo! I have vowed a fast unto the Beneficent, and may not speak this day to any mortal.

27. Then she brought him to her own folk, carrying him. They said: O Mary! Thou hast come with an amazing thing.

[3] John the Baptist.

28. O sister of Aaron![4] Thy father was not a wicked man nor was thy mother a harlot.

29. Then she pointed to him. They said: How can we talk to one who is in the cradle, a young boy?

30. He spake: Lo! I am the slave of Allah. He hath given me the Scripture and hath appointed me a Prophet,

31. And hath made me blessed wheresoever I may be, and hath enjoined upon me prayer and alms-giving so long as I remain alive,

32. And (hath made me) dutiful toward her who bore me, and hath not made me arrogant, unblest.

33. Peace on me the day I was born, and the day I die, and the day I shall be raised alive!

34. Such was Jesus, son of Mary: (this is) a statement of the truth concerning which they doubt.

35. It befitteth not (the Majesty of) Allah that He should take unto Himself a son. Glory be to Him! When He decreeth a thing, He saith unto it only: Be! and it is.

36. And lo! Allah is my Lord and your Lord. So serve Him. That is the right path.

37. The sects among them differ: but woe unto the disbelievers from the meeting of an awful Day.

38. See and hear them on the Day they come unto Us! Yet the evil-doers are to-day in error manifest.

39. And warn them of the Day of anguish when the case hath been decided. Now they are in a state of carelessness, and they believe not.

40. Lo! We inherit the earth and all who are thereon, and unto Us they are returned.

41. And make mention (O Muhammad) in the Scripture of Abraham. Lo! he was a saint, a Prophet.

42. When he said unto his father: O my father! Why worshippest thou that which heareth not nor seeth, nor can in aught avail thee?

43. O my father! Lo! there hath come unto me of knowledge that which came not unto thee. So follow me, and I will lead thee on a right path.

44. O my father! Serve not the devil. Lo! the devil is a rebel unto the Beneficent.

45. O my father! Lo! I fear lest a punishment from the Beneficent overtake thee so that thou become a comrade of the devil.

46. He said: Rejectest thou my gods, O Abraham? If thou cease not, I shall surely stone thee. Depart from me a long while!

47. He said: Peace be unto thee! I shall ask forgiveness of my Lord for thee. Lo! He was ever gracious unto me.

48. I shall withdraw from you and that unto which ye pray beside Allah,

[4] Has the Prophet confused Mary with Miriam? Perhaps he only refers to Mary's ancestry.

and I shall pray unto my Lord. It may be that, in prayer unto my Lord, I shall not be unblest.

49. So, when he had withdrawn from them and that which they were worshipping beside Allah, We gave him Isaac and Jacob. Each of them We made a Prophet.

50. And We gave them of Our mercy, and assigned to them a high and true renown.

51. And make mention in the Scripture of Moses. Lo! he was chosen, and he was a messenger (of Allah), a Prophet.

52. We called him from the right slope of the Mount, and brought him nigh in communion.

53. And We bestowed upon him of Our mercy his brother Aaron, a Prophet (likewise).

54. And make mention in the Scripture of Ishmael. Lo! he was a keeper of his promise, and he was a messenger (of Allah), a Prophet.

55. He enjoined upon his people worship and almsgiving, and was acceptable in the sight of his Lord.

56. And make mention in the Scripture of Idrîs.[5] Lo! he was a saint, a Prophet;

57. And We raised him to high station.

58. These are they unto whom Allah showed favour from among the Prophets, of the seed of Adam and of those whom We carried (in the ship) with Noah, and of the seed of Abraham and Israel, and from among those whom We guided and chose. When the revelations of the Beneficent were recited unto them, they fell down, adoring and weeping.

59. Now there hath succeeded them a later generation who have ruined worship and have followed lusts. But they will meet deception,

60. Save him who shall repent and believe and do right. Such will enter the Garden, and they will not be wronged in aught—

61. Gardens of Eden, which the Beneficent hath promised to His slaves in the Unseen. Lo! His promise is ever sure of fulfilment—

62. They hear therein no idle talk, but only Peace; and therein they have food for morn and evening.

63. Such is the Garden which We cause the devout among Our bondmen to inherit.

64. We (angels) come not down save by commandment of thy Lord. Unto Him belongeth all that is before us and all that is behind us and all that is between those two, and thy Lord was never forgetful—

65. Lord of the heavens and the earth and all that is between them! Therefore, worship thou Him and be thou steadfast in His service. Knowest thou one that can be named along with Him?

66. And man saith: When I am dead, shall I forsooth be brought forth alive?

[5] Enoch.

67. Doth not man remember that We created him before, when he was naught?

68. And, by thy Lord, verily We shall assemble them and the devils, then We shall bring them, crouching, around hell.

69. Then We shall pluck out from every sect whichever of them was most stubborn in rebellion to the Beneficent.

70. And surely We are best aware of those most worthy to be burned therein.

71. There is not one of you but shall approach it. That is a fixed ordinance of thy Lord.

72. Then We shall rescue those who kept from evil, and leave the evildoers crouching there.

73. And when Our clear revelations are recited unto them, those who disbelieve say unto those who believe: Which of the two parties (yours or ours) is better in position, and more imposing as an army?

74. How many a generation have We destroyed before them, who were more imposing in respect of gear and outward seeming!

75. Say: As for him who is in error, the Beneficent will verily prolong his span of life until, when they behold that which they were promised, whether it be punishment (in the world), or the Hour (of Doom), they will know who is worse in position and who is weaker as an army.

76. Allah increaseth in right guidance those who walk aright, and the good deeds which endure are better in thy Lord's sight for reward, and better for resort.

77. Hast thou seen him who disbelieveth in Our revelations and saith: Assuredly I shall be given wealth and children?

78. Hath he perused the Unseen, or hath he made a pact with the Beneficent?

79. Nay, but We shall record that which he saith and prolong for him a span of torment.

80. And We shall inherit from him that whereof he spake, and he will come unto Us, alone (without his wealth and children).

81. And they have chosen (other) gods beside Allah that they may be a power for them.

82. Nay, but they will deny their worship of them, and become opponents unto them.

83. Seest thou not that We have set the devils on the disbelievers to confound them with confusion?

84. So make no haste against them (O Muhammad). We do but number unto them a sum (of days).

85. On the Day when We shall gather the righteous unto the Beneficent, a goodly company.

86. And drive the guilty unto Hell, a weary herd,

87. They will have no power of intercession, save him who hath made a covenant with his Lord.

88. And they say: The Beneficent hath taken unto Himself a son.

89. Assuredly ye utter a disastrous thing,

90. Whereby almost the heavens are torn, and the earth is split asunder and the mountains fall in ruins,

91. That ye ascribe unto the Beneficent a son,

92. When it is not meet for (the Majesty of) the Beneficent that He should choose a son.

93. There is none in the heavens and the earth but cometh unto the Beneficent as a slave.

94. Verily He knoweth them and numbereth them with (right) numbering.

95. And each one of them will come unto Him on the Day of Resurrection, alone.

96. Lo! those who believe and do good works, the Beneficent will appoint for them love.

97. And We make (this Scripture) easy in thy tongue (O Muhammad), only that thou mayst bear good tidings therewith unto those who ward off (evil), and warn therewith the froward folk.

98. And how many a generation before them have We destroyed! Canst thou (Muhammad) see a single man of them, or hear from them the slightest sound?

The Event

Revealed at Mecca

IN THE NAME OF ALLAH, THE BENEFICENT, THE MERCIFUL.

1. When the event befalleth—
2. There is no denying that it will befall—
3. Abasing (some), exalting (others);
4. When the earth is shaken with a shock
5. And the hills are ground to powder
6. So that they become a scattered dust,
7. And ye will be three kinds:
8. (First) those on the right hand; what of those on the right hand?
9. And (then) those on the left hand; what of those on the left hand?
10. And the foremost in the race, the foremost in the race:
11. Those are they who will be brought nigh
12. In gardens of delight;
13. A multitude of those of old
14. And a few of those of later time,
15. On lined couches,

16. Reclining therein face to face.
17. There wait on them immortal youths
18. With bowls and ewers and a cup from a pure spring
19. Wherefrom they get no aching of the head nor any madness,
20. And fruit that they prefer
21. And flesh of fowls that they desire.
22. And (there are) fair ones with wide, lovely eyes,
23. Like unto hidden pearls,
24. Reward for what they used to do.
25. There hear they no vain speaking nor recrimination
26. (Naught) but the saying: Peace, (and again) Peace.
27. And those on the right hand; what of those on the right hand?
28. Among thornless lote-trees
29. And clustered plantains,
30. And spreading shade,
31. And water gushing,
32. And fruit in plenty
33. Neither out of reach nor yet forbidden,
34. And raised couches;
35. Lo! We have created them a (new) creation
36. And made them virgins,
37. Lovers, friends,
38. For those on the right hand;
39. A multitude of those of old
40. And a multitude of those of later time.
41. And those on the left hand: What of those on the left hand?
42. In scorching wind and scalding water
43. And shadow of black smoke,
44. Neither cool nor refreshing.
45. Lo! heretofore they were effete with luxury
46. And used to persist in the awful sin.
47. And they used to say: When we are dead and have become dust and bones, shall we then, forsooth, be raised again,
48. And also our forefathers?
49. Say (unto them, O Muhammad): Lo! those of old and those of later time
50. Will all be brought together to the tryst of an appointed day.
51. Then lo! ye, the erring, the deniers,
52. Ye verily will eat of a tree called Zaqqûm
53. And will fill your bellies therewith;
54. And thereon ye will drink of boiling water,
55. Drinking even as the camel drinketh.
56. This will be their welcome on the Day of Judgement.

57. We created you. Will ye then admit the truth?

58. Have ye seen that which ye emit?

59. Do ye create it or are We the Creator?

60. We mete out death among you, and We are not to be outrun,

61. That We may transfigure you and make you what ye know not.

62. And verily ye know the first creation. Why, then, do ye not reflect?

63. Have ye seen that which ye cultivate?

64. Is it ye who foster it, or are We the fosterer?

65. If We willed, We verily could make it chaff, then would ye cease not to exclaim:

66. Lo! we are laden with debt!

67. Nay, but we are deprived!

68. Have ye observed the water which ye drink?

69. Is it ye who shed it from the raincloud, or are We the shedder?

70. If We willed We verily could make it bitter. Why, then, give ye not thanks?

71. Have ye observed the fire which ye strike out;

72. Was it ye who made the tree thereof to grow, or were We the grower?

73. We, even We, appointed it a memorial and a comfort for the dwellers in the wilderness.

74. Therefore (O Muhammad), praise the name of thy Lord, the Tremendous.

75. Nay, I swear by the places of the stars—

76. And lo! that verily is a tremendous oath, if ye but knew—

77. That (this) is indeed a noble Qur'ân

78. In a Book kept hidden

79. Which none toucheth save the purified,

80. A revelation from the Lord of the Worlds.

81. Is it this Statement that ye scorn,

82. And make denial thereof your livelihood?

83. Why, then, when (the soul) cometh up to the throat (of the dying)

84. And ye are at that moment looking

85. —And We are nearer unto him than ye are, but ye see not—

86. Why then, if ye are not in bondage (unto Us),

87. Do ye not force it back, if ye are truthful?

88. Thus if he is of those brought nigh,

89. Then breath of life, and plenty, and a Garden of delight.

90. And if he is of those on the right hand,

91. Then (the greeting) "Peace be unto thee" from those on the right hand.

92. But if he is of the rejecters, the erring,

93. Then the welcome will be boiling water

94. And roasting at hell fire.

95. Lo! this is certain truth.

96. Therefore (O Muhammad) praise the name of thy Lord, the Tremendous.

Iron

Revealed at Al-Madinah

<small>IN THE NAME OF ALLAH, THE BENEFICENT, THE MERCIFUL.</small>

1. All that is in the heavens and the earth glorifieth Allah; and He is the Mighty, the Wise.

2. He is the Sovereignty of the heavens and the earth; He quickeneth and He giveth death; and He is Able to do all things.

3. He is the First and the Last, and the Outward and the Inward; and He is Knower of all things.

4. He it is Who created the heavens and the earth in six Days; then He mounted the Throne. He knoweth all that entereth the earth and all that emergeth therefrom and all that cometh down from the sky and all that ascendeth therein; and He is with you wheresoever ye may be. And Allah is Seer of what ye do.

5. His is the Sovereignty of the heavens and the earth, and unto Allah (all) things are brought back.

6. He causeth the night to pass into the day, and He causeth the day to pass into the night, and He is Knower of all that is in the breasts.

7. Believe in Allah and His messenger, and spend of that whereof He hath made you trustees; and such of you as believe and spend (aright), theirs will be a great reward.

8. What aileth you that ye believe not in Allah, when the messenger calleth you to believe in your Lord, and He hath already made a covenant with you, if ye are believers?

9. He it is Who sendeth down clear revelations unto His slave, that He may bring you forth from darkness unto light; and lo! for you, Allah is Full of Pity, Merciful.

10. And what aileth you that ye spend not in the way of Allah, when unto Allah belongeth the inheritance of the heavens and the earth? Those who spent and fought before the victory are not upon a level (with the rest of you). Such are greater in rank than those who spent and fought afterwards. Unto each hath Allah promised good. And Allah is Informed of what ye do.

11. Who is he that will lend unto Allah a goodly loan that He may double it for him and his may be a rich reward?

12. On the day when thou (Muhammad) wilt see the believers, men and women, their light shining forth before them and on their right hands, (and wilt hear it said unto them): Glad news for you this day: Gardens un-

derneath which rivers flow, wherein ye are immortal. That is the supreme triumph.

13. On the day when the hypocritical men and the hypocritical women will say unto those who believe: Look on us that we may borrow from your light! it will be said: Go back and seek for light! Then there will separate them a wall wherein is a gate, the inner side whereof containeth mercy, while the outer side thereof is toward the doom.

14. They will cry unto them (saying): Were we not with you? They will say: Yea, verily; but ye tempted one another, and hesitated, and doubted, and vain desires beguiled you till the ordinance of Allah came to pass; and the deceiver deceived you concerning Allah;

15. So this day no ransom can be taken from you nor from those who disbelieved. Your home is the Fire; that is your patron, and a hapless journey's end.

16. Is not the time ripe for the hearts of those who believe to submit to Allah's reminder and to the truth which is revealed, that they become not as those who received the Scripture of old but the term was prolonged for them and so their hearts were hardened, and many of them are evil-livers.

17. Know that Allah quickeneth the earth after its death. We have made clear Our revelations for you, that haply ye may understand.

18. Lo! those who give alms, both men and women, and lend unto Allah a goodly loan, it will be doubled for them, and theirs will be a rich reward.

19. And those who believe in Allah and His Messengers, they are the loyal; and the martyrs are with their Lord; they have their reward and their light; while as for those who disbelieve and deny Our revelations, they are owners of hell-fire.

20. Know that the life of the world is only play, and idle talk, and pageantry, and boasting among you, and rivalry in respect of wealth and children; as the likeness of vegetation after rain, whereof the growth is pleasing to the husbandman, but afterward it drieth up and thou seest it turning yellow, then it becometh straw. And in the Hereafter there is grievous punishment, and (also) forgiveness from Allah and His good pleasure, whereas the life of the world is but matter of illusion.

21. Race one with another for forgiveness from your Lord and a Garden whereof the breadth is as the breadth of the heavens and the earth, which is in store for those who believe in Allah and His messengers. Such is the bounty of Allah, which he bestoweth upon whom He will, and Allah is of infinite bounty.

22. Naught of disaster befalleth in the earth or in yourselves but it is in a Book before We bring it into being—Lo! that is easy for Allah—

23. That ye grieve not for the sake of that which hath escaped you, nor yet exult because of that which hath been given. Allah loveth not all prideful boasters,

24. Who hoard and who enjoin upon the people avarice, And whosoever turneth away, still Allah is the Absolute, the Owner of Praise.

25. We verily sent Our messengers with clear proofs, and revealed with them the Scripture and the Balance, that mankind may observe right measure; and He revealed iron, wherein is mighty power and (many) uses for mankind, and that Allah may know him who helpeth Him and His messengers, though unseen. Lo! Allah is Strong, Almighty.

26. And We verily sent Noah and Abraham and placed the Prophethood and the Scripture among their seed, and among them there is he who goeth right, but many of them are evil-livers.

27. Then We caused Our messengers to follow in their foot-steps; and We caused Jesus, son of Mary, to follow, and gave him the Gospel, and placed compassion and mercy in the hearts of those who followed him. But monasticism they invented—We ordained it not for them—only seeking Allah's pleasure, and they observed it not with right observance. So We give those of them who believe their reward, but many of them are evil-livers.

28. O ye who believe! Be mindful of your duty to Allah and put faith in His messenger. He will give you twofold of His mercy and will appoint for you a light wherein ye shall walk, and will forgive you. Allah is Forgiving, Merciful;

29. That the People of the Scripture[6] may know that they control naught of the bounty of Allah, but that the bounty is in Allah's hand to give to whom He will. And Allah is of infinite bounty.

The Dawn

Revealed at Mecca

IN THE NAME OF ALLAH, THE BENEFICENT, THE MERCIFUL.

1. By the Dawn
2. And ten nights,
3. And the Even and the Odd,
4. And the night when it departeth,
5. There surely is an oath for thinking man.
6. Dost thou not consider how thy Lord dealt with (the tribe of) A'âd,
7. With many-columned Iram,
8. The like of which was not created in the lands;
9. And with (the tribe of) Thamûd, who clove the rocks in the valley;
10. And with Pharaoh, firm of might,
11. Who (all) were rebellious (to Allah) in these lands,
12. And multiplied iniquity therein?
13. Therefore thy Lord poured on them the disaster of His punishment.

---

[6] Mohammed considered Jews and Christians to be People of the Book, or Scripture, and therefore on a higher plane than those infidels who worshipped many gods, and who ought therefore to be killed.

14. Lo! thy Lord is ever watchful.

15. As for man, whenever his Lord trieth him by honouring him, and is gracious unto him, he saith: My Lord honoureth me.

16. But whenever He trieth him by straitening his means of life, he saith: My Lord despiseth me.

17. Nay, but ye (for your part) honour not the orphan

18. And urge not on the feeding of the poor,

19. And ye devour heritages with devouring greed

20. And love wealth with abounding love.

21. Nay, but when the earth is ground to atoms, grinding, grinding,

22. And thy Lord shall come with angels, rank on rank,

23. And hell is brought near that day; on that day man will remember, but how will the remembrance (then avail him)?

24. He will say: Ah, would that I had sent before me (some provision) for my life!

25. None punisheth as He will punish on that day!

26. None bindeth as He then will bind.

27. But ah! thou soul at peace!

28. Return unto thy Lord, content in His good pleasure!

29. Enter thou among My bondmen!

30. Enter thou My Garden!

2. AL-BALÂDHURI: THE BATTLE OF THE YARMUK (636)[1]

The military dynamism of Islam, which immediately after Mohammed's death created a great Near Eastern and African empire, is one of the marvels of history. Islam profited from the mutual exhaustion of Byzantium and Persia after the great struggle in which the latter had been crushed by the Emperor Heraclius (reigned 610-641), and also from the religious and economic discontent of the reconquered eastern provinces of Byzantium, in which heresy and separatism were rampant. Crushed by the twin weights of Byzantine orthodoxy and taxation, the lands of the Near East welcomed new masters. It was in vain that Heraclius gathered a large army and sought to defend them against the onrushing Islamic tide. The Battle of the Yarmuk in Syria on 20 August 636 was a decisive victory for the Moslems. The account of al-Balâdhuri (d. c. 892) reprinted below indicates the episodic and personal character of early Islamic historiography but also emphasizes the

[1] *The Origins of the Islamic State,* being a translation from the Arabic . . . of the *Kitâb Futûh al-Buldân* of . . . Ahmad ibn-Jâbir al-Balâdhuri, trans. by P. K. Hitti and F. C. Murgotten, *Studies in History, Economics and Public Law,* LXVIII (New York, Columbia University Press, 1916 and 1924), I, 207-211.

hostility of Syria to Byzantium and the welcome which the inhabitants of the former province accorded to their invaders.

A description of the battle. Heraclius gathered large bodies of Greeks, Syrians, Mesopotamians and Armenians numbering about 200,000.[2] This army he put under the command of one of his choice men and sent as a vanguard Jabalah ibn-al-Aiham al-Ghassâni at the head of the "naturalized" Arabs [*musta'ribah*] of Syria of the tribes of Lakhm, Judhâm and others, resolving to fight the Moslems so that he might either win or withdraw to the land of the Greeks and live in Constantinople. The Moslems gathered together and the Greek army marched against them. The battle they fought at al-Yarmûk was of the fiercest and bloodiest kind. Al-Yarmûk [Hieromax] is a river. In this battle 24,000 Moslems took part. The Greeks and their followers in this battle tied themselves to each other by chains, so that no one might set his hope on flight. By Allah's help, some 70,000 of them were put to death, and their remnants took to flight, reaching as far as Palestine, Antioch, Aleppo, Mesopotamia and Armenia. In the battle of al-Yarmûk certain Moslem women took part and fought violently. Among them was Hind, daughter of 'Utbah and mother of Mu'âwiyah ibn-abi-Sufyân, who repeatedly exclaimed, "Cut the arms of these 'uncircumcised' with your swords!" Her husband abu-Sufyân had come to Syria as a volunteer desiring to see his sons, and so he brought his wife with him. He then returned to al-Madînah where he died, year 31, at the age of 88. Others say he died in Syria. When the news of his death was carried to his daughter, umm-Habîbah, she waited until the third day on which she ordered some yellow paint and covered with it her arms and face saying, "I would not have done that, had I not heard the Prophet say, 'A woman should not be in mourning for more than three days over anyone except her husband.'" It is stated that she did likewise when she received the news of her brother Yazîd's death. But Allah knows best.

Those who lost an eye or suffered martyrdom. Abu-Sufyân ibn-Harb was one-eyed. He had lost his eye in the battle of at-Ţâ'if. In the battle of al-Yarmûk, however, al-Ash'ath ibn-Ķais, Hâshim ibn-'Utbah ibn-abi-Wakkâs az-Zuhri (*i.e.*, al-Mirkâl) and Ķais ibn-Makshûh, each lost an eye. In this battle 'Âmir ibn-abi-Wakkâs az-Zuhri fell a martyr. It is this 'Âmir who once carried the letter of 'Umar ibn-al-Khaţţâb assigning abu-'Ubaidah to the governorship of Syria. Others say he was a victim of the plague; still others report that he suffered martyrdom in the battle of Ajnâdîn; but all that is not true.

Habîb ibn-Maslamah pursues the fugitives. Abu-'Ubaidah put Habîb ibn-Maslamah-l-Fihri at the head of a cavalry detachment charged with pursuing the fugitive enemy, and Habîb set out killing every man whom he could reach.

[2] The number of Heraclius' soldiers is obviously exaggerated.

The story of Jabalah. Jabalah ibn-al-Aiham sided with the Anṣâr[3] saying, "Ye are our brethren and the sons of our fathers," and professed Islâm. After the arrival of 'Umar ibn-al-Khaṭṭâb in Syria, year 17, Jabalah had a dispute with one of the Muzainah and knocked out his eye. 'Umar ordered that he be punished, upon which Jabalah said, "Is his eye like mine? Never, by Allah, shall I abide in a town where I am under authority." He then apostatized and went to the land of the Greeks. This Jabalah was the king of Ghassân and the successor of al-Ḥârith ibn-abi-Shimr.

According to another report, when Jabalah came to 'Umar ibn-al-Khaṭṭâb, he was still a Christian. 'Umar asked him to accept Islam and pay *ṣadaḳah*;[4] but he refused saying, "I shall keep my faith and pay *ṣadaḳah*." 'Umar's answer was, "If thou keepest thy faith, thou hast to pay poll-tax."[5] The man refused, and 'Umar added, "We have only three alternatives for thee: Islâm, tax or going whither thou willest." Accordingly, Jabalah left with 30,000 men to the land of the Greeks [Asia Minor]. 'Ubâdah ibn-aṣ-Ṣâmit gently reproved 'Umar saying, "If thou hadst accepted *ṣadaḳah* from him and treated him in a friendly way, he would have become Moslem."

In the year 21, 'Umar directed 'Umair ibn-Sa'd al-Anṣâri at the head of a great army against the land of the Greeks, and put him in command of the summer expedition which was the first of its kind. 'Umar instructed him to treat Jabalah ibn-al-Aiham very kindly and to try and appeal to him through the blood relationship between them, so that he should come back to the land of the Moslems with the understanding that he would keep his own faith and pay the amount of *ṣadaḳah* he had agreed to pay. 'Umair marched until he came to the land of the Greeks and proposed to Jabalah what he was ordered by 'Umar to propose; but Jabalah refused the offer and insisted on staying in the land of the Greeks. 'Umair then came into a place called al-Ḥimâr—a valley—which he destroyed putting its inhabitants to the sword. Hence the proverb, "In a more ruined state than the hollow of Ḥimâr."

Heraclius' adieu to Syria. When Heraclius received the news about the troops in al-Yarmûk and the destruction of his army by the Moslems, he fled from Antioch to Constantinople, and as he passed ad-Darb he turned and said, "Peace unto thee, O Syria, and what an excellent country this is for the enemy!"—referring to the numerous pastures in Syria.

The battle of al-Yarmûk took place in Rajab, year 15.

Hubâsh loses his leg. According to Hishâm ibn-al-Kalbi, among those who witnessed the battle of al-Yarmûk was Ḥubâsh ibn-Ḳais al-Ḳushairi, who killed many of the "uncircumcised" and lost his leg without feeling it. At last he began to look for it. Hence the verse of Sauwâr ibn-Aufa:

---

[3] "The helpers," a term first applied to those citizens of Medina who helped the Prophet after his flight from Mecca.

[4] The tax paid by a Moslem to furnish alms to the poor.

[5] A tax imposed on unbelievers.

Among us were ibn-'Attâb and the one who went seeki   ⁊: and among us was one who offered protection to the quarter,

—referring to dhu-l-Ruḳaibah.

Christians and Jews prefer Moslem rule. Abu-Ḥafṣ ad-Dimashḳi from Sa'id ibn-'Abd-al-'Azîz:—When Heraclius massed his troops aᵧ·ᵢnst the Moslems and the Moslems heard that they were coming to meet them at al-Yarmûk, the Moslems refunded to the inhabitants of Ḥimṣ the *kharâj*[6] they had taken from them saying, "We are too busy to support and protect you. Take care of yourselves." But the people of Hims replied, "We like your rule and justice far better than the state of oppression and tyranny in which we were. The army of Heraclius we shall indeed, with your *'âmil's* help, repulse from the city." The Jews rose and said, "We swear by the Thorah,   governor of Heraclius shall enter the city of Ḥimṣ unless we are first vanquished and exhausted!" Saying this, they closed the gates of the city and guaᵣded them. The inhabitants of the other cities—Christian and Jew—that had capitulated to the Moslems, did the same, saying, "If Heraclius and his followers win over the Moslems we would return to our previous condition, otherwise we shall retain our present state so long as numbers are with the Moslems." When by Allah's help the "unbelievers" were defeated and the Moslems won, they opened the gates of their cities, went out with the singers and music players who began to play, and paid the *kharâj*.

3.   IBN ABD-EL-HAKEM: THE MOORISH CONQUEST OF SPAIN (711)[1]

After submerging northern Africa, the great wave of Moslem conquest washed into Spain in 711 and subsequently threatened France; it was not checked until the victory of Charles Martel near Poitiers in 733. The Spanish invasion took place under the leadership of the Berber Tarik, who landed near the rock which now bears his name, Jabal (mount of) Tarik or Gibraltar. Tarik's superior, Musa ibn-Nusayr, was jealous of his subordinate's exploit and joined the invasion in 712. Within seven years the conquest of the peninsula was complete. It became one of the centers of Moslem civilization, and the Umayyad caliphate of Cordova reached a peak of glory in the tenth century. Spain was then probably the most civilized

[6] This word originally meant tribute in general but later referred to land tax paid both by unbelievers and by converts to Islam as distinct from poll tax paid only by unbelievers.

[1] Ibn Abd-el-Hakem, *History of the Conquest of Spain,* trans. by John Harris Jones (Göttingen, W. Fr. Kaestner, 1858), pp. 18-22.

land in all of Europe. Christian reconquest began in earnest in the eleventh
century   until 1492 was the last great Moslem stronghold, Granada, re-
captured.

The selection below is taken from the *History of the Conquest of Spain* by
the Egyptian Ibn Abd-el-Hakem (d. 870 or 871), who also wrote a history of Egypt.
His account is a mingling of legend and fact, as might be expected from a history
written a century and a half after the events it describes.

Musa Ibn Nosseyr[2] sent his son Merwan to Tangiers, to wage a holy
war upon her coast. Having, then, exerted himself together with his friends,
he returned, leaving to Tarik Ibn Amru the command of his army which
amounted to 1,700. Others say that 12,000 Berbers besides 16 Arabs
were with Tarik: but that is false. It is also said that Musa Ibn Nosseyr
marched out of Ifrikiya[3] upon an expedition into Tangiers, and that he was
the first governor who entered Tangiers, where parts of the Berber tribes Botr
and Beranes resided. These had not yet submitted themselves. When he approached Tangiers, he scattered his light troops. On the arrival of his cavalry
in the nearest province of Sus, he subdued its inhabitants, and made them
prisoners, they yielding him obedience. And he gave them a governor whose
conduct was agreeable to them. He sent Ibn Beshr Ibn Abi Artah to a citadel,
three days' journey from the town of Cairwan. Having taken the former, he
made prisoners of the children, and plundered the treasury. The citadel was
called Beshr, by which name it is known to this day. Afterwards Musa deposed
the viceroy whom he had placed over Tangiers, and appointed Tarik Ibn
Zeiyad governor. He, then, returned to Cairwan, Tarik with his female slave
of the name Umm-Hakim setting out for Tangiers. Tarik remained some time
in this district, waging a holy war. This was in the year 92. The governor of
the straits between this district and Andalus was a foreigner called Ilyan, Lord
of Septa. He was also the governor of a town called Alchadra, situated on the
same side of the straits of Andalus as Tangiers. Ilyan[4] was a subject of Roderic
the Lord of Andalus,[5] who used to reside in Toledo. Tarik put himself in
communication with Ilyan, and treated him kindly, until they made peace
with each other. Ilyan had sent one of his daughters to Roderic, the Lord of
Andalus, for her improvement and education; but she became pregnant by
him. Ilyan having heard of this, said, I see for him no other punishment or
recompense, than that I should bring the Arabs against him. He sent to Tarik,
saying, I will bring thee to Andalus; Tarik being at that time in Tlemsen, and
Musa Ibn Nosseyr in Cairwan. But Tarik said I cannot trust thee until thou
send me a hostage. So he sent his two daughters, having no other children.

[2] Governor of North Africa.
[3] Africa.
[4] Count of Ceuta.
[5] King of the Visigoths.

Tarik allowed them to remain in Tlemsen, guarding them closely. After that Tarik went to Ilyan who was in Septa on the straits. The latter rejoicing at his coming, said, I will bring thee to Andalus. But there was a mountain called the mountain of Tarik[6] between the two landing places, that is, between Septa and Andalus. When the evening came, Ilyan brought him the vessels, in which he made him embark for that landing-place, where he concealed himself during the day, and in the evening sent back the vessels to bring over the rest of his companions. So they embarked for the landing-place, none of them being left behind: whereas the people of Andalus did not observe them, thinking that the vessels crossing and recrossing were similar to the trading vessels which for their benefit plied backwards and forwards. Tarik was in the last division which went across. He proceeded to his companions, Ilyan together with the merchants that were with him being left behind in Alchadra, in order that he might the better encourage his companions and countrymen. The news of Tarik and of those who were with him, as well as of the place where they were, reached the people of Andalus. Tarik, going along with his companions, marched over a bridge of mountains to a town called Cartagena. He went in the direction of Cordova. Having passed by an island in the sea, he left behind his female slave of the name of Umm-Hakim, and with her a division of his troops. That island was then called Umm-Hakim. When the Moslems settled in the island, they found no other inhabitants there, than vinedressers. They made them prisoners. After that they took one of the vine-dressers, slaughtered him, cut him in pieces, and boiled him, while the rest of his companions looked on. They had also boiled meat in other cauldrons. When the meat was cooked, they threw away the flesh of that man which they had boiled; no one knowing that it was thrown away: and they ate the meat which they had boiled, while the rest of the vinedressers were spectators. These did not doubt but that the Moslems ate the flesh of their companion; the rest being afterwards sent away, informed the people of Andalus that the Moslems feed on human flesh, acquainting them with what had been done to the vinedresser.

As Abd-Errahman has related to us on the authority of his father Abd-Allah Ibn Abd-El-Hakem, and of Hisham Ibn Ishaak: There was a house in Andalus, the door of which was secured with padlocks, and on which every new king of the country placed a padlock of his own, until the accession to power of the king against whom the Moslems marched. They therefore begged him to place a padlock on it, as the kings before him were wont to do. But he refused saying, I will place nothing on it, until I shall have known what is inside; he then ordered it to be opened; but behold inside were portraits of the Arabs, and a letter in which it was written: "When this door shall be opened, these people will invade this country."

.   .   .   .   .

[6] Gibraltar.

When Tarik landed, soldiers from Cordova came to meet him; and seeing the small number of his companions they despised him on that account. They then fought. The battle with Tarik was severe. They were routed, and he did not cease from the slaughter of them till they reached the town of Cordova. When Roderic heard of this, he came to their rescue from Toledo. They then fought in a place of the name of Shedunia, in a valley which is called this day the valley of Umm-Hakim.[7] They fought a severe battle; but God, mighty and great, killed Roderic and his companions. Mugheyth Errumi, a slave of Welid, was then the commander of Tarik's cavalry. Mugheyth Errumi went in the direction of Cordova, Tarik passing over to Toledo. He, then, entered it, and asked for the table, having nothing else to occupy himself. This, as the men of the Bible relate, was the table of Suleyman Ibn Dawid, may the blessing of God be upon him.

As Abd Errahman has related to us on the authority of Yahya Ibn Bukeir, and the latter on the authority of Leyth Ibn Sâd: Andalus having been conquered for Musa Ibn Nosseyr, he took from it the table of Suleyman Ibn Dawid, and the crown. Tarik was told that the table was in a citadel called Faras, two days' journey from Toledo, and the governor of this citadel was a nephew of Roderic. Tarik, then, wrote to him, promising safety both for himself and family. The nephew descended from the citadel, and Tarik fulfilled his promise with reference to his safety. Tarik said to him, deliver the table, and he delivered it to him. On this table were gold and silver, the like of which one had not seen. Tarik, then, took off one of its legs together with the pearls and the gold it contained, and fixed to it a similar leg. The table was valued at two hundred thousand dinars, on account of the pearls that were on it. He took up the pearls, the armour, the gold, the silver, and the vases which he had with him, and found that quantity of spoils, the like of which one had not seen. He collected all that. Afterwards he returned to Cordova, and having stopped there, he wrote to Musa Ibn Nosseyr informing him of the conquest of Andalus, and of the spoils which he had found. Musa then wrote to Welid Abd Ed-Malik[8] informing him of that, and throwing himself upon his mercy. Musa wrote to Tarik ordering him not to leave Cordova until he should come to him. And he reprimanded him very severely. Afterwards Musa Ibn Nosseyr set out for Andalus, in Rajab of the year 93, taking with him the chiefs of the Arabs, the commanders, and the leaders of the Berbers to Andalus. He set out being angry with Tarik, and took with him Habib Ibn Abi Ubeida Elfihri, and left the government of Cairwan to his son Abd Allah who was his eldest son. He then passed through Alchadra, and afterwards went over to Cordova. Tarik then met him, and tried to satisfy him, saying: "I am merely thy slave, this conquest is thine." Musa collected of the money a sum, which exceeded all description. Tarik delivered to him all that he had plundered.

[7] On July 11, 711, at the mouth of the Barbate River.
[8] The Umayyad Caliph of Damascus.

4.   NIZĀM-AL-MULK: THE JUST KING (c. 1090)[1]

Nizām-al-Mulk was the chief minister of two great rulers of the Seljūq Turks, Alp Arslan (reigned 1063-1072), who destroyed the Byzantine army under Romanus IV at Manzikert (1071), and Malik-shah (reigned 1072-1092), who campaigned throughout the Near and Middle East. At the request of Malik-shah, Nizām wrote a manual of government called *Rules for Kings,* from which the following extract is taken. In view of his zeal for order, it is ironic that he should have died at the hands of those famous anarchists, the Assassins (1092).

It is for kings to observe His[2] pleasure (His name be glorified) and the pleasure of The Truth is in the charity which is done to His creatures and in the justice which is spread among them. A kingdom which is blessed by its people will endure and increase from day to day, while its king will enjoy power and prosperity; in this world he will acquire good fame, in the next world salvation, and his reckoning will be the easier. Great men have said [in Arabic], "A kingdom may last while there is irreligion, but it will not endure when there is oppression." . . .

Tradition tells that when Joseph the prophet (the prayers of Allah and His peace be upon him) went out from this world, they were carrying him to Abraham's tomb (upon him be peace) to bury him near his forefathers, when Gabriel (upon him be peace) came and said, "Stop where you are; this is not his place; for at the resurrection he will have to answer for the sovereignty which he has exercised." Now if the case of Joseph the prophet was such, consider what the position of others will be.

It has come down in a tradition from The Prophet (may Allah bless him and save him) that on the day of the resurrection, when anyone is brought forward who [in his life] wielded power and command over God's creatures, his hands will be bound; if he has been just, his justice will loose his hands and send him to paradise; but if he has been unjust, his injustice will cast him into hell as he is, with his hands bound in chains.

There is also a tradition that on resurrection day whoever had any com-

[1] Reprinted by permission of Routledge and Kegan Paul Ltd. from Nizām-al-Mulk, *The Book of Government or Rules for Kings,* trans. by H. Darke (London, Routledge and Kegan Paul Ltd., 1960), pp. 12-13, 34-43.
    [2] Allah's.

mand in this world over God's creatures, even over the inhabitants of his own
house or over his own underlings, will be questioned about it; likewise the
shepherd who tended his sheep will be required to answer for that too.

They say that at the time of his father's leaving this world 'Abd Allah ibn
'Umar ibn al Khattab (may Allah be pleased with them both) asked, "O
father, where and when shall I see you again?" 'Umar said, "In the next
world." 'Abd Allah said, "I would it were sooner." He said, "You will see me
in a dream tonight, tomorrow night, or the next night." Twelve years passed
by without his appearing in a dream. Then one night he saw him in a dream
and said, "O father, did you not say that within three nights I should see
you?" He said, "O son, I was occupied, because in the country around Baghdad a bridge had become dilapidated and officials had not attended to repairing it. One day a sheep's forefoot fell into a hole on that bridge and was
broken. Till now I have been answering for that."

Of a certainty The Master of the World[3] (may Allah perpetuate his
reign) should know that on that great day he will be asked to answer for all
those of God's creatures who are under his command, and if he tries to transfer [his responsibility] to someone else he will not be listened to. Since this is
so it behoves the king not to leave this important matter to anyone else, and
not to disregard the state of God's creatures. To the best of his ability let him
ever acquaint himself, secretly and openly, with their conditions; let him protect them from extortionate hands, and preserve them from cruel tyrants, so
that the blessings resulting from those actions may come about in the time of
his rule, if Allah wills. . . .

They say that when Qubad the king died Nushirwan (The Just), who
was his son, succeeded to the throne; he was only eighteen years old, yet he
reigned as king. He was a youth whose character had been trained in justice
right from infancy; he recognized evil things as evil and he knew what was
good. He always used to say, "My father is weak in judgment and simple
hearted; he is quickly deceived. He has left the country to the hands of officials and they are doing whatever they please; so the country is being ruined
and the treasury emptied; they are embezzling the revenue, and the shame
and guilt will be for ever upon his neck." Qubad completely succumbed to the
wiles of Mazdak; similarly he was deceived by two men—a governor and a
tax-collector—who together had ruined their province and impoverished the
peasantry by illegal extortions; such was his love of money that when they
proffered him a purse of dinars he was seduced and satisfied; he had not sufficient discernment to question them and to say [to the one], "You are the governor and the commander of this province. I assigned you such proportion of
the provincial revenue as would suffice for the pay, rations and clothing of
you and your retinue; I am sure that you will have extracted the full amount
from the people. Then what is this surplus which you have brought to me? I
know that you did not inherit it from your father; it is all what you have ille-

[3] Malik-shah.

gally extorted from the people." Nor did he speak likewise to the tax-collector, saying, "The revenue of the province is so much; some of it you have used for [encashing] drafts and some you have sent to the treasury. This surplus which I see you have—where did you obtain that? Is it not part of your illegal extortions?" He never investigated such matters nor took suitable measures against the offenders so that others might have made a practice of honesty.

When three or four years of his reign had passed, the assignees and officials were still practising their wonted oppression, and complainants were clamouring at the king's threshold. Nushirwan The Just held court for the redress of wrongs and summoned all the nobles; he sat upon the throne and first gave thanks to God; then he said, "You know that God (to Him be power and glory) has granted me this kingdom; furthermore I inherited it from my father; and thirdly my uncle rebelled against me and I did battle with him and regained the throne by the sword. As God has bestowed the world upon me, so have I assigned it to you, and to each one have I given authority; I did not leave without a portion anyone who had deserved well of this dynasty; the nobles who had received high rank and command from my father were maintained in their rank and station, and I did not in any way reduce their degree or subsistence. I have constantly exhorted you to treat the people well and to gather only the due amount of taxes; I have guarded your honour but you have cared for nothing and listened to nothing; you do not fear God nor do you spare His creatures. Wherefore I fear retribution; I do not wish that your iniquity and injustice should redound upon the days of my reign. The world is free of enemies; you have prosperity and ease; therefore you ought to concentrate on thanksgiving to God for the benefits which He has bestowed upon you and upon us; for injustice brings about the decline of empires and ingratitude causes the stoppage of benefits. Henceforth there must be no ill-treatment of God's creatures; you must keep the peasants light-burdened and never oppress the weak; respect learned men, consort with the good, avoid the bad, and do no harm to those who mind their own business. I call upon God and the angels to be my witnesses that if any man follows a path contrary to this, I will not suffer him further." All said, "We will do as you say and obey your command."

A few days later they all returned to their posts. They engaged in the same injustice and oppression; they looked upon Nushirwan as a mere boy and each one in his arrogance imagined that it was he who had set Nushirwan upon the throne, and that he could at his own will regard him or not regard him as king. Nushirwan held his peace and continued to treat them with all external tokens of civility. So five years passed.

Now there was a certain army-commander, incomparably wealthy and affluent, whom Nushirwan The Just had made governor of Adharbaygan; in all the kingdom there was no more powerful commander, and nobody could match him in arms, horses and other paraphernalia. This man was seized with the desire to build a mansion and a garden in the city where he was stationed; in the environs of the city there was a piece of land belonging to an old woman, of such an extent that the income from it sufficed for her to pay the royal quota and for the cultivator to take his share, while enough remained to provide her with four loaves of bread for every day of the year; one loaf she exchanged for other eatables, and one for oil for her lamp; then she ate one loaf for breakfast and one for supper; people took pity on her and gave her clothing; she never went outside her house but passed her life in retirement and poverty. Now it suited this army-commander to include that piece of land in the rest of his property; he sent someone to the wretched old woman to say, "Sell this piece of land as I have need of it." The poor old woman said, "I will not sell it as I need it more; I have only this piece of land in all the world; it gives me my sustenance, and nobody sells his own sustenance." The man said, "I will pay you for it or else I will give you in exchange another piece of land which will provide just as much income and produce." The old woman said, "This land is my lawful property; I inherited it from my mother and father; the water-supply is near to it, and the neighbours are agreeable and kind to me. Any land which you may give me will not have these particular features. Keep your hands off my land." The army-commander did not listen to the old woman but he arbitrarily and forcibly seized the land and extended his garden wall around it so that it became part of his estate. The wretched old woman was helpless and reduced to indigence; she resigned herself to accepting payment for the land or else a substitute. She threw herself in front of the man and said, "Either give me the price or a substitute." He did not even look at her, but completely ignored her. The wretched old woman gave up hope and went away; and thereafter they did not admit her into his house. But every time the army-commander mounted and went out for recreation or hunting the old woman sat in his way; when he approached her, she called out and demanded payment for the land. He gave no answer but passed by at a distance. If she spoke to his retainers or companions or chamberlains, they said, "Very well; we will speak to him about it." But nobody ever did so. Two years passed after this.

The wretched old woman was reduced to extreme destitution; she found no justice and gave up hope of ever getting it from the man. She said to herself, "How long shall I hammer cold iron? Over every authority God has placed a higher authority; with all his tyranny this man is but a servant and minion of Nushirwan The Just. I will contrive by whatever means I can, no matter what hardships I may suffer, to make my way to Mada'in, throw myself in front of Nushirwan, and acquaint him of my case; maybe I shall obtain justice from him." She told no one of her designs, but secretly set out and with great trouble and difficulty went from Adharbaygan to Mada'in; when she saw Nushirwan's palace she said to herself, "They will never let me go in there; they refused to let me enter the house of the governor of Adharbaygan, and he is a mere servant of this sovereign; so how should they allow me to enter the palace of him who is the lord of the world? I had better find a lodging in this vicinity and enquire when the king will go out riding; perhaps I can throw myself at his feet and present my petition."

By chance the army-commander who had seized the old woman's land came to the court, and King Nushirwan decided to go hunting. The old woman found out that the king was going to a certain hunting-ground on such-and-such a day. She set off and by constant enquiry and strenuous effort made her way to the hunting-ground; she sat down behind a straw [screen] and slept the night. The next day Nushirwan arrived; the nobles and retainers scattered over the country and began the chase. Nushirwan stayed behind with one arms-bearer; he was just riding off to the hunt, when the old woman, seeing the king alone, got up from behind the screen and approached him; she handed him the petition and said, "O king, if you rule the world, give justice to this poor wretch; read her petition and learn her case." When Nushirwan saw the old woman and heard her speak, he knew that she would not have come to the hunting-ground except out of dire necessity; he rode towards her, took her petition and read it. Tears came into his eyes and he said to her, "Do not worry any more; up to now this has been your affair; now that we know about it, it has become our responsibility. We shall satisfy your want; then we shall send you home. Rest a few days here as you have come a long way." He looked round and saw one of his grooms coming along mounted on a riding-mule; he said, "Dismount and set this woman on your mule; take her to a village, hand her over to the headman and tell him to look after her; then come back quickly. When we return from hunting take her from the village to the city and keep her in your own house. Allow her two maunds of bread and one maund of meat, daily, and let her have five gold dinars a month from our treasury, until such time as I call for her." The groom did so.

As he returned from the chase King Nushirwan spent the whole day pondering how he should contrive a means of examining this case without the knowledge of any of the courtiers. So one afternoon at the time of the siesta, when everyone was asleep and the palace was deserted, he ordered a servant to go to such-and-such a tent and summon a certain page. The servant went and brought the page; the king said, "O page, you know that I have many worthy pages; I have particularly chosen you to be entrusted with a certain task. You must draw some money from the treasury for your expenses, and go to Adharbaygan; you should lodge in a certain quarter of a certain city and stay for twenty days; you will pretend to the inhabitants that you have come in search of a runaway page. You should associate with all kinds of people, and as you mix with them in drunkenness and sobriety, in the course of conversation enquire about an old woman called so-and-so, who used to live in their district and seems to have disappeared; find out where she went and what she did with the piece of land which she had; listen to what each person says, remember it well and bring back a verified report. This is the true object of your mission; but tomorrow I shall summon you to the court before the nobles and say to you in a loud voice for all to hear: Go, draw money for expenses from the treasury, and travel to Adharbaygan; each city and district that you reach, take note and enquire about the state of the cereals and fruits this year; see whether any celestial calamity has befallen or not, and at the same time look at the condition of the pastures and hunting-grounds. Come back without delay and report what you find without letting anyone know why I sent you." The page said, "I will obey your command."

The next day Nushirwan did thus. The page departed and went to that city. He stayed there twenty days, enquiring about the old woman from everyone he talked to. They all said, "That old woman was of good family and gentle manners; formerly we used to see her with her husband and children; but the husband and children all died and she was left alone in reduced circumstances with only a piece of land which she inherited. She gave the land to a peasant to cultivate and the produce from it was just enough for her to pay the royal quota and the peasant's share; the portion which remained sufficed until the next harvest to provide her with a ration of four loaves a day; she exchanged one loaf for other eatables and one for oil for her lamp; then she ate one loaf for breakfast and one for supper. Now the governor desired to make a garden with a pavilion and a fine view. He forcibly seized her plot of land and incorporated it in his estate; he neither paid for it nor offered a substitute. For a year the old woman kept going to his house, crying out and demanding payment; nobody listened to her, and now it is some time since anyone saw her in this city; we do not know where she has gone, whether she is dead or alive."

The page returned to the capital. Nushirwan The Just had begun audience; the page entered and bowed; Nushirwan said, "Ah! tell us what you found." He said, "Thanks to Your Majesty the crops are good everywhere this year; no calamity has befallen; the pastures are fresh and the hunting-grounds well stocked." The king said, "Praise be to Allah! You have brought good news." When the people had dispersed and the palace was empty of strangers, the page related the story of the old woman according to what he had heard. Nushirwan was convinced that what the old woman had said was true. All that day and night he could not sleep from anxiety and distress. Next day early he called for the great chamberlain and instructed him that, when the nobles began to arrive, if a certain one came in, he was to keep him in the vestibule until he told him what to do.

When all the nobles and priests arrived at the audience-hall, the chamberlain did as Nushirwan had ordered. Nushirwan appeared and gave audience. After some time he turned to the nobles and priests and said, "I wish to ask you something; answer me truthfully according to your lights and judgment." They said, "We will obey." He said, "This man (of such-and-such a name) who is the army-commander of Adharbaygan, how great is his wealth in gold coin?" They said, "He probably has 2,000,000 dinars which he does not need." He said, "How about household furnishings and chattels?" They said, "He has

500,000 dinars' worth of gold and silver articles." He said, "And jewels?" They said, "600,000 dinars' worth." He said, "What about landed property, estates and farms?" They said, "In Khurasan, 'Iraq, Pars and Adharbaygan there is not a district or city where he does not possess a dozen estates, mills, caravanserais, hot-baths and farms." He said, "How many horses and mules has he?" They said, "Thirty thousand." He said, "Sheep?" They said, "Two hundred thousand." He said, "Camels?" They said, "Thirty thousand." He said, "Slaves and hirelings?" They said, "He owns 1,700 Turkish, Rumi and Abyssinian pages and 400 slave-girls." He said, "A man who has this amount of wealth and every day eats twenty different dishes of lamb, sweetmeats and rich concoctions, while another human being, a devout servant of God (to Him be power and glory), weak, friendless, helpless, having in all the world only two loaves of dry bread to eat, one for morning and one for evening—supposing the rich man unlawfully seized the other's two dry loaves and deprived him of them, what would he deserve?" All said, "He would deserve every punishment; whatever penalty he were made to suffer, it would be less than justice." Nushirwan said, "I require you immediately to strip the skin from that man's body, throw his flesh to the dogs, stuff the skin with straw and hang it upon the palace gate. Then let it be proclaimed for seven days that hereafter if any man commits oppression, taking even a bag of straw, a chicken or a handful of grass wrongfully from somebody else, and if a complainant comes to the court, the same will happen to him as happened to this man." They did as Nushirwan commanded.

He told the groom to bring the old woman. Then he said to the nobles, "This is the injured party; and there is the oppressor who has met his reward." To the page whom he had sent to Adharbaygan he said, "O page, why did I send you to Adharbaygan?" He said, "To investigate the case of this old woman and her complaint, and to bring Your Majesty a true and exact report." Then Nushirwan said to the nobles, "So that you may know that I have not inflicted this punishment wantonly, [I warn you that] hereafter I shall not deal with oppressors except by the sword; I shall protect the ewes and lambs from the wolves, I shall restrain grasping hands, I shall remove evil-doers from the face of the earth and fill the world with justice and equity, for this is the task for which I was born. If it were right for men to do as they wished, God would not have created the king and appointed him over them. So now strive to do no act that would lead to your suffering the same fate as this criminal." All those present were so awed by the king's majesty and authority that they nearly died of fear. He said to the old woman, "I have punished him who wronged you, and his mansion and the garden which contains your piece of land are now granted to you; I am also giving you animals and money so that you can return home to your own city in safety with my warrant, and I trust that you will remember me in your prayers." Then he addressed the company, saying, "Why is it that the door of my palace is open for oppressors and closed to the oppressed? Soldiers and peasants are all my underlings and labourers; nay, the peasants are the givers and the soldiers are the takers; so the door ought to be open wider for the giver than for the taker. Now one of the current irregularities, injustices and unofficial practices is that when a complainant comes to the court, he is not allowed to come before me and state his case. If the old woman had gained access to me here, she would not have needed to go to the hunting-ground." Then the king commanded that a chain should be set up with bells attached to it, within the reach of even a child of seven years old, so that any complainants who came to the court would not need to see a chamberlain; they would pull the chain and the bells would ring; Nushirwan would hear it and redress their grievances. This was done.

When the nobles and army chiefs left the palace and returned to their homes, they straightaway summoned their stewards and underlings and said, "See how much you have unjustly extorted in the last two years, whose blood you have shed, and whom you have harmed in drunkenness and sobriety; we must all stand together in this and satisfy our creditors before anyone goes to the court and complains against us." So they all set to and politely summoned their creditors or called at their houses and satisfied every one either with apologies or indemnities; they also took signed statements to the effect that so-and-so had received satisfaction from so-and-so and had no further claim upon him. By this single exercise of his authority Nushirwan The Just reduced his whole kingdom to order; he eliminated oppression and all the world was so relieved that seven years passed without anyone coming to the court to complain of injustice.

Seven years later one afternoon when the palace was empty and everyone had gone, and the guards were asleep, the bells began to ring; Nushirwan heard them and at once sent two servants to see who had come to complain. When they reached the palace gate they saw an old donkey, lean and scabby, which had come inside the gate and was rubbing its back on the chain. The servants went back and said, "There is no complainant, but only a scabby donkey which is rubbing itself on the chain." Nushirwan said, "O fools that you are! it is not as you think; when you look at it well, even this ass has come to seek justice. I desire you both to go, take the ass into the middle of the bazaar; ask everyone about its history and let me know." The servants went out, took the donkey into the bazaar and asked the people if there was anyone who could tell them about it. All said, "Yes, by Allah, there is hardly anybody in the city who does not know this donkey." They said, "What do you know about it?" They said, "It belongs to a certain washerman, and for about twenty years we have seen him with it; every day he used to put people's clothes on its back and take them to the washing-place, and bring them back in the evening. As long as the donkey was young and could do its work, he used to feed it; now that it has grown old and incapable of work, he has disowned it and turned it out of his house; it is now a year and a half since he set it loose;

night and day it wanders through the streets, bazaars and quarters of the city; people feed it out of charity, but for two days it has failed to get any food and is roaming in vain."

Since the servants heard the same story from everyone they asked, they soon went back and informed the king. Nushirwan said, "Did I not tell you this ass had come to seek redress? Look after it well tonight and tomorrow bring the washerman to me together with four headmen from his quarter, and I will deal with him as necessary." The next day the servants did so; they brought the ass and the washerman together with four headmen in front of Nushirwan at the time of audience; Nushirwan said to the washerman, "As long as this poor donkey was young and could work for you, you used to feed it and look after it; now that it has grown old and can no longer work, you have cut off its fodder, given it its freedom, and turned it out of your house. So where are his rights for his twenty years' service?" He ordered the man to be given forty lashes, and said, "As long as this donkey is alive, every day in the presence of these four men you must give it as much straw and barley as it can eat, and if you fail and I come to know of it, I shall punish you severely, so that you may know that kings have always been concerned for the rights of the weak and watchful of the doings of officers, assignees and pages, for the sake of their reputation in this world and salvation in the next."

5.   IBN AL-QALĀNISI: THE ASSASSINS (c. 1100-1130)[1]

The rise of a fanatical religious sect, the Bātinīs, in northern Syria about 1090, shows how far the fragmentation of Islam could go. The Bātinīs were the schismatic offshoot of a schism, that of the Fātimids, established in northwest Africa in 909 and in Egypt in 972, chief competitors of the Abbāsid Caliphs of Baghdad for the leadership of Islam. The Bātinīs were terrorists, who murdered Abbāsids, Fātimids, Turks, and Crusaders with a fine impartiality. They spread all over the Middle East and were not crushed until the coming of the Mongols in the thirteenth century. Their popular name, the Assassins, comes from the probably apocryphal stories told about them by the Crusaders. The word *assassin* is derived from the word *hashish*, which the Bātinīs were supposed to take in order to nerve themselves for murder and martyrdom.

[1] *The Damascus Chronicle of the Crusades,* extracted and trans. by H. A. R. Gibb from the *Chronicle* of Ibn al-Qalānisī (London, Luzac & Company Ltd., 1932), pp. 57-58, 145-146, 179-180, 187-195.

A good picture of their early activities is given by Ibn al-Qalānisī (c. 1070-1160) in his *Damascus Chronicle*, a valuable contemporary account of the wars between the Moslems and the first Crusaders.

In this year[2] also news was received from Hims that its lord, the amīr Janāh al-Dawla Husain Atābek on descending from the citadel to the mosque for the Friday prayer, surrounded by his principal officers with full armour, and occupying his place of prayer, according to custom, was set upon by three Persians belonging to the Bātinīya. They were accompanied by a shaikh, to whom they owed allegiance and obedience, and all of them were dressed in the garb of ascetics. When the shaikh gave the signal they attacked the amīr with their knives and killed both him and a number of his officers. There were in the mosque at the time ten Sūfīs,[3] Persians and others; they were suspected of complicity in the crime, and were straightway executed in cold blood, every man of them, although they were innocent. The people of Hims were greatly perturbed at this event, and at once dispersed in panic. Most of the Turks amongst the inhabitants fled to Damascus, and everything fell into confusion. The townsfolk then wrote to the king Shams al-Mulūk at Damascus, begging him to send an officer to take over the town and be responsible for its defence, before the news reached the Franks and their covetous desires extended to it. The king Shams al-Mulūk and Zahīr al-Dīn Atābek thereupon set out with the 'askar from Damascus, reached Hims, took possession of it, and occupied the citadel. At the same time the Franks arrived at Hims and encamped at al-Rastan, with the intention of cutting off and besieging the town, but on learning what had taken place, they kept at a discreet distance and eventually withdrew.

Now the person known as al-Hakīm al-Munajjim the Bātinī, a member of the entourage of the king Fakhr al-Mulūk Rudwān, lord of Aleppo, was the first to profess the doctrines of the Bātinīya in Aleppo and Syria, and it was he who commissioned the three men to kill Janāh al-Dawla at Hims. The news of his death arrived fourteen days after this event. . . .

The Bātinīya had by now[4] become strong in Aleppo and their power there was formidable. Ibn Badī', the chief of the gens d'armes in Aleppo, and the principal men of the town were afraid of them because of their numbers, the strength of their corporate organization, and the protection which they assured by their numbers to those of their sect who sought their help. Al-Hakīm al-Munajjim and Abū Tāhir the goldsmith were the first who openly professed this detestable doctrine in Syria, in the days of the king Rudwān. They sought to gain his sympathy by deceitful devices and intrigues, and were supported

---

[2] A.H. 496 (15 October 1102–4 October 1103).

[3] A great ascetic and quietistic movement in Islam, the Sūfīs represented a reaction against official Moslem theology in the direction of a more mystical religion.

[4] By 1114.

by a great host of the Ismā 'īlīs of Sarmīn, the Jawr, Jabal al-Summāq, and
Banū 'Ulaim. Ibn Badī', the prefect of Aleppo, set himself to speak with the
king Alp-Arslān son of Rudwān about their movement, and reached a decision
with him to use rigorous measures against them and root them out. In pursu-
ance of this design, he arrested Abū Tāhir the goldsmith and all the adherents
of his sect, about two hundred souls. Abū Tāhir the goldsmith was immediately put to death, along with the missionary Ismā 'īl, and the brother of al-
Hakīm al-Munajjim, and the other leaders in their movement who have been
referred to. The remainder were imprisoned and their properties were confiscated. Some of these were interceded for, some were set free, some were
thrown from the top of the citadel, and some were executed. A number escaped, fled to the Franks,[5] and dispersed throughout the country. . . .

In this year[6] also the position of Bahrām, the propagandist of the Bātinīya,
grew so formidable that he became a factor to be reckoned with in Aleppo and
Syria. He lived in extreme concealment and secrecy, and continually dis-
guised himself, so that he moved from city to city and castle to castle without
anyone being aware of his identity, until he appeared in Damascus in pursu-
ance of an agreement which Najm al-Dīn Il-Ghāzī son of Ortuq had made
with the amīr Zahīr al-Dīn Atābek, and with a letter containing strong recom-
mendations on his behalf. He was received with honour as a measure of precaution against his malice and that of his organization, and every consideration
was shown him, and protection was assured him after suffering many
vicissitudes of fortune. He moved about from place to place and gained a
following among the ignorant and witless mob, and foolish peasantry, men
lacking both intelligence and religion, who sought in him and his party a
means of protecting themselves and injuring others. He found an ally in the
Wazīr Abū 'Alī Tāhir b. Sa 'd al-Mazdaqānī, who, even though he was not of
his way of thinking, assisted him to spread his malicious devices and to manifest his secret objects. When his organization came into the open and extended
far and wide, and this wazīr of Zahīr al-Dīn consented to become an accomplice in his activities and to strengthen his hands in his operations, he requested of Zahīr al-Dīn Atābek a castle in which to take refuge and a fortress
in which to defend himself. Zahīr al-Dīn accordingly delivered up to him the
frontier fort of Bānyās in Dhu'l-Qa 'da 520 (November to December, 1126),
and when he had established himself in it, he was joined there by his rabble
of varlets, half-wits, peasants, low fellows and vile scum, whom he had seduced
by his lying and his false pretensions, and had won over to his side by his
intrigues and deceits. This public establishment of their cause created a
grievous calamity and a public terror; men of learning, piety, and religious
authority, the people of the Sunna and the Tradition of the Fathers, and true
Believers of honourable and peaceful life were sore distressed, and none of
them dared say a word about these people or complain about any man of them,

[5] The Crusaders.
[6] A.D. 1126.

in order to ward off their malice and guard against their vengeance upon him. For they set about killing all those who opposed them, and supporting all who gave them assistance in their impious ways, so that neither Sultan nor Wazīr would condemn them, nor could any general or amīr break the edge of their malice. . . .

A sufficient account has already been given of Bahrām, the missioner of the Bātinīya, and the cause which necessitated the deliverance to him of the frontier castle of Bānyās. When he had established himself in Bānyās he set about fortifying it and rebuilding what of it was in ruins or out of repair. In all directions he dispatched his missionaries, who enticed a great multitude of the ignorant folk of the provinces and foolish peasantry from the villages and the rabble and scum, persons without intelligence to restrain them from mischief or fear of God to prevent them from wrong-doing. Their evil power was thereby increased and the true nature of their false doctrine made manifest; their hands and tongues were lengthened with slander and abuse against the men of repute amongst the subjects, and with greed and spoliation against lonely travellers on the highways, whom they seized with violence and used despitefully, and with the slaying of men outrageously and unjustly. They were assisted to these depths of misdoing by the wazīr Abū 'Alī Tāhir b. Sa 'd al-Mazdaqānī, who carried his partisanship to extreme lengths. But he suffered the dire consequences and bitter penalty of his action when an agreement was established between him and Bahrām the missioner to furnish [one another with] aid and support—an agreement made in flat disregard of and disobedience to God, and inspired by the desire to take joint action against those who sought to injure them and pursue a common aim against those who had evil designs upon them. Tāj al-Mulūk[7] was by no means pleased at this nor did he consent to it; but sound statesmanship, a strong spirit of forbearance, and penetrating knowledge moved him to close his eyes, with whatever pain, to their activities and to bear patiently their rankling injury. Meanwhile he secretly meditated taking steps against them, without disclosing his design until such time as he should find an opportunity which facilitated his object and a clear predominance over the enemies of God, whereupon the opportunity would be seized and the quarry hunted down.

Now it chanced that Bahrām the missioner, since it was the will of God that he should perish, conceived the idea of slaying Baraq b. Jandal, one of the chiefs in Wādī'l-Taim, not for any cause which impelled him to do so, or for any crime which required him to take action against him, but in sheer disregard of the fate of tyrants who shed inviolate human blood and in culpable ignorance of the warning of God to those who seek to do so and venture upon it in His words "And whoso slayeth a Believer of set purpose, his recompense shall be Hell, to dwell therein to eternity; God shall be wrath with him and shall curse him, and shall make ready for him a mighty chastisement." So Bahrām used deceit with Baraq until he came into his hands, when he put

[7] Son and successor of Zahīr al-Din as atābek or regent at Damascus.

him in fetters and killed him in cold blood. There was general lamentation at the murder in this way of such a man notwithstanding his youth, his gallantry, and personal beauty, and imprecations and reproofs were openly uttered against his murderer in all gatherings and assemblies, and by all, both far and near. His brother Dahhāk b. Jandal, with his clan and family, impelled by the ardour of their Muslim pride and their passion for the honour of the family to seek revenge for his blood, assembled and made a compact together and swore to one another to remain steadfast in meeting their enemies, to devote themselves to the pursuit of their vendetta and to spend their lifeblood and their souls in attaining their revenge. They set about making preparations to this end with steadfastness and watchfulness for an opportunity, until their predestined doom laid Bahrām and his band by the heels, and God decreed their uprooting and extirpation.

With forces gathered together from all quarters, and swelled by adherents who came in from every side, Bahrām marched out from Bānyās in the year 522[8] and made in the direction of Wādī'l-Taim in order to crush these persons of whom we have spoken, but they were prepared to meet him and watching for an opportunity to engage him in battle. When they were made aware of his approach to them, they rose to meet him in a body like lions rising from their lairs to defend their cubs, and flew at them as mountain-hawks at partridges. On approaching his broken faction and Godforsaken host they charged upon them when they were in their camp and off their guard. Shouting the battlecry, they took them unawares, and ere the horseman could mount his steed or the footsoldier could seize his weapons death overtook the greater part of the Bātinīs, by smiting with the sword, abrading with the poniards of fate, sprinkling with the arrows of destruction, and stoning with the rocks of predestination.

Bahrām meanwhile was in his tent, surrounded by a company of his partners in his folly and error, ignorant of what had encompassed him and his sectaries. On hearing the uproar and shouting they had leapt up to seize their weapons, but the men of Wādī'l-Taim rushed upon them with their keen swords and death-dealing poniards and killed the whole company. Bahrām's head and hand were cut off, after he had been dissected by swords and knives, and one of the slayers who took these, along with his ring, to Egypt, carrying the joyful tidings of his death and destruction, was vested with a robe of honour and rewarded. The news of this event spread far and wide, and all the people were united in joy and congratulation at their destruction, and derived the fullest share of pleasure from this victory.

In consequence of this, the numbers of the Bātinīs were diminished and their power of offence was weakened. The place of Bahrām was taken by his friend Ismā 'īl the Persian, his comrade in error and violence, and his accomplice in intrigue and rebellion, who set about enticing the witless, exactly as Bahrām had done, and even surpassed him in folly to an extent which made plain the weakness of his intelligence and his malignity. Round him gathered

[8] A.D. 1128.

the remnants of the abominable sect from all provinces and districts, and all those of them who were scattered throughout the country. The wazīr Abū 'Alī Tāhir b. Sa 'd al-Mazdaqānī maintained towards Ismā 'īl the same policy as he had observed towards Bahrām, by assisting him to achieve his purposes, in order to guard himself against their malice and out of desire for his own safety, not knowing that the end of such actions is bitter repentance and wide digression from the path of security. As it has been said, "Many an one who gives himself up is saved by his surrender, and many an one who guards against evil finds therein his bane." The complaints of the people, men of rank and commons alike, continued to multiply, and their losses at the hands of the deluded fanatics to succeed one another, until Tāj al-Mulūk, son of Zahīr al-Dīn Atābek, set about their extirpation and whetted the blade of his determination to purify the provinces of them. He considered that the most advisable step necessitated by his plans for attaining this object was to make away in the first instance with the wazīr Abū 'Alī, since he was the most certain mark at which to aim and the first to be sought. He therefore laid upon one of his household officers in whom he had confidence the duty of killing him, and arranged with him that he should strike his head with a sword when he himself gave him the signal. On Wednesday 17th Ramadān 523 (4th September, 1129), the wazīr presented himself as usual with all the amīrs and commanders in the Rose Pavilion at the Palace of the Citadel at Damascus, and various matters were transacted and discussed in the council with Tāj al-Mulūk and those present, until the hour of their withdrawal and return to their houses. The wazīr rose to withdraw after them, according to his custom, and at that moment Tāj al-Mulūk gave the signal to his antagonist, who struck his head several blows with his sword and killed him. His head was then cut off, carried with his dead body to the ashheap at the Iron Gate, and thrown upon it, that all the people might see the act of God upon one who plotted and sought other helpers than Him. His body was burned with fire some days later, and reduced to ashes strewn by the winds. "This is the reward for that which his hands wrought, and God is not unjust towards His creatures."

The report of this spread immediately, and the town bands at Damascus, assisted by the mob and the refuse of the city, rose with swords and naked poniards and put to death all the Bātinīs and their adherents upon whom they could lay hands, and every person connected with them or related to them. They pursued them into their dwellings, fetched them out of their places, and dispatched them all either by dismemberment with swords or by slaughter with poniards, and they were thrown out upon the dungheaps like abandoned carrion. A large number of individuals among them who had taken refuge with various high quarters in order to protect themselves, and who hoped for safety through their intercession, were forcibly seized and their blood was shed without fear of consequences. By the next morning the quarters and streets of the city were cleared of the Bātinīs and the dogs were yelping and quarrelling over their limbs and corpses. "Verily in this is a sign to men of intelligence."

Amongst those who were captured was the man known as Shādī the freedman, the pupil of Abū Tāhir the Bātinī goldsmith who was formerly at Aleppo. This accursed freedman was the root of all the trouble and evil, and was repaid with the severest punishment, at which the hearts of many of the Believers were comforted. He was crucified, along with a few others of the sect, on the battlements of the wall of Damascus, in order that it might be seen how God had dealt with the oppressors and brought signal chastisement upon the infidels. The chamberlain Yūsuf b. Fīrūz, military governor of the town, and its worthy mayor, Thiqat al-Mulk Abū'l-Dhuwād Mufarrij b. al-Hasan ibn al-Sūfī, had displayed the utmost zeal in urging on the destruction of the abominable sectaries. They adopted in consequence elaborate precautions against the sudden onslaught of emissaries who might be sent against them from the Bātinīya of Alamūt,[9] the centre of the Bātinīya,[10] by wearing iron and surrounding themselves with large numbers of guards carrying quantities of weapons ready for action. So disaster came upon the evildoers and rejectors of God, and felicity to the upright and heedful of admonition.

As for Ismā 'īl the missioner, who was living at Bānyās, and those who were with him, when they heard the report of this disaster, they were filled with despair and humiliation and began to lay the blame upon one another, while their supporters dispersed throughout the country. Ismā 'īl himself, knowing that disaster threatened him if he remained at Bānyās and being unable to put up an obstinate resistance, sent to the Franks, promising to deliver up Bānyās to them, in order to seek safety with them. He surrendered it to them accordingly, and he with a number of others came into their hands and slunk away from Bānyās into the Frankish territories in the utmost abasement and wretchedness. Ismā 'īl was smitten by the disease of diarrhoea, and dying of it was buried in Bānyās at the beginning of the year 524. So this district was rid of them and purified from their uncleanness.

6.   AL-GHAZĀLI: FROM *DELIVERANCE FROM ERROR* (c. 1110)[1]

Appointed to teach at the University of Baghdad by Nizām-al-Mulk, Abu Hamid Muhammad al-Ghazālī (1058-1111) renounced the pursuit of learning and ambition to join the Sūfī movement. This was a reaction against the rigid ortho-

---

[9] A castle in northwestern Persia, which remained the mother-settlement of the Bātinīs from its capture by them in 1090 until the coming of the Mongols.

[10] A.D. 1130.

[1] W. Montgomery Watt, *The Faith and Practice of Al-Ghazālī* (London, George Allen & Unwin Ltd., 1953), pp. 27-30, 54-60.

doxy of traditional theology and was characterized by asceticism, mysticism, and neo-Platonic ideas. Al-Ghazali's brief autobiographical work, *Deliverance from Error,* from which the following extracts are taken, gives a vivid impression both of the intellectual and religious ferment in eleventh century Islam and of the mind of one of its greatest thinkers.

I commenced, then, with the science of Theology, and obtained a thorough grasp of it. I read the books of sound theologians and myself wrote some books on the subject. But it was a science, I found, which, though attaining its own aim, did not attain mine. Its aim was merely to preserve the creed of orthodoxy and to defend it against the deviations of heretics.

Now God sent to His servants by the mouth of His messenger, in the Qur'an and Traditions, a creed which is the truth and whose contents are the basis of man's welfare in both religious and secular affairs. But Satan too sent, in the suggestions of heretics, things contrary to orthodoxy; men tended to accept his suggestions and almost corrupted the true creed for its adherents. So God brought into being the class of theologians, and moved them to support traditional orthodoxy with the weapon of systematic argument by laying bare the confused doctrines invented by the heretics at variance with traditional orthodoxy. This is the origin of theology and theologians.

In due course a group of theologians performed the task to which God invited them; they successfully preserved orthodoxy, defended the creed received from the prophetic source and rectified heretical innovations. Nevertheless in so doing they based their arguments on premises which they took from their opponents and which they were compelled to admit by naïve belief, or the consensus of the community, or bare acceptance of Qur'an and Traditions. For the most part their efforts were devoted to making explicit the contradictions of their opponents and criticizing them in respect of the logical consequences of what they admitted.

This was of little use in the case of one who admitted nothing at all save logically necessary truths. Theology was not adequate to my case and was unable to cure the malady of which I complained. It is true that, when theology appeared as a recognized discipline and much effort had been expended in it over a considerable period of time, the theologians, becoming very earnest in their endeavours to defend orthodoxy by the study of what things really are, embarked on a study of substances and accidents with their nature and properties. But, since that was not the aim of their science, they did not deal with the question thoroughly in their thinking and consequently did not arrive at results sufficient to dispel universally the darkness of confusion due to the different views of men. I do not exclude the possibility that for others than myself these results have been sufficient; indeed, I do not doubt that this has been so for quite a number. But these results were mingled with naïve belief in certain matters which are not included among first principles.

My purpose here, however, is to describe my own case, not to disparage those who sought a remedy thereby, for the healing drugs vary with the disease. How often one sick man's medicine proves to be another's poison!

After I had done with theology I started on philosophy. I was convinced that a man cannot grasp what is defective in any of the sciences unless he has so complete a grasp of the science in question that he equals its most learned exponents in the appreciation of its fundamental principles, and even goes beyond and surpasses them, probing into some of the tangles and profundities which the very professors of the science have neglected. Then and only then is it possible that what he has to assert about its defects is true.

So far as I could see none of the doctors of Islam had devoted thought and attention to philosophy. In their writings none of the theologians engaged in polemic against the philosophers, apart from obscure and scattered utterances so plainly erroneous and inconsistent that no person of ordinary intelligence would be likely to be deceived, far less one versed in the sciences.

I realized that to refute a system before understanding it and becoming acquainted with its depths is to act blindly. I therefore set out in all earnestness to acquire a knowledge of philosophy from books, by private study without the help of an instructor. I made progress towards this aim during my hours of free time after teaching in the religious sciences and writing, for at this period I was burdened with the teaching and instruction of three hundred students in Baghdad. By my solitary reading during the hours thus snatched God brought me in less than two years to a complete understanding of the sciences of the philosophers. Thereafter I continued to reflect assiduously for nearly a year on what I had assimilated, going over it in my mind again and again and probing its tangled depths, until I comprehended surely and certainly how far it was deceitful and confusing and how far true and a representation of reality. . . .

When I had finished with these sciences, I next turned with set purpose to the method of mysticism (or Sūfism). I knew that the complete mystic "way" includes both intellectual belief and practical activity; the latter consists in getting rid of the obstacles in the self and in stripping off its base characteristics and vicious morals, so that the heart may attain to freedom from what is not God and to constant recollection of Him.

The intellectual belief was easier to me than the practical activity. I began to acquaint myself with their belief by reading their books, such as *The Food of the Hearts* by Abū Tālib al-Makkī (God have mercy upon him), the works of al-Hārith al-Muhāsibī, the various anecdotes about al-Junayd, ash-Shiblī and Abū Yazīd al-Bistāmī (may God sanctify their spirits), and other discourses of their leading men. I thus comprehended their fundamental teachings on the intellectual side, and progressed, as far as is possible by study and oral instruction, in the knowledge of mysticism. It became clear to me, however, that what is most distinctive of mysticism is something which cannot be apprehended by study, but only by immediate experience, by ecstasy and by a moral change. What a difference there is between *knowing* the definition of health and satiety, together with their causes and presuppositions, and *being* healthy and satisfied! What a difference between being acquainted with the definition of drunkenness—namely, that it designates a state arising from the domination of the seat of the intellect by vapours arising from the stomach—and being drunk. Indeed, the drunken man while in that condition does not know the definition of drunkenness nor the scientific account for it; he has not the very least scientific knowledge of it. The sober man, on the other hand, knows the definition of drunkenness and its basis, yet he is not drunk in the very least. Again the doctor, when he is himself ill, knows the definition and causes of health and the remedies which restore it, and yet is lacking in health. Similarly there is a difference between knowing the true nature and causes and conditions of the ascetic life and actually leading such a life and forsaking the world.

I apprehended clearly that the mystics were men who had real experiences, not men of words, and that I had already progressed as far as was possible by way of intellectual apprehension. What remained for me was not to be attained by oral instruction and study but only by immediate experience and by walking in the mystic way.

Now from the sciences I had laboured at and the paths I had traversed in my investigation of the revelational and rational sciences (that is, presumably, theology and philosophy), there had come to me a sure faith in God most high, in prophethood (or revelation), and in the Last Day. These three credal principles were firmly rooted in my being, not through any carefully argued proofs, but by reason of various causes, coincidences and experiences which are not capable of being stated in detail.

It had already become clear to me that I had no hope of the bliss of the world to come save through a Godfearing life and the withdrawal of myself from vain desire. It was clear to me too that the key to all this was to sever the attachment of the heart to worldly things by leaving the mansion of deception and returning to that of eternity, and to advance towards God most high with all earnestness. It was also clear that this was only to be achieved by turning away from wealth and position and fleeing from all time-consuming entanglements.

Next I considered the circumstances of my life, and realized that I was caught in a veritable thicket of attachments. I also considered my activities, of which the best was my teaching and lecturing, and realized that in them I was dealing with sciences that were unimportant and contributed nothing to the attainment of eternal life.

After that I examined my motive in my work of teaching, and realized that it was not a pure desire for the things of God, but that the impulse moving me was the desire for an influential position and public recognition. I saw for certain that I was on the brink of a crumbling bank of sand and in imminent danger of hell-fire unless I set about to mend my ways.

I reflected on this continuously for a time, while the choice still remained open to me. One day I would form the resolution to quit Baghdad and get rid of these adverse circumstances; the next day I would abandon my resolution. I put one foot forward and drew the other back. If in the morning I had a genuine longing to seek eternal life, by the evening the attack of a whole host of desires had reduced it to impotence. Worldly desires were striving to keep me by their chains just where I was, while the voice of faith was calling, "To the road! to the road! What is left of life is but little and the journey before you is long. All that keeps you busy, both intellectually and practically, is but hypocrisy and delusion. If you do not prepare *now* for eternal life, when will you prepare? If you do not now sever these attachments, when will you sever them?" On hearing that, the impulse would be stirred and the resolution made to take to flight.

Soon, however, Satan would return. "This is a passing mood," he would say; "do not yield to it, for it will quickly disappear; if you comply with it and leave this influential position, these comfortable and dignified circumstances where you are free from troubles and disturbances, this state of safety and security where you are untouched by the contentions of your adversaries, then you will probably come to yourself again and will not find it easy to return to all this."

For nearly six months beginning with Rajab 488 A.H. (=July 1095 A.D.), I was continuously tossed about between the attractions of worldly desires and the impulses towards eternal life. In that month the matter ceased to be one of choice and became one of compulsion. God caused my tongue to dry up so that I was prevented from lecturing. One particular day I would make an effort to lecture in order to gratify the hearts of my following, but my tongue would not utter a single word nor could I accomplish anything at all.

This impediment in my speech produced grief in my heart, and at the same time my power to digest and assimilate food and drink was impaired; I could hardly swallow or digest a single mouthful of food. My powers became so weakened that the doctors gave up all hope of successful treatment. "This trouble arises from the heart," they said, "and from there it has spread through the constitution; the only method of treatment is that the anxiety which has come over the heart should be allayed."

Thereupon, perceiving my impotence and having altogether lost my power of choice, I sought refuge with God most high as one who is driven to Him, because he is without further resources of his own. He answered me, He who "answers him who is driven (to Him by affliction) when he calls upon Him" (Qur'an 27, 63). He made it easy for my heart to turn away from position and wealth, from children and friends. I openly professed that I had resolved to set out for Mecca, while privately I made arrangements to travel to Syria. I took this precaution in case the Caliph and all my friends should oppose my resolve to make my residence in Syria. This stratagem for my departure from Baghdad I gracefully executed, and had it in my mind never to return there. There was much talk about me among all the religious leaders of 'Iraq, since none of them would allow that withdrawal from such a state of life as I was in could have a religious cause, for they looked upon that as the culmination of a religious career; that was the sum of their knowledge.

Much confusion now came into people's minds as they tried to account for my conduct. Those at a distance from 'Iraq supposed that it was due to some apprehension I had of action by the government. On the other hand those who were close to the governing circles and had witnessed how eagerly and assiduously they sought me and how I withdrew from them and showed no great regard for what they said, would say, "This is a supernatural affair; it must be an evil influence which has befallen the people of Islam and especially the circle of the learned."

I left Baghdad, then. I distributed what wealth I had, retaining only as much as would suffice myself and provide sustenance for my children. This I could easily manage, as the wealth of 'Iraq was available for good works, since it constitutes a trust fund for the benefit of the Muslims. Nowhere in the world have I seen better financial arrangements to assist a scholar to provide for his children.

In due course I entered Damascus, and there I remained for nearly two years with no other occupation than the cultivation of retirement and solitude, together with religious and ascetic exercises, as I busied myself purifying my soul, improving my character and cleansing my heart for the constant recollection of God most high, as I had learnt from my study of mysticism. I used to go into retreat for a period in the mosque of Damascus, going up the minaret of the mosque for the whole day and shutting myself in so as to be alone.

At length I made my way from Damascus to the Holy House (that is, Jerusalem). There I used to enter into the precinct of the Rock every day and shut myself in.

Next there arose in me a prompting to fulfil the duty of the Pilgrimage, gain the blessings of Mecca and Medina, and perform the visitation of the Messenger of God most high (peace be upon him), after first performing the visitation of al-Khalīl, the Friend of God (God bless him).[2] I therefore made the journey to the Hijaz. Before long, however, various concerns, together with the entreaties of my children, drew me back to my home (country); and so I came to it again, though at one time no one had seemed less likely than myself to return to it. Here, too, I sought retirement, still longing for solitude and the purification of the heart for the recollection (of God). The events of the interval, the anxieties about my family, and the necessities of my livelihood altered the aspect of my purpose and impaired the quality of my solitude, for I experienced pure ecstasy only occasionally, although I did not cease to hope for that; obstacles would hold me back, yet I always returned to it.

[2] That is, Abraham, who is buried in the cave of Machpelah under the mosque at Hebron, which is called 'al-Khalīl' in Arabic; similarly the visitation of the Messenger is the formal visit to his tomb at Medina. [Translator's note.]

I continued at this stage for the space of ten years, and during these periods of solitude there were revealed to me things innumerable and unfathomable. This much I shall say about that in order that others may be helped: I learnt with certainty that it is above all the mystics who walk on the road of God; their life is the best life, their method the soundest method, their character the purest character; indeed, were the intellect of the intellectuals and the learning of the learned and the scholarship of the scholars, who are versed in the profundities of revealed truth, brought together in the attempt to improve the life and character of the mystics, they would find no way of doing so; for to the mystics all movement and all rest, whether external or internal, brings illumination from the light of the lamp of prophetic revelation; and behind the light of prophetic revelation there is no other light on the face of the earth from which illumination may be received.

V

MONARCHY IN THE WEST

Strong monarchy was to be the salvation of the medieval West, both against external attacks and internal disintegration. Its first major success was among the Franks, where a succession of powerful eighth-century rulers culminated in Charlemagne, whose domains included what is now France, Saxony, Switzerland, Bavaria, and northern and central Italy. This great king aroused the wonder both of his contemporaries and of posterity. His coronation in 800 at the hands of Pope Leo III was later regarded as marking the birth of the medieval empire, and despite the subsequent break in political continuity, German emperors thought of themselves as his rightful heirs. His military triumphs over Avars, Slavs, Saxons, and Frisians were remembered with nostalgia amid the swooping raids of Vikings and Moslems and the bloody invasions of the Magyars. His masterful way with his own subjects, laymen and ecclesiastics alike, commanded admiration in a period when the privileges of the aristocracy were hardening. Finally, his support of learning and demand for an educated clergy left a rich cultural legacy to later generations. It was due, at least in part, to his patronage that manuscripts were copied and illuminated and an important portion of the heritage of the classical and patristic worlds was preserved to nourish the intellectual revival of the eleventh and twelfth centuries.

King Alfred of Wessex and the Emperors Otto I and Otto III of Germany seem quite consciously to have modeled themselves on Charlemagne. In a sterner age and without such scholars as Charles had been able to attract to his court, Alfred himself had to serve as the schoolmaster of his kingdom and at the same time beat off the Danish onslaught; his reign prepared the way for the golden age of Anglo-Saxon England in the tenth century. On a much larger scale, Otto I attacked the problems of tenth-century Germany. Like Charlemagne, he was crowned in Rome by the Pope, and he, too, dominated the church in his realm. He was not merely the first among equals in the manner of his immediate predecessors but put down the revolts of the dukes with a strong hand. His victories over the Magyars and Slavs and the fortified marches he established paralleled the eastern campaigns and marches of Charles. Moreover, the monasteries and their learning prospered under him and his successors.

The reign of his grandson, Otto III, was brief, but not too brief to reveal the further growth of imperial ideology and ambitions. By the early eleventh century the Kingdom of Germany represented by far the greatest concentration of power in western Europe. The latter region still had a very long way to go before achieving a reasonable degree of political stability, but the rule of these strong kings did much to start it moving in that direction.

1. EINHARD: PORTRAIT OF CHARLEMAGNE (c. 830)[1]

Einhard, the biographer of Charlemagne (reigned 768-814), lived from c. 775 to 840 and received his education in the great monastic house of Fulda. He came to court around 791 and lived there until 828, eventually becoming the private secretary of Louis the Pious. Although his *Life* was written several years after Charlemagne's death in 814, it was based on personal knowledge and friendship. Despite Einhard's rather pedantic habit of describing Charles with phrases used by Suetonius in his *Lives of the Caesars*, his biography remains on the whole a fundamental and reliable source.

Thus did Charles defend and increase as well as beautify his kingdom, as is well known; and here let me express my admiration of his great qualities and his extraordinary constancy alike in good and evil fortune. I will now forthwith proceed to give the details of his private and family life.

After his father's death, while sharing the kingdom with his brother, he 768-

[1] Einhard, *Life of Charlemagne*, trans. by E. E. Turner (New York, American Book Company, 1880), pp. 47-71.

bore his unfriendliness and jealousy most patiently, and, to the wonder of all, could not be provoked to be angry with him. Later he married a daughter **770** of Desiderius, King of the Lombards, at the instance of his mother; but he repudiated her at the end of a year for some reason unknown, and married **771** Hildegard, a woman of high birth, of Suabian origin. He had three sons by her—Charles, Pepin, and Lewis—and as many daughters—Hruodrud, Bertha, and Gisela.[2] He had three others daughters besides these—Theoderada, Hiltrud, and Ruodhaid—two by his third wife, Fastrada, a woman of East Frankish (that is to say, of German) origin, and the third by a concubine, whose name for the moment escapes me. At the death of Fastrada, he married Liut- **794** gard, an Alemannic woman, who bore him no children. After her death he **800** had three concubines[3]—Gersuinda, a Saxon, by whom he had Adaltrud; Regina, who was the mother of Drogo and Hugh; and Ethelind, by whom he had Theodoric. Charles's mother, Berthrada, passed her old age with him in great honour; he entertained the greatest veneration for her; and there was never any disagreement between them except when he divorced the daughter of King Desiderius, whom he had married to please her. She died soon after **783** Hildegard, after living to see three grandsons and as many granddaughters in her son's house, and he buried her with great pomp in the Basilica of St. Denis, where his father lay. He had an only sister,[4] Gisela, who had consecrated herself to a religious life from girlhood, and he cherished as much affection for her as for his mother. She also died a few years before him in the **810** nunnery where she had passed her life.

The plan that he adopted for his children's education was, first of all, to have both boys and girls instructed in the liberal arts, to which he also turned his own attention. As soon as their years admitted, in accordance with the custom of the Franks, the boys had to learn horsemanship, and to practise war and the chase, and the girls to familiarize themselves with cloth-making, and to handle distaff and spindle, that they might not grow indolent through idleness, and he fostered in them every virtuous sentiment. He only lost three of all his children before his death, two sons and one daughter, Charles, who was the eldest, Pepin, whom he had made King of Italy, and Hruodrud, his oldest daughter, whom he had betrothed to Constantine,[5] Emperor of the Greeks. Pepin left one son, named Bernard,[6] and five daughters, Adelaide, Atula, Guntrada, Berthaid, and Theoderada. The King gave a striking proof of his fatherly affection at the time of Pepin's death: he appointed the grandson to **810** succeed Pepin, and had the granddaughters brought up with his own daugh-

---

[2] And also one son, Lothair, and two daughters, Adelaide and Hildegard, who died young.
[3] Some manuscripts say four.
[4] He had actually three sisters.
[5] Constantine VI (reigned 780-797), blinded and deposed by his mother Irene.
[6] Bernard was blinded by command of Charlemagne's successor Louis the Pious. Since the old Frankish custom was to cut off the hair of a possible rival to the throne, this deed seems to indicate influence on the Franks from the superior culture of Byzantium.

ters. When his sons and his daughter died, he was not so calm as might have
been expected from his remarkably strong mind, for his affections were no
less strong, and moved him to tears. Again, when he was told of the death of   795
Hadrian, the Roman Pontiff, whom he had loved most of all his friends, he
wept as much as if he had lost a brother, or a very dear son. He was by nature
most ready to contract friendships, and not only made friends easily, but
clung to them persistently, and cherished most fondly those with whom he had
formed such ties. He was so careful of the training of his sons and daughters
that he never took his meals without them when he was at home, and never
made a journey without them; his sons would ride at his side, and his daughters follow him, while a number of his body-guard, detailed for their protection, brought up the rear. Strange to say, although they were very handsome
women, and he loved them very dearly, he was never willing to marry any of
them to a man of their own nation or to a foreigner, but kept them all at home
until his death, saying that he could not dispense with their society.[7] Hence,
though otherwise happy, he experienced the malignity of fortune as far as
they were concerned; yet he concealed his knowledge of the rumours current
in regard to them, and of the suspicions entertained of their honour.

By one of his concubines he had a son, handsome in face, but hunch-
backed, named Pepin, whom I omitted to mention in the list of his children.
When Charles was at war with the Huns, and was wintering in Bavaria, this   792
Pepin shammed sickness, and plotted against his father in company with some
of the leading Franks, who seduced him with vain promises of the royal authority. When his deceit was discovered, and the conspirators were punished,
his head was shaved, and he was suffered, in accordance with his wishes, to
devote himself to a religious life in the monastery of Prüm. A formidable conspiracy against Charles had previously been set on foot in Germany, but all   785-
the traitors were banished, some of them without mutilation, others after their
eyes had been put out. Three of them only lost their lives; they drew their
swords and resisted arrest, and, after killing several men, were cut down, because they could not be otherwise overpowered. It is supposed that the cruelty
of Queen Fastrada was the primary cause of these plots, and they were both
due to Charles's apparent acquiescence in his wife's cruel conduct, and devia-
tion from the usual kindness and gentleness of his disposition. All the rest of
his life he was regarded by every one with the utmost love and affection, so
much so that not the least accusation of unjust rigour was ever made against
him.

He liked foreigners, and was at great pains to take them under his protection. There were often so many of them, both in the palace and the kingdom,
that they might reasonably have been considered a nuisance; but he, with his
broad humanity, was very little disturbed by such annoyances, because he felt

---

[7] Charlemagne probably wanted to prevent troublesome political entanglements. Two
daughters produced illegitimate children, one of which was the historian Nithard, son of
Bertha and of the poet and abbot Angilbert.

himself compensated for these great inconveniences by the praises of his generosity and the reward of high renown.

Charles was large and strong, and of lofty stature, though not disproportionately tall (his height is well known to have been seven times the length of his foot); the upper part of his head was round, his eyes very large and animated, nose a little long, hair fair, and face laughing and merry. Thus his appearance was always stately and dignified, whether he was standing or sitting; although his neck was thick and somewhat short, and his belly rather prominent; but the symmetry of the rest of his body concealed these defects. His gait was firm, his whole carriage manly, and his voice clear, but not so strong as his size led one to expect. His health was excellent, except during the four years preceding his death, when he was subject to frequent fevers; at the last he even limped a little with one foot. Even in those years he consulted rather his own inclinations than the advice of physicians, who were almost hateful to him, because they wanted him to give up roasts, to which he was accustomed, and to eat boiled meat instead. In accordance with the national custom, he took frequent exercise on horseback and in the chase, accomplishments in which scarcely any people in the world can equal the Franks. He enjoyed the exhalations from natural warm springs, and often practised swimming, in which he was such an adept that none could surpass him; and hence it was that he built his palace at Aix-la-Chapelle, and lived there constantly during his latter years until his death. He used not only to invite his sons to his bath, but his nobles and friends, and now and then a troop of his retinue or body-guard, so that a hundred or more persons sometimes bathed with him.

He used to wear the national, that is to say, the Frank, dress—next his skin a linen shirt and linen breeches, and above these a tunic fringed with silk; while hose fastened by bands covered his lower limbs, and shoes his feet, and he protected his shoulders and chest in winter by a close-fitting coat of otter or marten skins. Over all he flung a blue cloak, and he always had a sword girt about him, usually one with a gold or silver hilt and belt; he sometimes carried a jewelled sword, but only on great feast-days or at the reception of ambassadors from foreign nations. He despised foreign costumes, however handsome, and never allowed himself to be robed in them, except twice in Rome, when he donned the Roman tunic, chlamys, and shoes; the first time at the request of Pope Hadrian,[8] the second to gratify Leo,[9] Hadrian's successor. On great feast-days he made use of embroidered clothes, and shoes bedecked with precious stones; his cloak was fastened by a golden buckle, and he appeared crowned with a diadem of gold and gems: but on other days his dress varied little from the common dress of the people.

Charles was temperate in eating, and particularly so in drinking, for he abominated drunkenness in anybody, much more in himself and those of his household; but he could not easily abstain from food, and often complained

[8] Hadrian I (772-795).
[9] Leo III (795-816).

that fasts injured his health. He very rarely gave entertainments, only on great feast-days, and then to large numbers of people. His meals ordinarily consisted of four courses, not counting the roast, which his huntsmen used to bring in on the spit; he was more fond of this than of any other dish. While at table, he listened to reading or music. The subjects of the readings were the stories and deeds of olden time: he was fond, too, of St. Augustine's books, and especially of the one entitled "The City of God." He was so moderate in the use of wine and all sorts of drink that he rarely allowed himself more than three cups in the course of a meal. In summer, after the midday meal, he would eat some fruit, drain a single cup, put off his clothes and shoes, just as he did for the night, and rest for two or three hours. He was in the habit of awaking and rising from bed four or five times during the night. While he was dressing and putting on his shoes, he not only gave audience to his friends, but if the Count of the Palace told him of any suit in which his judgment was necessary, he had the parties brought before him forthwith, took cognizance of the case, and gave his decision, just as if he were sitting on the judgment-seat. This was not the only business that he transacted at this time, but he performed any duty of the day whatever, whether he had to attend to the matter himself, or to give commands concerning it to his officers.

Charles had the gift of ready and fluent speech, and could express whatever he had to say with the utmost clearness. He was not satisfied with command of his native language merely, but gave attention to the study of foreign ones, and in particular was such a master of Latin that he could speak it as well as his native tongue; but he could understand Greek better than he could speak it. He was so eloquent, indeed, that he might have passed for a teacher of eloquence. He most zealously cultivated the liberal arts, held those who taught them in great esteem, and conferred great honours upon them. He took lessons in grammar of the deacon Peter of Pisa, at that time an aged man. Another deacon, Albin of Britain, surnamed Alcuin, a man of Saxon extraction, who was the greatest scholar of the day, was his teacher in other branches of learning. The King spent much time and labour with him studying rhetoric, dialectics, and especially astronomy; he learned to reckon, and used to investigate the motions of the heavenly bodies most curiously, with an intelligent scrutiny. He also tried to write, and used to keep tablets and blanks in bed under his pillow, that at leisure hours he might accustom his hand to form the letters; however, as he did not begin his efforts in due season, but late in life, they met with ill success.

He cherished with the greatest fervour and devotion the principles of the Christian religion, which had been instilled into him from infancy. Hence it was that he built the beautiful basilica at Aix-la-Chapelle, which he adorned with gold and silver and lamps, and with rails and doors of solid brass. He had the columns and marbles for this structure brought from Rome and Ravenna, for he could not find such as were suitable elsewhere. He was a constant worshipper at this church as long as his health permitted, going morning and evening, even after nightfall, besides attending mass; and he took care that all the services there conducted should be administered with the utmost possible propriety, very often warning the sextons not to let any improper or unclean thing be brought into the building, or remain in it. He provided it with a great number of sacred vessels of gold and silver, and with such a quantity of clerical robes that not even the doorkeepers, who fill the humblest office in the church, were obliged to wear their every-day clothes when in the exercise of their duties. He was at great pains to improve the church reading and psalmody, for he was well skilled in both, although he neither read in public nor sang, except in a low tone and with others.

He was very forward in succouring the poor, and in that gratuitous generosity which the Greeks call alms, so much so that he not only made a point of giving in his own country and his own kingdom, but when he discovered that there were Christians living in poverty in Syria, Egypt, and Africa, at Jerusalem, Alexandria, and Carthage, he had compassion on their wants, and used to send money over the seas to them. The reason that he zealously strove to make friends with the kings beyond seas was that he might get help and relief to the Christians living under their rule. He cherished the Church of St. Peter the Apostle at Rome above all other holy and sacred places, and heaped its treasury with a vast wealth of gold, silver, and precious stones. He sent great and countless gifts to the popes; and throughout his whole reign the wish that he had nearest at heart was to re-establish the ancient authority of the city of Rome under his care and by his influence, and to defend and protect the Church of St. Peter, and to beautify and enrich it out of his own store above all other churches. Although he held it in such veneration, he only repaired to Rome to pay his vows and make his supplications four times during the whole forty-seven years that he reigned.

When he made his last journey thither, he had also other ends in view. 800 The Romans had inflicted many injuries upon the Pontiff Leo, tearing out his eyes and cutting out his tongue, so that he had been compelled to call upon the King for help. Charles accordingly went to Rome, to set in order the 24 Nov. affairs of the Church, which were in great confusion, and passed the whole winter there. It was then that he received the titles of Emperor and Augustus, 25 Dec. to which he at first had such an aversion that he declared that he would not have set foot in the Church the day that they were conferred, although it was a great feast-day, if he could have foreseen the design of the Pope. He bore very patiently with the jealousy which the Roman emperors[10] showed upon his assuming these titles, for they took this step very ill; and by dint of frequent embassies and letters, in which he addressed them as brothers, he made their haughtiness yield to his magnanimity, a quality in which he was unquestionably much their superior.

[10] Charlemagne never called himself "Roman Emperor," thereby recognizing implicitly that this title belonged to the rulers of Byzantium.

It was after he had received the imperial name that, finding the laws of his people very defective (the Franks have two sets of laws, very different in many particulars), he determined to add what was wanting, to reconcile the discrepancies, and to correct what was vicious and wrongly cited in them. However, he went no further in this matter than to supplement the laws by a few capitularies, and those imperfect ones; but he caused the unwritten laws of all the tribes that came under his rule to be compiled and reduced to writing. He also had the old rude songs that celebrate the deeds and wars of the ancient kings written out for transmission to posterity. He began a grammar of his native language. He gave the months names in his own tongue, in place of the Latin and barbarous names by which they were formerly known among the Franks. He likewise designated the winds by twelve appropriate names; there were hardly more than four distinctive ones in use before.

Towards the close of his life, when he was broken by ill-health and old age, he summoned Lewis, King of Aquitania, his only surviving son by Hildegard, and gathered together all the chief men of the whole kingdom of the Franks in a solemn assembly. He appointed Lewis, with their unanimous consent, to rule with himself over the whole kingdom, and constituted him heir to the imperial name; then, placing the diadem upon his son's head, he bade him be proclaimed Emperor and Augustus. This step was hailed by all present with great favour, for it really seemed as if God had prompted him to it for the kingdom's good; it increased the King's dignity, and struck no little terror into foreign nations. After sending his son back to Aquitania, although weak from age he set out to hunt, as usual, near his palace at Aix-la-Chapelle, and passed the rest of the autumn in the chase, returning thither about the first of November. While wintering there, he was seized, in the month of January, with a high fever, and took to his bed. As soon as he was taken sick, he prescribed for himself abstinence from food, as he always used to do in case of fever, thinking that the disease could be driven off, or at least mitigated, by fasting. Besides the fever, he suffered from a pain in the side, which the Greeks call pleurisy; but he still persisted in fasting, and in keeping up his strength only by draughts taken at very long intervals. He died January twenty-eighth, the seventh day from the time that he took to his bed, at nine o'clock in the morning, after partaking of the holy communion, in the 72d[11] year of his age and the 47th of his reign.

His body was washed and cared for in the usual manner, and was then carried to the church, and interred amid the greatest lamentations of all the people. There was some question at first where to lay him, because in his lifetime he had given no directions as to his burial; but at length all agreed that he could nowhere be more honourably entombed than in the very basilica that he had built in the town at his own expense, for love of God and our Lord Jesus Christ, and in honour of the Holy and Eternal Virgin, His Mother. He was buried there the same day that he died, and a gilded arch was erected

[11] In the 71st year.

above his tomb with his image and an inscription. The words of the inscription were as follows: "In this tomb lies the body of Charles, the Great and Orthodox Emperor, who gloriously extended the kingdom of the Franks, and reigned prosperously for forty-seven years.[12] He died at the age of seventy, in the year of our Lord 814, the 7th Indiction, on the 28th day of January."

2. CHARLEMAGNE: CAPITULARIES[1]

Charlemagne's capitularies, or decrees (the name comes from the *capitula* or chapters into which they were divided), give a many-sided picture of his activities as a ruler. The following three selections emphasize his concern with clerical discipline and education. Better instruction for the clergy, schools in the monasteries where boys could learn to read, correction and revision of sacred and secular books: such improvements would benefit the service both of God and of the Emperor. They were intended not only to strengthen the Church but also to provide the kingdom with an educated ruling class.

The fourth selection tells how Charles created a new group of royal officials, the *missi dominici*. Armed with exceptional authority, they made yearly circuits of assigned districts of the empire and served as messengers, judges, and inspectors. They represented an attempt to check the growing decentralization and feudal tendencies of the time. Charlemagne's wars, however, helped to encourage those tendencies, and even the most intelligent governmental innovation was powerless to do more than delay their growth.

ON THE CULTIVATING OF LETTERS (780-800)

. . . We, together with our faithful, have considered it to be useful that the bishoprics and monasteries entrusted by the favor of Christ to our control, in addition to the order of monastic life and the intercourse of holy religion, in the culture of letters also ought to be zealous in teaching those who by the gift of God are able to learn, according to the capacity of each individual, so that just as the observance of the rule imparts order and grace to honesty of morals, so also zeal in teaching and learning may do the same for sentences, so that those who desire to please God by living rightly should not neglect to please him also by speaking correctly. For it is written: "Either from thy words

---

[12] Really only 45 years and four months.

[1] "Laws of Charles the Great," trans. by D. C. Munro, *Translations and Reprints from the Original Sources of European History*, Series I, Vol. VI, No. 5 (Philadelphia, University of Pennsylvania Press, 1900), pp. 12-18.

thou shalt be justified or from thy words thou shalt be condemned." For although correct conduct may be better than knowledge, nevertheless knowledge precedes conduct. Therefore, each one ought to study what he desires to accomplish, so that so much the more fully the mind may know what ought to be done, as the tongue hastens in the praises of omnipotent God without the hindrances of errors. For since errors should be shunned by all men, so much the more ought they to be avoided as far as possible by those who are chosen for this very purpose alone, so that they ought to be the especial servants of truth. For when in the years just passed letters were often written to us from several monasteries in which it was stated that the brethren who dwelt there offered up in our behalf sacred and pious prayers, we have recognized in most of these letters both correct thoughts and uncouth expressions; because what pious devotion dictated faithfully to the mind, the tongue, uneducated on account of the neglect of study, was not able to express in the letter without error. Whence it happened that we began to fear lest perchance, as the skill in writing was less, so also the wisdom for understanding the Holy Scriptures might be much less than it rightly ought to be. And we all know well that, although errors of speech are dangerous, far more dangerous are errors of the understanding. Therefore, we exhort you not only not to neglect the study of letters, but also with most humble mind, pleasing to God, to study earnestly in order that you may be able more easily and more correctly to penetrate the mysteries of the divine Scriptures. Since, moreover, images, tropes and similar figures are found in the sacred pages, no one doubts that each one in reading these will understand the spiritual sense more quickly if previously he shall have been fully instructed in the mastery of letters. Such men truly are to be chosen for this work as have both the will and the ability to learn and a desire to instruct others. And may this be done with a zeal as great as the earnestness with which we command it. For we desire you to be, as it is fitting that soldiers of the church should be, devout in mind, learned in discourse, chaste in conduct and eloquent in speech, so that whosoever shall seek to see you out of reverence for God, or on account of your reputation for holy conduct, just as he is edified by your appearance, may also be instructed by your wisdom, which he has learned from your reading or singing, and may go away joyfully giving thanks to omnipotent God. . . .

GENERAL LETTER (786-800)

Charles, confiding in the aid of God, King of the Franks and Lombards, and Patrician of the Romans, to the religious lectors subject to our power.

Since the divine clemency always guards us at home and abroad, in the issues of war or in the tranquillity of peace, though human insignificance is in no way able to pay back His benefits, nevertheless, because our God is inestimable in His mercy, He approves benignly the goodwill of those devoted to His service. Therefore, because we take care constantly to improve the condition of our churches, we have striven with watchful zeal to advance the cause of learning, which has been almost forgotten by the negligence of our ancestors; and, by our example, also we invite those whom we can to master the study of the liberal arts. Accordingly, God aiding us in all things, we have already corrected carefully all the books of the Old and New Testaments, corrupted by the ignorance of the copyists.

Incited, moreover, by the example of our father Pippin, of venerated memory, who by his zeal decorated all the churches of the Gauls with the songs of the Roman church, we are careful by our skill to make these churches illustrious by a series of excellent lectionaries. Finally, because we have found the lectionaries for the nocturnal offices, compiled by the fruitless labor of certain ones, in spite of their correct intention, unsuitable because they were written without the words of their authors and were full of an infinite number of errors, we cannot suffer in our days discordant solecisms to glide into the sacred lessons among the holy offices, and we purpose to improve these lessons. And we have entrusted this work to Paul the deacon,[2] our friend and client. We have directed him to peruse carefully the sayings of the catholic fathers and to choose, so to speak, from the most broad meadows of their writings certain flowers, and from the most useful to form, as it were, a single garland. He, desiring to obey devoutly our highness, has read through the treatises and sermons of the different catholic fathers, has chosen from each the best, and has presented to us in two volumes lessons suitable for the whole year and for each separate festival, and free from error. We have examined the text of all these with our wisdom, we have established these volumes by our authority, and we deliver them to your religion to be read in the churches of Christ.

GENERAL ADMONITION (789)

And we also demand . . . that the ministers of the altar of God shall adorn their ministry by good manners, and likewise the other orders who observe a rule and the congregations of monks. We implore them to lead a just and fitting life, just as God Himself commanded in the Gospel. "Let your light so shine before men that they may see your good works and glorify your Father which is in heaven," so that by their example many may be led to serve God; and let them join and associate to themselves not only children of servile

[2] Paul the Deascon (c. 720 - c. 800), a noble Lombard who wrote a famous history of his people, visited Charlemagne in 782 and remained in France about four years.

condition, but also sons of free men. And let schools be established in which boys may learn to read. Correct carefully the Psalms, the signs in writing, the songs, the calendar, the grammar, in each monastery or bishopric, and the catholic books; because often some desire to pray to God properly, but they pray badly because of the incorrect books. And do not permit your boys to corrupt them in reading or writing. If there is need of writing the Gospel, Psalter and Missal, let men of mature age do the writing with all diligence.

. . . . .

GENERAL CAPITULARY FOR THE *MISSI* (802)

Concerning the embassy sent out by the lord emperor. Therefore, the most serene and most Christian lord emperor Charles has chosen from his nobles the wisest and most prudent men, both archbishops and some of the other bishops also, and venerable abbots and pious laymen, and has sent them throughout his whole kingdom, and through them by all the following chapters has allowed men to live in accordance with the correct law. Moreover, where anything which is not right and just has been enacted in the law, he has ordered them to inquire into this most diligently and to inform him of it; he desires, God granting, to reform it. And let no one, through his cleverness or astuteness, dare to oppose or thwart the written law, as many are wont to do, or the judicial sentence passed upon him, or to do injury to the churches of God or the poor or the widows or the wards or any Christian. But all shall live entirely in accordance with God's precept, justly and under a just rule, and each one shall be admonished to live in harmony with his fellows in his business or profession; the canonical clergy ought to observe in every respect a canonical life without heeding base gain, nuns ought to keep diligent watch over their lives, laymen and the secular clergy ought rightly to observe their laws without malicious fraud, and all ought to live in mutual charity and perfect peace. And let the *missi* themselves make a diligent investigation whenever any man claims that an injustice has been done to him by any one, just as they desire to deserve the grace of omnipotent God and to keep their fidelity promised to Him, so that entirely in all cases everywhere, in accordance with the will and fear of God, they shall administer the law fully and justly in the case of the holy churches of God and of the poor, of wards and widows and of the whole people. And if there shall be anything of such a nature that they, together with the provincial counts, are not able of themselves to correct it and to do justice concerning it, they shall, without any ambiguity, refer this, together with their reports, to the judgment of the emperor; and the straight path of justice shall not be impeded by any one on account of flattery or gifts from any one, or on account of any relationship, or from fear of the powerful. . . .

3. CHARLEMAGNE AND ALCUIN: THREE LETTERS[1]

The first of these letters, written by Charlemagne to Offa, King of Mercia, in 796, gives interesting evidence of early trade between England and France. The second, from Alcuin, the English monk who was head of Charlemagne's Palace School and one of the foremost figures in the Carolingian "Renaissance" of learning, to King Offa, written in 796, tells of Charlemagne's horror at the murder of King Ethelred of Northumbria by his own subjects and of the Frankish monarch's contempt for the whole "perfidious and perverse race" of the Northumbrians. The third, from Alcuin to Charlemagne, written between 796 and 797, is a plea for books to make the abbey of St. Martin at Tours, of which Alcuin was abbot, the equal of his old home, York, as a center of learning. Alcuin was successful in founding at Tours a famous library and school.

CHARLEMAGNE TO OFFA, KING OF MERCIA (796)

Charles, by the grace of God, king of the Franks and Lombards and patrician of the Romans, to the revered man his dearest brother, Offa, king of the Mercians, sends greeting of present prosperity and eternal blessedness in Christ.

Between royal dignities and exalted personages of the world, the keeping of the laws of friendship joined in the unity of peace, and of the concord of holy love, with the deepest affection of heart, is wont to be of profit to many. And if we are commanded by our Lord's precept to untie the knots of enmity, how much more ought we to take care to secure the links of love? Hence, most beloved brother, mindful of the ancient pact between us, we have sent these letters to your Reverence, that the treaty established in the root of faith may flourish in the fruit of love. Having perused your brotherly letters, which have at divers times been brought to us by the hands of your messengers, and endeavouring to reply adequately to the several suggestions of your authority, we first give thanks to the Almighty God for the sincerity of the catholic faith which we found laudably set down in your pages; recognizing you to be not only a most strong protector of your earthly country, but also a most devout defender of the holy faith.

[1] Reprinted by permission of Eyre & Spottiswoode Ltd. and Oxford University Press, Inc. from *English Historical Documents,* I, ed. by D. Whitelock (London, Eyre & Spottiswoode, 1955), pp. 781-784, 786.

Concerning pilgrims, who for the love of God and the salvation of their souls desire to reach the thresholds of the blessed Apostles, as we granted formerly, they may go in peace free from all molestation, bearing with them the necessities for their journey. But we have discovered that certain persons fraudulently mingle with them for the sake of commerce, seeking gain, not serving religion. If such are found among them, they are to pay the established toll at the proper places; the others may go in peace, immune from toll.

You have written to us also about merchants, and by our mandate we allow that they shall have protection and support in our kingdom, lawfully, according to the ancient custom of trading. And if in any place they are afflicted by wrongful oppression, they may appeal to us or to our judges, and we will then order true justice to be done. Similarly our men, if they suffer any injustice in your dominion, are to appeal to the judgment of your equity, lest any disturbance should arise anywhere between our men.

Regarding the priest Odberht, who desires on his return from Rome to live abroad for the love of God, as he often says, and did not come to accuse you, I inform you, dear brother, that we have sent him to Rome with the other exiles who in fear of death have taken refuge under the wings of our protection; so that in the presence of the apostolic lord and your archbishop—since, as your letters have informed us, they had bound themselves by a vow—their cause may be heard and judged, that equitable judgment may be effective where pious intercession failed. What could be safer for us than that the opinion of the apostolic authority should determine a case in which the views of others disagree?

As for the black stones which your Reverence begged to be sent to you, let a messenger come and consider what kind you have in mind, and we will willingly order them to be given, wherever they are to be found, and will help with their transport. But as you have intimated your wishes concerning the length of the stones, so our people make a demand about the size of the cloaks, that you may order them to be such as used to come to us in former times.

Moreover, we make known to your love that we have sent a gift from our dalmatics and palls to the various episcopal sees of your kingdom and of Ethelred's, in alms for the apostolic lord, Hadrian, our father and your friend; beseeching you to order diligent intercession for his soul, not having any doubt that his blessed soul is at rest, but to show our trust and love towards a friend most dear to us. So, also, the blessed Augustine has taught, that intercessions of ecclesiastical piety ought to be made for all; asserting that to intercede for a good man profits him who does it. Also from the treasure of earthly riches, which the Lord Jesus Christ has granted us with freely bestowed kindness, we have sent something to each of the metropolitan cities; also to your love, for joy and thanksgiving to Almighty God, we have sent a belt, and a Hunnish sword and two silk palls.

To the end that everywhere among Christian people the divine clemency may be preached and the name of our Lord Jesus Christ be glorified in eternity, we pray that you cause assiduous intercessions to be made for us and for our faithful subjects, nay more, for all Christian people; that the most merciful goodness of the heavenly King may deign to protect, exalt and extend the kingdom of the Holy Church. May Almighty God deign to preserve in long-lasting prosperity the excellence of your dignity unimpaired for the protection of his Holy Church, most longed-for brother.

ALCUIN TO OFFA, KING OF MERCIA (796)

To the most excellent man and to us most dear, Offa, king of the Mercians, his humble friend Alcuin sends greeting.

Be it known to your reverend love that the lord king, Charles, has often spoken to me of you in a most loving and loyal way, and in him you certainly have a most faithful friend. Thus he is sending envoys to Rome for the judgment of the apostolic pope and of Archbishop Aethelheard. He is also sending fitting gifts to you. Moreover, he is sending presents to all the episcopal sees in alms for himself and for the apostolic pope, that you should order prayers to be offered for them. Do you act faithfully, as you are always wont to act towards your friends.

Similarly, he had sent gifts both to King Ethelred and to his episcopal sees. But alas, the pity! When the gifts and letters had been given into the messenger's hands, the sad news came to us by the messengers who had returned from Ireland by way of you, of the treachery of the people and of his murder. King Charles withdrew his generous gifts, and was so greatly enraged against that nation, holding "that perfidious and perverse race, murderers of their lords," as he called them, worse than pagans, that whatever benefit he could have taken away from them, or whatever evil he could have contrived, he would have put into effect, if I had not interceded for them.

I was prepared to come to you with the gifts of King Charles and return to my country. But it seemed better, for the sake of the peace of my people, for me to remain abroad; for I do not know what I could do among them, where no one can be safe or prevail with any wholesome counsel. Look at the most holy places laid waste by the pagans, altars defiled by perjuries, monasteries profaned by adulteries, the earth polluted with the blood of kings and princes. What can I do other than groan with the prophet: "Woe to the sinful nation, a people laden with iniquity, a wicked seed, ungracious children; they have forsaken the Lord; they have blasphemed the holy Saviour of the world in their wickedness." And if what was read in your Highness's letter be true, that the iniquity started from the elders of the people, where then is safety and fidelity to be hoped for, if the turbulent torrent of iniquity flowed from the place where the purest fountain of truth and faith was wont to spring?

You, most wise ruler of the people of God, correct very diligently your people from perverse habits and instruct it in the precepts of God, that the land given to us by God may not be destroyed for the sins of the people. Be a father to the Church of Christ, a brother to the priests of God, and kind and just to all the people, moderate and peaceful in all your bearing and speech, and ever devout in the praise of God; that the divine clemency may preserve you in long-lasting prosperity, and may deign by the grace of his goodness to exalt, enlarge and crown in eternity with the benefits of everlasting piety, your kingdom, nay more, that of all the English.

I implore you that you order the several churches of your Reverence to intercede for me, your servant and fellow-worker for your honour. The charge of the church of St. Martin has come into my keeping, all unworthy as I am, not by my wishes but to a certain measure by necessity and from the advice of many. Yet know that I am free faithfully to offer prayers for you there, and wherever I can.

Be with all love and care a friend of God and fill your days with his commands. Endeavour that an eternal reward may follow you and the heavenly blessing your descendants. Again and again I implore you for the love of God to take thought for the country, lest it perish; and for the churches of God, lest they be destroyed; and that truth with mercy may increase in it. For by the true saying of Solomon, the throne of the kingdom shall be strengthened in truth and mercy; these things may confirm you and your throne for ever, that you may rule happily in this world and live in glory with Christ in the heavenly kingdom.

May you flourish, by the favour of the Lord Christ, in all felicity, and may you advance in all goodness, for the consolation of the Holy Church of God, and the joy of Christian people, O Lord most excellent and to us most dear.

I pray you, greet with my love that most noble youth[2] and instruct him diligently in the fear of God; and may the hope of many not come to naught in him. Remember the proverb of Solomon: "For in what way a boy is reared, when he is old he will not depart from it." Greet also the queen and lady of the royal household. May she live happy, rejoicing in an offspring of a happy father. And also I pray that you greet in my name all your Highness's children. May the right hand of Almighty God ever protect, direct and guard you all.

I pray you to receive with your accustomed goodness the pupils we have trained and taught, and the messengers of the royal dignity. They indeed bear a peaceful message in their mouth and hands. Through them you can demand of me what you wish.

ALCUIN TO CHARLEMAGNE (796-797)

I, your Flaccus,[3] according to your exhortation and encouragement, am occupied in supplying to some under the roof of St. Martin the honey of the

---

[2] Offa's son.

[3] The members of Charlemagne's circle took pleasure in calling themselves by classical names, and in this instance Alcuin uses the surname of Horace in writing to his imperial Maecenas.

sacred Scriptures; am eager to inebriate others with the old wine of ancient learning; begin to nourish others on the fruits of grammatical subtlety; long to illumine some with the order of the stars, like the painted ceiling of a great man's house; becoming many things to many men, that I may instruct many to the profit of the Holy Church of God and to the adornment of your imperial kingdom, that the grace of the Almighty be not void in me, nor the bestowal of your bounty in vain.

But I, your servant, miss to some extent the rarer books of scholastic learning which I had in my own country through the excellent and devoted zeal of my master[4] and also through some toil of my own. I tell these things to your Excellency, in case it may perchance be agreeable to your counsel, which is most eager for the whole of knowledge, that I send some of our pupils to choose there what we need, and to bring into France the flowers of Britain; that not in York only there may be a "garden enclosed," but in Tours the "plants of Paradise with the fruit of the orchard," that the south wind may come and blow through the gardens by the River Loire, and the aromatical spices thereof may flow; and finally, that there may come to pass what follows in the Canticle from which I have taken this metaphor: "Let my beloved come into his garden and eat the fruit of his apple-trees"; and he may say to his young men; "'Eat, friends, and drink and be inebriated, my dearly beloved.' I sleep, and my heart watcheth"; or that admonitory utterance of the prophet Isaiah on the teaching of wisdom: "All you that thirst, come to the waters. And you that have no money, make haste, buy and eat. Come ye: buy wine and milk without money and without any price."

4. THE *ANGLO-SAXON CHRONICLE:* VIKING ATTACKS (878-887)[1]

The *Anglo-Saxon Chronicle*, which covers the period A.D. 494 to 1154 and which is one of the most important sources for our knowledge of early English history, was probably begun at the direction of King Alfred (reigned 871-899), under whom the first section, down to 892, was put together. It continued to be compiled for nearly three centuries by monks working in such ecclesiastical centers as Winchester, Canterbury, and Peterborough. Often its entries are merely dry and bare annalistic fragments, but they sometimes contain remarkably interesting discussions of historical figures and events. On the subject of Viking incursions and the wars of King Alfred against them, they give, as might be ex-

[4] Ethelbert, Archbishop of York (767-780).

[1] Reprinted by permission of Eyre & Spottiswoode Ltd. and the Rutgers University Press from *Anglo-Saxon Chronicle,* ed. and trans. by D. Whitelock (London, Eyre & Spottiswoode, 1961), pp. 49-52.

pected, considerable information, touching also on Viking raids against the continent.

The excerpts quoted below relate some of the most important military events of Alfred's reign: his victory over the Danes at Edington in 878, the peace he made with them at Chippenham by which the Danish king Guntram became a Christian, and Alfred's war against the Danes at sea in 885. Alfred himself was not so successful a warrior-king as his successors, Edward the Elder (reigned 899-925) and Athelstan (reigned 925-939), who succeeded in subjugating the Danes of central and eastern England and in defeating the Vikings in the north. But it was Alfred who in the dark earlier period succeeded in preserving the independence of the Kingdom of the West Saxons (Wessex) and in administering the first major check to the invaders. His reorganization of the Wessex peasant army, the *fyrd*, his building of a network of fortresses, and his emphasis on sea power were of the utmost importance in laying the basis for the creation of a large and flourishing English kingdom in the tenth century.

In this year in midwinter after twelfth night the enemy army came   878 stealthily to Chippenham, and occupied the land of the West Saxons and settled there, and drove a great part of the people across the sea, and conquered most of the others; and the people submitted to them, except King Alfred. He journeyed in difficulties through the woods and fen-fastnesses with a small force.

And the same winter the brother of Ivar and Healfdene was in the kingdom of the West Saxons [in Devon], with 23 ships. And he was killed there and 840 men of his army with him. And there was captured the banner which they called "Raven."

And afterwards at Easter, King Alfred with a small force made a stronghold at Athelney, and he and the section of the people of Somerset which was nearest to it proceeded to fight from that stronghold against the enemy. Then in the seventh week after Easter he rode to "Egbert's stone" east of Selwood, and there came to meet him all the people of Somerset and of Wiltshire and of that part of Hampshire which was on this side of the sea, and they rejoiced to see him. And then after one night he went from that encampment to Iley, and after another night to Edington, and there fought against the whole army and put it to flight, and pursued it as far as the fortress, and stayed there a fortnight. And then the enemy gave him preliminary hostages and great oaths that they would leave his kingdom, and promised also that their king should receive baptism, and they kept their promise. Three weeks later King Guthrum with 30 of the men who were the most important in the army came [to him] at Aller, which is near Athelney, and the king stood sponsor to him at his baptism there; and the unbinding of the chrism[2] took place at Wedmore.

---

[2] Unbinding of the white cloth worn around the head for eight days after it had been anointed with chrism or holy oil.

And he was twelve days with the king, and he honoured him and his companions greatly with gifts.

In this year the army went from Chippenham to Cirencester, and stayed 879 there for one year. And the same year a band of vikings assembled and encamped at Fulham by the Thames. And the same year there was an eclipse of the sun for one hour of the day.

In this year the army went from Cirencester into East Anglia, and settled 880 there and shared out the land. And the same year the army which had encamped at Fulham went overseas into the Frankish empire to Ghent and stayed there for a year.

In this year the army went farther inland into the Frankish empire, and 881 the Franks fought against them,[3] and the Danish army provided itself with horses after that battle.

In this year the army went farther into the Frankish empire along the 882 Meuse, and stayed there a year. And the same year King Alfred went out with ships to sea and fought against four crews of Danish men, and captured two of the ships—and the men were killed who were on them—and two crews surrendered to him. And they had great losses in killed or wounded before they surrendered.

In this year the army went up the Scheldt to Condé, and stayed there for 883 a year. And Pope Marinus sent some wood of the Cross to King Alfred. And that same year Sigehelm and Athelstan took to Rome the alms which King Alfred had promised thither, and also to India[4] to St. Thomas and St. Bartholomew, when the English were encamped against the enemy army at London; and there, by the grace of God, their prayers were well answered after that promise.

In this year the army went up the Somme to Amiens, and stayed there a 884 year.

In this year the aforesaid army divided into two, one part going east, the 885 other part to Rochester, where they besieged the city and made other fortifications round themselves. And nevertheless the English defended the city until King Alfred came up with his army. Then the enemy went to their ships and abandoned their fortification, and they were deprived of their horses there, and immediately that same summer they went back across the sea. That same year King Alfred sent a naval force from Kent into East Anglia. Immediately they came into the mouth of the Stour, they encountered 16 ships of vikings and fought against them, and seized all the ships and killed the men. When they turned homeward with the booty, they met a large naval force of vikings and fought against them on the same day, and the Danes had the victory. . . .

And that same year the Danish army in East Anglia violated their peace with King Alfred.

[3] Probably the Battle of Saucourt, won by the Franks in August, 881.
[4] Some manuscripts say Indea.

In this year the Danish army which had gone east went west again, and   886
then up the Seine, and made their winter quarters there at the town of Paris.[5]

That same year King Alfred occupied London; and all the English people
that were not under subjection to the Danes submitted to him. And he then
entrusted the borough to the control of Ealdorman Ethelred.[6]

In this year the Danish army went up past the bridge at Paris, then up   887
along the Seine to the Marne, and then up the Marne as far as Chézy, and
stayed there and in the Yonne area, spending two winters in those two places.

5.   ASSER: KING ALFRED AS A PATRON OF LEARNING (c. 893)[1]

Alfred was forced to devote most of his energies during an anxious and
troubled reign to the tasks of war and legislation. He campaigned indefatigably
against the Danes; he carefully revised the legal code of the West Saxons. Drawing many laws from earlier kings, such as Ine of Kent and Offa of Mercia, he also
devised new laws of his own. Somehow he found time also to be both patron of
and participant in a modest but very significant revival of learning. He translated
or had translated into the Anglo-Saxon vernacular such works as Pope Gregory I's
Cura Pastoralis, of which a copy was sent to every bishop in his realm; Orosius'
account of ancient history, the Seven Books against the Pagans, with the addition
of the latest geographical information about northern lands as found in the accounts of Othere's voyage to the White Sea and Wulfstan's to the Baltic; an
abridged version of Bede's History of the English Church; and Boethius' famous
work The Consolation of Philosophy. He was concerned not only to remedy the
defects of his own early education but also to improve that of his subjects, and especially to raise the level of literacy of the English church.

Asser's Life of King Alfred has much the same value as a source of information about the reign and character of this monarch as Einhard's for Charles the
Great. Asser was one of Alfred's helpers in translating Latin works into Anglo-
Saxon; beyond this and the fact that he died early in the tenth century very little
is known about him. Some doubts have been cast on the authenticity of his Life,
but it is generally regarded as a contemporary and valuable source.

Now, he was loved by his father and mother, and indeed by everybody,
with a united and immense love, more than all his brothers, and was always

[5] They did not, however, succeed in capturing the town because of its strong island
position in the Seine.

[6] Lord of the Mercians.

[1] Reprinted by permission of Eyre & Spottiswoode and Oxford University Press, Inc.
from English Historical Documents, I, ed. by D. Whitelock (London, Eyre & Spottiswoode, 1955), pp. 266-269.

brought up in the royal court, and as he passed through his childhood and boyhood he appeared fairer in form than all his brothers, and more pleasing in his looks, his words and his ways. And from his cradle a longing for wisdom before all things and among all the pursuits of this present life, combined with his noble birth, filled the noble temper of his mind; but alas, by the unworthy carelessness of his parents and tutors, he remained ignorant of letters until his twelfth year, or even longer. But he listened attentively to Saxon poems day and night, and hearing them often recited by others committed them to his retentive memory. A keen huntsman, he toiled unceasingly in every branch of hunting, and not in vain; for he was without equal in his skill and good fortune in that art, as also in all other gifts of God, as we have ourselves often seen.

When, therefore, his mother one day was showing him and his brothers a certain book of Saxon poetry which she held in her hand, she said: "I will give this book to whichever of you can learn it most quickly." And moved by these words, or rather by divine inspiration, and attracted by the beauty of the initial letter of the book, Alfred said in reply to his mother, forestalling his brothers, his elders in years though not in grace: "Will you really give this book to one of us, to the one who can soonest understand and repeat it to you?" And, smiling and rejoicing, she confirmed it, saying: "To him will I give it." Then taking the book from her hand he immediately went to his master, who read it. And when it was read, he went back to his mother and repeated it.

After this he learnt the daily course, that is, the services of the hours, and then certain psalms and many prayers. He collected these into one book and carried it about with him everywhere in his bosom as I have myself seen day and night, for the sake of prayer, through all the changes of this present life, and was never parted from it. But alas, what he principally desired, the liberal arts, he did not obtain according to his wish, because, as he was wont to say, there were at that time no good scholars in all the kingdom of the West Saxons.

He often affirmed with frequent laments and sighs from the bottom of his heart, that among all his difficulties and hindrances in this present life this was the greatest: that, during the time when he had youth and leisure and aptitude for learning, he had no teachers; but when he was more advanced in years, he did have teachers and writers to some extent, when he was not able to study, because he was harassed, nay, rather disturbed, day and night both with illnesses unknown to all the physicians of this island, and with the cares of the royal office at home and abroad, and also with the invasions of pagans by land and sea. Yet, among all the difficulties of this present life, from infancy unto the present day, he has never abandoned that same insatiable longing, and even now still yearns for it.

Sons and daughters were born to him by the aforesaid wife, namely Aethelflaed, the first-born, and after her Edward, then Aethelgifu, next Aelfthryth, then Aethelweard, besides those who were snatched away in infancy by an early death. . . . Aethelflaed, when she reached marriageable age, was joined in matrimony to Ethelred, ealdorman of the Mercians. Aethelgifu, devoted to God as a virgin, subjected and consecrated to the rules of the monastic life, entered the service of God. Aethelweard, the youngest, was given over by the divine counsel and the admirable prudence of the king to the pleasures of literary studies, along with almost all the children of noble birth of the whole country, and also many of humble birth, under the diligent care of masters. In that school, books of both languages, Latin, that is, and English, were assiduously read, and they had leisure for writing; so that before they had the strength for manly pursuits, namely hunting and other pursuits which are fitting for noblemen, they were zealous and skilled in the liberal arts. Edward and Aelfthryth were always brought up in the royal court, with great care from their tutors and nurses, and, indeed, with great affection from all; and until this day they continue there, showing humility, affability and gentleness to all, whether their countrymen or foreigners, and great obedience to their father. Nor, indeed, are they allowed to live idly and carelessly without a liberal education among the other occupations of this present life which are fitting for nobles; for they have learnt carefully psalms and Saxon books, and especially Saxon poems, and they frequently make use of books.

Meanwhile the king, in the midst of wars and frequent hindrances of this present life, and also of the raids of the pagans and his daily infirmities of body, did not cease, single-handed, assiduously and eagerly with all his might, to govern the kingdom, to practise every branch of hunting, to instruct his goldsmiths and all his craftsmen, and his falconers, hawkers and dog-keepers, to erect buildings to his own new design more stately and magnificent than had been the custom of his ancestors, to recite Saxon books, and especially to learn by heart Saxon poems, and command others to do so. He also was in the habit of hearing daily the divine office, the Mass, and certain prayers and psalms, and of observing both the day and the night hours, and of visiting churches at night-time, as we have said, in order to pray without his followers knowing. Moreover, he showed zeal for almsgiving, and generosity both to his countrymen and to strangers from all nations, and very great and matchless kindness and pleasantness towards all men, and skill in searching into things unknown. And many Franks, Frisians, men of Gaul, pagans, Welsh, Scots and Bretons willingly submitted to his lordship, both noblemen and men of humble rank; and he ruled them all in accordance with his own honourable nature just like his own people, and loved and honoured them, and enriched them with money and rights. Also he was accustomed to listen to the Holy Scripture recited by native clergy, but also, if by chance someone had come from elsewhere, to listen with equal earnestness and attention to prayers along with foreigners. He also loved his bishops and all the ecclesiastical order, his ealdormen and his nobles, his officials and all members of his household, with a wonderful affection. And he himself never ceased among other occupations, day and night, to train their sons, who were being brought up in the royal household, in all good behaviour, and to educate them in letters, loving them no less than his own sons. Yet, as if he had no comfort in all these things and as if he suffered no other disquiet from within or without, he complained in anxious sadness by day and night to God and to all who were bound to him in close affection, and lamented with repeated sighs, that Almighty God had not made him skilled in divine wisdom and the liberal arts; emulating in this the pious and most illustrious and rich Solomon, king of the Hebrews, who, despising all present glory and riches, sought first wisdom from God, and also found both, wisdom and present glory, as it is written: "Seek therefore first the kingdom of God and his justice, and all these things shall be granted unto you." But God, who always sees into the inmost thoughts, and prompts our designs and all good desires, and also most amply ordains that good desires may be obtained, and who never prompts anyone to desire well without also ordaining what each man well and justly desires to have, stirred up the king's mind from within, not without; as it is written: "I will hear what the Lord God will speak in me." Whenever he could, he would acquire assistants in his good design, who could help him to the desired wisdom, that he might obtain what he longed for. Forthwith, like the prudent bee, which arises in the summertime at dawn from its beloved cells and, directing its course in swift flight through the unknown ways of the air, alights upon many and various blossoms of herbs, plants and fruits, and finds and carries home what pleases it most, he turned afar the gaze of his mind, seeking abroad what he had not at home, that is, in his own kingdom.

And then God, suffering no longer his so good and just complaint, sent for the king's goodwill some consolations, certain lights, as it were, namely Waerferth, bishop of the church of Worcester, a man well versed in the divine Scriptures, who at the king's command first translated clearly and beautifully from Latin into the Saxon language the books of the "Dialogues" of Pope Gregory and his disciple Peter, sometimes giving a paraphrase; and then Plegmund, a Mercian by race, archbishop of the church of Canterbury, a venerable man, endowed with wisdom; also Athelstan and Waerwulf, priests and chaplains, learned men, of Mercian race. King Alfred summoned these four to him from Mercia, and advanced them with great honours and authority in the kingdom of the West Saxons, in addition to those which Archbishop Plegmund and Bishop Waerferth possessed in Mercia. By the teaching and wisdom of all these men, the king's desire was ceaselessly increased and fulfilled. For by day and night, whenever he had any free time, he ordered books to be read before him by such men, nor indeed did he allow himself to be without one of them. Therefore he obtained a knowledge of almost all books, although he could not as yet by himself understand anything from books, for he had not yet begun to read anything.

But, since in this matter the royal avarice, praiseworthy as it was, was still unsatisfied, he sent messengers across the sea to Gaul to acquire teachers.

From there he summoned Grimbald, priest and monk, a venerable man, an excellent singer, most learned in every way in ecclesiastical studies and the divine Scriptures, and adorned with all good qualities; and also John, likewise a priest and monk, a man of very keen intelligence and most learned in all branches of the art of literature, and skilled in many other arts. By their teaching the king's mind was much enriched, and he endowed and honoured them with great authority.

6. WIDUKIND OF CORVEY: BATTLE OF THE LECHFELD (955)[1]

Otto I (reigned 936-973), the first king of Germany to be crowned Emperor in Rome, destroyed an invading Magyar army on the Lechfeld in one of the decisive battles of European history. A contemporary, but not eyewitness, account of it was given by the monk Widukind in his *History of the Saxons*, a people to which both he and Otto belonged. Their homeland in northern Germany had become one of the main ducal subdivisions of the German kingdom, but Widukind's "national" pride was still narrowly Saxon in scope. For example, he was uninterested in Otto's imperial coronation but he dwelt lovingly on instance after instance of his people's military prowess. In describing the battle on the Lech, however, his patriotism had to be concentrated on the person of King Otto, for few Saxon soldiers were involved in the fight; they were engaged in a simultaneous war with the Slavs.

Having entered Saxony about the Kalends of July [1 July 955], he [Otto] was met by Hungarian ambassadors. They were allegedly visiting him on account of friendship and the old treaty; in reality, however, as it seemed to some, they wished to know the outcome of the civil war. After he had kept them with him for a few days and sent them away in peace with some small gifts, he heard the following news from envoys of his brother, who was Duke of the Bavarians: "Behold, the Hungarians are swarming over your borders

---

[1] Trans. by C. T. Davis from Widukind, *Rerum Gestarum Saxonicarum*, III, 44, 46-49, ed. by G. Waitz and K. A. Kehr, 5th ed. revised by Paul Hirsch and H.-E. Lohman, *Scriptores Rerum Germanicarum in Usum Scholarum ex Mon. Germ. Hist. separatim editi* (Hannover, Hahnsche Buchhandlung, 1935), pp. 123-125, 127-129.

and are resolved to begin a war with you." Having learned these things, the King, as though he felt no fatigue as a result of the preceding war, set forth against the enemy. He took with him, however, very few Saxons, since they already faced war with the Slavs. Having pitched camp outside Augsburg, he was joined by the army of the Franconians and Bavarians. Duke Conrad[2] also arrived at the camp with a strong cavalry force. His coming encouraged the soldiers not to postpone battle. He was naturally audacious, but also possessed prudence, a rare quality among the bold. Irresistible in combat both on foot and horseback, he was dear to his companions in peace and war. Then the marauding parties of each army gave notice that the armies were close together. The soldiers in camp were ordered to fast and to be ready for battle on the morrow. At daybreak,[3] having pledged peace and fealty first to their leader and then to each other, they raised their banners and left the camp, about eight legions strong. They were led through rough and difficult country, lest the enemy should have the opportunity to demoralize the march with their arrows, which they use ferociously, protected by the forest. The Bavarians made up the first, second, and third legions, commanded by the prefect of Duke Henry. He himself was not present at the war, for he had been suffering from the sickness of which he died. The fourth legion was made up of the Franconians, led by Duke Conrad. In the fifth, the largest, called the royal legion, was the emperor himself, surrounded with men selected from all the thousands of soldiers, and with eager youths. There as well was the angel [Michael], with whom is victory, hidden by the dense host. The Swabians comprised the sixth and seventh legions; they were commanded by Burchard, to whom the brother of the King had given a daughter in marriage. In the eighth were the Bohemians, a thousand picked soldiers, better provided with arms than luck, with whom were left all the baggage and transport, for it seemed that the rear would be the safest place. But affairs did not go according to plan. For the Hungarians quickly crossed the Lech River, and circling round the army began to harass the last legion with arrows. Then with loud cries they launched an attack, killed some, took others prisoner, captured all the baggage, and forced the other soldiers of the legion to flee. They likewise attacked the seventh and sixth legions, and having overcome many of them, forced the rest into flight. The King, however, when he realized that the battle was going badly and that the last line to his rear was in peril, sent the Duke with the fourth legion into the fray. He freed the captives, recovered the booty, and repulsed the plundering enemy hosts. Having routed the foes who were looting on all sides, Duke Conrad returned to the king with triumphant banners. Thus in a marvelous manner, when the veteran soldiers accustomed to conquer were faltering, new soldiers almost ignorant of warfare achieved the victory.

[2] Duke of Franconia.
[3] 10 August 955.

. . . . .

When the king saw that he had now before him the whole weight of the battle, he spoke thus to his companions in order to encourage them:

That it is needful for us, my soldiers, to be of good courage amid such exigencies, you yourselves see, who face no distant foe, but one already upon us. Gloriously employing your tireless hands and your never defeated arms beyond my territory and empire, I have conquered everywhere; now in my own land and kingdom shall I yield? We are outmatched, I know, in numbers, but not in valor or in arms. We have perceived that they are in large part totally destitute of weapons, and also of that which is the greatest solace to us, the help of God. They rely only on audacity; we have hope and divine protection. Let those who are now already lords of almost the whole of Europe feel ashamed to submit to such enemies. It is better, my soldiers, if the end is near, to die gloriously in war than captive to drag out a servile life, and certainly better than to die by the rope like wretched beasts. I should speak longer, my soldiers, if I knew how to increase your courage and boldness with words. Now not with words but with swords let us begin our colloquy.

Having said these things, he grasped his shield and holy lance and himself first turned his horse against the enemy, performing the office of a stalwart soldier and dauntless emperor. The more audacious of the foe resisted at first; then, seeing their comrades flee, they gave way to terror and were cut down in the mêlée. Of the remainder, some entered neighboring villages on their exhausted horses and, surrounded by our warriors, were burned together with the walls; others swam across the nearby river, but, unable to ascend the farther bank, were swept away by the waters and so perished. On that same day their camp was captured and all their prisoners freed; on the next two days most of the surviving multitude in the neighboring cities were annihilated, so that none or few escaped. It was no bloodless victory, however, that was won from so savage a people.

Indeed, Duke Conrad, fighting bravely, heated by his fervid spirit and the hot sun, which that day was overpowering, loosed the thongs [of his cuirass] in order to breathe and fell, pierced in the throat by an arrow. His body was reverently gathered up at the King's command and brought to Worms and there buried, amid the grief and tears of all the Franconians over the death of a man so great and famous for every virtue of soul and body.

Three of the captured Hungarian generals, brought before Duke Henry, suffered an evil death, their just punishment. They were executed by hanging.

Honored in a great triumph, the King was hailed by his army as emperor and father of his country. He then decreed that worship and fitting praises should be offered to God in every church, and sent legates to command his venerable mother to do the same. The victor returning to Saxony was received by his people joyfully, with dancing and much festivity. Nor indeed had any other king for two hundred years before him celebrated such a victory.

7. OTTO III AND GERBERT: THREE LETTERS[1]

The close relationship between the brilliant young emperor Otto III and the famous scholar Gerbert has always fascinated students of medieval history. One wonders how much of Otto's preoccupation with the Roman past was due to the lessons of his old teacher, who did more to appropriate and propagate the cultural heritage of the ancient world than any other man of his time.

Gerbert (c. 940-1003) was born in or near Aurillac in southern France. He was educated there in the monastery of St. Gerald and also studied in Catalan Spain. After visits to the imperial and papal courts, he went in 972 to Rheims to study logic. He rapidly became one of the best-known teachers in Europe, emphasizing rhetorical training and the instruction provided by Boethius' textbooks on logic, arithmetic, and music. He was much interested in the classical authors and searched out manuscripts of their works with all the eagerness of a Renaissance scholar. Indeed, the following passage from one of his letters might express the sentiments of a fifteenth-century humanist:

Since philosophy does not separate ways of conduct and ways of speaking, I have always added the fondness for speaking well to the fondness for living well. . . . To us, busied in affairs of state, both are necessary. For speaking effectively to persuade, and restraining the minds of angry persons from violence by smooth speech are both of the greatest usefulness. For this activity, which must be prepared beforehand, I am diligently forming a library.[2]

Gerbert also had a great reputation as a mathematician and revived the study of the abacus. Probably his main contribution to medieval education, however, was his placing the study of logic on a firmer basis than it had known since the fifth century. Otto III had good reason to respect his old master.

In 997, at the time of this exchange of letters, Gerbert was Archbishop of Rheims; two years later he would be raised to the papacy by the favor of his old pupil. This example of the imperial patronage of learning combined with the wide fame of Gerbert's teaching indicates that western Europe was on the verge of being ready to learn new lessons and to enter a new cultural age.

OTTO TO GERBERT (21 OCTOBER 997)

Otto himself writes Gerbert, most skilled of masters and crowned in the three branches of philosophy.[3]

[1] *The Letters of Gerbert*, trans. by H. P. Lattin, *Records of Civilization*, No. LX (New York, Columbia University Press, 1961), pp. 294-299.
[2] *Ibid.*, p. 90.
[3] Natural, moral, rational.

We wish to attach to our person the excellence of your very loving self, so revered by all, and we seek to affiliate with ourself the perennial steadfastness of such a patron because the extent of your philosophical knowledge has always been for Our Simplicity an authority not to be scorned. Not to be ambiguous but to enjoy plain speaking with you, we have firmly resolved and arranged that this letter shall make clear to you our desire as to the extent of our choice and the singleness of our request in order that your expert knowledge may be zealous in correcting us, though not more than usual, unlearned and badly educated as we are, both in writing and speaking, and that with respect to the commonwealth you may offer advice of the highest trustworthiness.

We desire you to show your aversion to Saxon ignorance by not refusing this suggestion of our wishes, but even more we desire you to stimulate Our Greek Subtlety to zeal for study, because if there is anyone who will arouse it, he will find some shred of the diligence of the Greeks in it. Thanks to this, we humbly ask that the flame of your knowledge may sufficiently fan our spirit until, with God's aid, you cause the lively genius of the Greeks[4] to shine forth.

Pray explain to us the book on arithmetic[5] so that when fully taught by its lessons we may learn something of the attainments of the ancients.

Whether it pleases you to act upon this invitation, or displeases you, may Your Paternity not postpone making a reply to us by letter.

Farewell.

> Verses have I never made
> Nor in such study ever stayed.
> When to its practice myself I apply
> And can write successfully,
> As many men as has Lorraine,
> To you, then, songs I'll send the same.

GERBERT TO OTTO (25 OCTOBER 997)

Gerbert, archbishop of Rheims, by the grace of God, [sends] whatever is worthy so great an emperor to the ever august glorious Lord Otto.

Not because of our merits, though perchance because of solemn vows, are we able to make answer to your surpassing kindness that deems us worthy of perpetual obedience to you. If we are aglow with the slightest spark of knowledge, it redounds to your glory through the excellence of your father who nourished it and the magnificence of your grandfather who matched it.

What shall I say? We are not bringing our own treasures to yours, but

---

[4] Otto's mother was a Byzantine princess.
[5] Probably the treatise by Boethius on this subject.

rather are giving back what we once received, some of which you have enjoyed already,[6] some of which you are very soon to enjoy as is evidenced by the honest and useful invitation, so worthy of Your Majesty. For, unless you were not firmly convinced that the power of numbers contained both the origins of all things in itself and explained all from itself, you would not be hastening to a full and perfect knowledge of them with such zeal. Furthermore, unless you were embracing the seriousness of moral philosophy, humility, the guardian of all virtues, would not thus be impressed upon your words.

Not silent, moreover, is the subtlety of a mind conscious of itself since, as I might say, oratorically you have shown its oratorical capabilities as flowing from itself and its Greek fountain. I do not know what more evidence of the divine there can be than that a man, Greek by birth, Roman by empire, as if by hereditary right seeks to recapture for himself the treasures of Greek and Roman wisdom.

Therefore, Caesar, we obey the imperial edicts not only in this, but also in all things whatsoever Your Divine Majesty has decreed. For we who consider nothing sweeter among human affairs than your command cannot fail in obedience to you.

GERBERT TO OTTO (26 DECEMBER 997)

Bishop Gerbert sends the homage of service that he owes to the ever august Caesar, glorious Lord Otto, emperor of the Romans.

While we lingered in Germany during the hotter part of the year, obligated as heretofore and henceforth by allegiance to the emperor, some hidden spark of your divine mind secretly struck fire in us and refined the flux of our thoughts into words. It revealed to everyone qualities discussed in very difficult phrases by Aristotle and the greatest men. One such was the wonderful ability of any mortal to have such depths of thoughts midst the strifes of war being prepared against the Sarmatians [Slavs], since from them flowed such noteworthy penetrating ideas like streams from the purest source.

For you remember, and we continually recall to mind many noble and learned scholars who used to be with us, among whom were some bishops, notable in wisdom and distinguished for their eloquence. However, we saw none of them who explained any of these questions properly, because certain problems too removed from use produced beforehand no hesitancy in them, and certain problems frequently aired could not be solved. Therefore, you in your divine prudence, regarding ignorance unworthy of the sacred palace, commanded me to discuss what others had argued in various ways in a [tract] *De rationali et ratione uti.*

[6] In conversations earlier in the year with Gerbert.

At that time, indeed, both a lassitude of body and more serious matters postponed this. Now that good health has been restored, and I am now midst public and private cares on this very Italian journey, and in all allegiance about to be your inseparable companion, I shall set forth briefly my conclusions on this question lest Greece shall boast of herself alone both in imperial philosophy and in Roman power.

Ours, ours is the Roman Empire. Italy, fertile in fruits, Lorraine and Germany, fertile in men, offer their resources, and even the strong kingdoms of the Slavs are not lacking to us.[7] Our august emperor of the Romans art thou, Caesar, who, sprung from the noblest blood of the Greeks, surpass the Greeks in empire and govern the Romans by hereditary right, but both you surpass in genius and eloquence.

Therefore, in the presence of so keen a judge let us first state certain preliminaries, or rather sophistical statements of scholars, then investigate the findings of philosophers on these points, and thence the many-sided and thorny dialectic will offer the conclusion of the proposed question.

[The text of the tract *De rationali et ratione uti* appears here.]

I have set forth, O Caesar, that which, though remote from the seriousness of a priest, still is not foreign to an emperor's zeal for learning, for I prefer to displease others than not to please you, not only in this respect but in all things worthy of your command. May you, therefore, read this in the midst of your mathematical exercises. Whether I may have offered anything worthy of the sacred palace, the [intellectual] efforts of the nobles[8] will give the answer, and logic, when consulted, will not be silent, nor, indeed, let me fear any censure if I have worked to accomplish what could please the sacred ears.

8. OTTO III: AN IMPERIAL DONATION (1001)[1]

The young emperor Otto III (reigned 983-1002) had an extremely exalted conception of the imperial office. Perhaps influenced by his Byzantine mother, Theophano, he adopted the title *Servant of the Apostles,* and evidently regarded himself, like the Emperor at Constantinople, as overlord of spiritual as well as temporal affairs. He tried to establish his imperial capital at Rome and rewarded his old teacher Gerbert with the Papacy. Gerbert took the name Sylvester II, evi-

[7] Otto had made an alliance with the Polish Duke Boleslav Chobry and had recently conquered various Slavic tribes.

[8] Gerbert seems to have had in mind a palace school like Charlemagne's.

[1] Trans. by C. T. Davis from the Latin text in P. E. Schramm, *Kaiser, Rom und Renovatio* (Leipzig and Berlin, Warburg-Institut, 1929), ii, 65-67.

dently hoping that his pupil's munificence would rival the legendary generosity of Constantine to Pope Sylvester I, as reflected in the spurious Donation of Constantine. But Otto declared the latter to be a malicious forgery invented and used by previous popes. (Its validity, however, continued to be accepted in most quarters throughout the Middle Ages.) Otto also made a much more conditional grant to the papal see than those of such predecessors as Charlemagne and Otto I. He apparently retained some control even over the eight counties of the Pentapolis which he bestowed on St. Peter. The text of his donation, dated 23 January 1001, is given below.

1. In the name of the holy and indivisible Trinity, Otto the servant of the Apostles and, according to the will of God the Saviour, Emperor of the Romans, Augustus.

2. We profess Rome to be the head of the world, and acknowledge that the Roman Church is the mother of all churches, but by the negligence and ignorance of the pontiffs the titles of her glory have long been obscured.

3. For not only did they sell and alienate to certain low knaves what clearly belonged to the household of St. Peter outside the city, but (grievous to relate), if they possessed anything within this our imperial city, they transferred it to the common coffers[2] in order to spread it about more promiscuously, money being the only consideration. They despoiled the very altars of St. Peter and St. Paul, and their attempts to make reparation led always to confusion. Since the papal laws were indeed confused, and the Roman church already in an abject state, certain of the pontiffs committed such great infringements that they annexed a very large part of our empire to their apostolic holdings. At this point they did not inquire what and how much they lost through their own sins, or care how much they poured out in voluntary frivolity. They forgot what was theirs, inasmuch as they themselves had squandered it. Turning, as it were, their own guilt upon our empire, they moved energetically against alien property, which belonged to us and our empire.

4. These are indeed the glosses that they themselves invented, with which John the Deacon, nicknamed Stubfinger, wrote an edict in golden letters; under the name of the great Constantine he fashioned a long-standing lie.[3]

5. These are moreover the glosses by which they say that a certain Charles[4] has bestowed our imperial property on St. Peter. But to this we an-

[2] Probably Otto is referring sarcastically here to the common fund for public purposes to which all were supposed to contribute.

[3] John the Deacon was ordered by Pope John XII (reigned 955-964) to make an ornamented copy of the Donation for Otto I's visit to Rome in 962. Shortly afterward, the scribe fell into papal disfavor and his hands were mutilated. He then entered Otto I's service and revealed the forgery.

[4] Charles the Bald came to Rome in 875-876 and again in 877; he renewed earlier donations to the Pope.

swer that this Charles could not legally give away anything, since he had already been put to flight by a better Charles,[5] and was already deprived of empire, already destitute and reduced to nothing. Therefore he gave what he did not have; he gave certainly, in the only way that he could, as one who acquired something dishonestly, and did not hope to possess it long.

6. Rejecting therefore these forged edicts and fanciful writings, out of our liberality we give to St. Peter what is ours; we do not give him what is his as if it were ours. For just as we have because of our love for St. Peter chosen our teacher Lord Sylvester as Pope, and by the will of God have ordained and made him *Serenissimus,* so for love of the same Lord Pope Sylvester, we confer gifts on St. Peter from our imperial patrimony, so that our teacher may have something to offer to our Lord Peter from his disciple.

7. Therefore we offer and give eight counties[6] to St. Peter out of love for our master Lord Sylvester the Pope, that he may have and hold them to the honor of God and of St. Peter with spiritual benefit to him and to us and that he may rule them to the augmenting of his apostolic patrimony and our empire. These therefore we give him to rule: Pesaro, Fano, Senigallia, Ancona, Fossombrone, Cagli, Iesi, and Osimo, that no one may ever dare to make any trouble for him and St. Peter, or vex him with any sort of craftiness.

8. Whosoever shall presume to do this, let him lose all that he has, and let St. Peter have his property.

9. That this, moreover, shall be preserved in eternity by everyone, we have confirmed this edict with our own long conquering (God willing) hand and have ordered it to be sealed with our own seal, that it may be valid for him and his successors.

9. GERMANIC LAW: COMPURGATION AND THE ORDEAL[1]

The sophistication of Otto III and Gerbert and their awareness of the heritage of Rome must not make us forget that the culture of western Europe was still largely tribal, characterized by kin right and blood feud, and only slightly disciplined by the restraints of customary law. These restraints, however, were gradually becoming more effective as kings and their ecclesiastical allies took the lead in extending and strengthening them. Testimony to their work may be found in

[5] Carloman came into Italy and drove away Charles the Bald in 877.

[6] These counties, which are listed below, are the eight counties of the Pentapolis, already bestowed on the Papacy by earlier emperors.

[1] Trans. by A. C. Howland, *Translations and Reprints from the Original Sources of European History,* Series I, Vol. IV, No. 4 (Philadelphia, University of Pennsylvania Press, 1898), pp. 6, 10-13.

the various written "codes" put together between the seventh and eleventh centuries. These were collections of decisions which clarified and supplemented particular points, but did not replace the larger body of oral tradition. They reflected, however, a far-reaching process of legal change. Although the existence of the kin or clan was still the basic fact of social life, the duty of the king to maintain order and punish violence was increasingly acknowledged. It was obviously necessary to find some way of limiting the blood feud; kings and clerics were understandably eager to provide legal substitutes for it. It is in this light that compurgation and the ordeal should be viewed.

A man accused of a crime was often allowed to purge himself by bringing to court a group of compurgators or "oath-helpers" whose number and rank were commensurate with the offence involved and who were prepared to swear to his innocence. Another, though riskier, method of purging was offered by the ordeal, in which God's judgment was invoked. This proved later to be a major obstacle to more rational legal procedures and aroused the hostility of both secular and ecclesiastical officials. Ordeals were prohibited by the Fourth Lateran Council in 1215. Long after this, however, popular attachment to them remained strong.

FRISIAN LAW: PENALTY FOR PERJURY (c. 800)

He who seeks the composition for homicide, let him swear on the relics of the saints that he will not accuse any one of this except those whom he suspects of the murder; and then let him accuse of homicide one, two, or even three or four or however many there may have been that wounded him who was killed. But, though there were twenty or thirty, yet no more than seven can be accused, and let each one of these who has been accused swear with his twelfth hand,[2] and after the oath let him show himself innocent by the judgment of God in the ordeal of boiling water. Let the one who swore first go first to the ordeal, and so on in order. He who shall be found guilty by the ordeal, let him pay the composition for homicide, and to the king double his *wergild;* let the others who were his oath-helpers pay the fine for perjury as has been previously enacted.[3]

GREGORY OF TOURS: AN ORDEAL OF HOT WATER (c. 580)[4]

An Arian presbyter disputing with a deacon of our religion made venemous assertions against the Son of God and the Holy Ghost, as is the habit of that sect. But when the deacon had discoursed a long time concerning the reasonableness of our faith and the heretic, blinded by the fog of unbelief, continued to reject the truth, according as it is written, "Wisdom shall not enter

---

[2] With eleven compurgators.
[3] One wergild, i.e., the value of the dead man. Set by law in accordance with his social rank.
[4] Gregory of Tours, *In Gloria Martyrum,* c. 80.

the mind of the wicked," the former said: "Why weary ourselves with long discussions? Let acts approve the truth; let a kettle be heated over the fire and someone's ring be thrown into the boiling water. Let him who shall take it from the heated liquid be approved as a follower of the truth, and afterwards let the other party be converted to the knowledge of this truth. And do thou also understand, O heretic, that this our party will fulfil the conditions with the aid of the Holy Ghost; thou shalt confess that there is no discordance, no dissimilarity in the Holy Trinity." The heretic consented to the proposition and they separated after appointing the next morning for the trial. But the fervor of faith in which the deacon had first made this suggestion began to cool through the instigation of the enemy. Rising with the dawn he bathed his arm in oil and smeared it with ointment. But nevertheless he made the round of the sacred places and called in prayer on the Lord. What more shall I say? About the third hour they met in the market place. The people came together to see the show. A fire was lighted, the kettle was placed upon it, and when it grew very hot the ring was thrown into the boiling water. The deacon invited the heretic to take it out of the water first. But he promptly refused, saying, "Thou who didst propose this trial art the one to take it out." The deacon all of a tremble bared his arm. And when the heretic presbyter saw it besmeared with ointment he cried out: "With magic arts thou hast thought to protect thyself, that thou hast made use of these salves, but what thou hast done will not avail." While they were thus quarreling there came up a deacon from Ravenna named Iacinthus and inquired what the trouble was about. When he learned the truth he drew his arm out from under his robe at once and plunged his right hand into the kettle. Now the ring that had been thrown in was a little thing and very light so that it was thrown about by the water as chaff would be blown about by the wind; and searching for it a long time he found it after about an hour. Meanwhile the flame beneath the kettle blazed up mightily so that the greater heat might make it difficult for the ring to be followed by the hand; but the deacon extracted it at length and suffered no harm, protesting rather that at the bottom the kettle was cold while at the top it was just pleasantly warm. When the heretic beheld this he was greatly confused and audaciously thrust his hand into the kettle saying, "My faith will aid me." As soon as his hand had been thrust in all the flesh was boiled off the bones clear up to the elbow. And so the dispute ended.

HINCMAR OF RHEIMS: THE ORDEAL OF COLD WATER (860)[5]

Now the one about to be examined is bound by a rope and cast into the water because, as it is written, each one shall be holden with the cords of his

[5] Hincmar, *De Divortio Lotharii et Teutbergae, c. 6.*

iniquity. And it is evident that he is bound for two reasons; to wit, that he may not be able to practice any fraud in connection with the judgment, and that he may be drawn out at the right time if the water should receive him as innocent, so that he perish not. For as we read that Lazarus, who had been dead four days (by whom is signified each one buried under a load of crimes), was buried wrapped in bandages and, bound by the same bands, came forth from the sepulchre at the word of the Lord and was loosed by the disciples at his command; so he who is to be examined by this judgment is cast into the water bound, and is drawn forth again bound, and is either immediately set free by the judgment of the judges, being purged, or remains bound till the time of his purgation and is then examined by the court. . . . And in this ordeal of cold water whoever, after the invocation of God, who is the Truth, seeks to hide the truth by a lie, cannot be submerged in the waters above which the voice of the Lord God has thundered; for the pure nature of the water recognizes as impure and therefore rejects as inconsistent with itself such human nature as has once been regenerated by the waters of baptism and is again infected by falsehood.[6]

ANONYMOUS ENGLISH DOOM: THE ORDEAL OF HOT IRON (c. 930)

If anyone shall have given pledge to undergo the ordeal of iron . . . let him go three days beforehand to the priest whose duty it is to bless him with the sign of the cross; and let him live upon bread, water, salt and herbs, and hear mass each one of the three days; and let him make his offering and go to the holy communion on the day when he is to be examined by the ordeal; and before he is examined let him swear that by the law of the realm he is innocent of the charge. . . . Concerning the ordeal we enjoin in the name of God and by the command of the archbishop and of all our bishops that no one enter the church after the fire has been brought in with which the ordeal is to be heated except the priest and him who is to undergo judgment. And let nine feet be measured off from the stake to the mark, by the feet of him who is to be tried. . . . And when the ordeal is ready let two men from each side go in and certify that it is as hot as we have directed it to be. Then let an equal number from both sides enter and stand on either side of the judgment place along the church, and let them all be fasting and abstinent from their wives on the preceding night. And let the priest sprinkle them all with water and let them bow themselves everyone to the holy water and let the holy Gospel and the cross be given them all to kiss. And no one shall mend the fire any longer than the beginning of the hallowing, but let the iron lie on the coals until the last collect. Afterwards let it be placed on a

[6] If the accused sank, he was therefore innocent; if he floated, he was guilty.

frame, and let no one speak except to pray diligently to God, the Father Omnipotent, to deign to manifest His truth in the matter. And let the accused drink of the holy water and then let the hand with which he is about to carry the iron be sprinkled, and so let him go [to the ordeal.] Let the nine feet that were measured off be divided into three sections. In the first division let him hold his right foot, close to the stake. Then let him move his right foot across the second into the third division, where he shall cast the iron in front of him and hasten to the holy altar. Then let his hand be sealed up, and on the third day let examination be made whether it is clean or foul[7] within the wrapper. And whoever shall transgress these laws, be the ordeal of no worth in his case, but let him pay the king a fine of one hundred and twenty shillings.

[7] If the burn had become infected, the accused was guilty.

1336 Schoolcraft